Pelican Books
Progress and Disillusion

Raymond Aron, who is Professor of Sociology at the
University of Paris and Director of Studies at the École
Pratique des Hautes Études, is known throughout the
English-speaking world as France's leading social
theorist. Among his many books published in English
are *Peace and War, The Dawn of Universal History, The
Industrial Society, 18 Lectures on Industrial Society*, and
volume 1 of *Main Currents in Sociological Thought*,
which dealt with the theories of Montesquieu, Comte,
Tocqueville, and Marx.

D0550081

Raymond Aron

# Progress and Disillusion

The Dialectics of Modern Society

Penguin Books

Penguin Books Ltd, Harmondsworth,
Middlesex, England
Penguin Books Australia Ltd, Ringwood,
Victoria, Australia

First published in the U.S.A. by Frederick A. Praeger 1968
First published in Great Britain by Pall Mall Press 1968
Published in Pelican Books 1972
Copyright © Encyclopaedia Britannica, 1968

*Progress and Disillusion: The Dialectics of Modern
Society* is a *Britannica Perspective* prepared to
commemorate the 200th anniversary of
*Encyclopaedia Britannica*.

Made and printed in Great Britain by
Hazell Watson & Viney Ltd,
Aylesbury, Bucks
Set in Monotype Times

# Contents

# Introduction

The three words *social, socialism*, and *sociology* are of relatively recent usage.

The famous *Encyclopédie* of Diderot and D'Alembert, – titled *Analytical Dictionary of the Arts, Sciences and Professions*, which appeared between 1751 and 1772, defined the term *social* as 'a word newly introduced in the language to designate those attributes that render a man useful in society, and fit him for human intercourse: "the social virtues"'. During the first half of the nineteenth century the word *socialism* appeared, but Littré's dictionary gave it only a few lines, defining it as the term applied to doctrines that are not content merely with political reform but advocate the modification of the very structure of society. *Sociology* was coined by Auguste Comte in the 1830s to denote a new science, that of society as such, in its unity and development.

In the eyes of Comte two arguments justified his neologism. It was important to apply to human society the positivist method to which the physical, chemical, and biological sciences owed their brilliant achievements. But this positivist science was by no means to be confused with the studies of jurists and economists, who were still, according to Comte, metaphysicians, more given to conceptual analysis and abstract reasoning than to the observation of facts and the establishment of categories. Moreover, jurists and economists could not become sociologists merely by adopting the positivist method; they would still need to perceive the *unity*, the *total* image that characterizes each society and, ultimately, the entire history of mankind. The sociologist, as envisioned by Comte, is the product of the need for a *scientific* knowledge of the *social* totality.

Actually, Comte was mistaken about the historical significance of his work and goal. His predecessors had been unaware of the distinctive nature of sociology, not because they failed to recognize the unity of society but because they did not distinguish equally the diverse activities of man or the various segments of the social order.

Aristotle's *Politics* contains chapters that deal with disciplines we call today economics and sociology. 'Social animal' is as good a definition of *zoon politicon* as 'political animal'. Man, according to Aristotle, is fated to live in society; he needs other men in order to fulfil his spiritual essence, and society presupposes a multiplicity of families assembled in a single city (*polis*). A city, in turn, is ordered according to hierarchical relationships of command and obedience – relationships that may assume different modes, each of which determines a regime, a *politeia*. Aristotle's *Politics* overlooks neither the family, the means of production, nor trade; the concept of *polis* constitutes the principle of totalization because society and politics (in the modern sense of these terms) are not separable; thus it is primarily the regime that distinguishes each city.

A famous article by Jean-Jacques Rousseau in the *Encyclopédie* defined economics in such a way as to embrace the study of all of politics and society:

> Economy or *oeconomie*, a word derived from *oikos*, meaning a house, and *nomos*, meaning law, ordinarily signifies merely the wise and legitimate management of a house for the common good of the entire family. The meaning of the term has since been extended to mean the management of the larger family of the state. In order to distinguish between these two meanings, in the latter case we speak of *general* or *political economy,* and in the former, of *domestic* or *special economy*.

No inkling is given of the distinction to be made between the three disciplines – sociology, economics, politics. Rousseau, indifferent to the conflict between facts and values, between observation and judgement, probes solely the wise government of the family and the state.

The isolation of the *social* as such, and the birth of sociology, did not originate in an awareness of the unity of society – Western thinkers have never misjudged this unity – but, on the contrary, in an intuition of historical crisis and of a dissension of sorts between the various segments of society. The *social* seems autonomous when society itself breaks up. The doctrines we today call social, socialist, or sociological, and which multiplied so rapidly at the beginning of the last century, are all based on the idea of a separation or even a conflict between society and the state. The Saint-Simonians and Auguste Comte, meditating on the French Revolution, emphasized the lack of harmony between the organization of modern society and the centuries-old political regime. They saw science, industry, labour, and the creation of goods as the true reality of modern society, with the real power held by bankers, scientists, engineers, and industrialists. Kings and their courtiers, the diplomats and the jurists, the parliamentarians and the ministers of state were no more than survivors of another age, holding on to an authority that becomes more and more illusory and to privileges that are less and less justifiable.

The Saint-Simonian formula, restated by Karl Marx, that the *administration of things will be substituted for the government of peoples* is both an interpretation of modernity and a vision of the future. Marx's intellectual journey takes this as its point of departure: an acknowledgement of the divorce between civil *society (bürgerliche Gesellschaft)* and the state. The individual viewed as a worker, as a member of civil society, is enclosed in his own individuality; at the same time he is subject to the requirements of producing goods and to the arbitrary will of the owners of the means of production. As a citizen he possesses his atom of sovereignty, and thereby partakes of the universal. But he expresses his citizenship only at intervals, by dropping a ballot in the ballot box – a ridiculous gesture that symbolizes his freedom yet does not free him from servitude. The revolution, as envisioned by Marx, would re-establish the unity of worker and citizen, assuring, in the course of time, that freedom and universality which bourgeois democracy grants solely in the empyrean of the state. Hegel believed that the distinction between civil society and the state was inevitable; he filled the breach between the individuality of the workers and the universality of the state with agencies of mediation: professional groups, representative institutions, bureaucracy, even that incarnation of the totality, the king. In Marx's eyes, the separation between civil society and the state, between the worker and the citizen, is such that no mediation whatever is possible – at least in a capitalist regime. If the workers are to become citizens, they must themselves assume responsibility, as partners in production, for the organization of society. And the state will wither away when it loses its repressive function, which was its *raison d'être* before the advent of industrial society.

This idea of the separation of society and the state also is to be found in many forms among the enemies of socialism, the liberals of various schools. Economists have a tendency to congratulate themselves on the autonomy the economy has acquired, and thus to view it as a characteristic feature of modern society. The merchant republic prospers on its own, with the sole proviso that the state must protect it against those who would violate its laws or otherwise threaten it, whether from without or from within. Even a liberal thinker like Tocqueville in the light of his American experience depicts the antithesis of a *society*, essentially and inevitably democratic, where distinctions of estate or order are in the process of disappearing, and a *state* which is either despotic or free, depending on the circumstances. American society, he believed, bears within itself the principles of its own organization and perpetuation, even though the state remains indispensable. In this sense, one might say that a *social order* exists apart from the political order. A French writer of liberal persuasions, Prévost-Paradol, who threw in his lot with Napoleon III on the eve of the catastrophe of 1870 (and who was later to commit suicide in Washington a few days after his arrival to take up the post of French ambassador), thirty years after Tocqueville developed this thesis, wrote that the French Revolution had created a *social order*, but not a state or a political system that could be adapted to that order.

More than a century has passed since Auguste Comte christened the science of society as such with the title sociology, and Karl Marx bestowed the name of socialism upon the scientific interpretation of capitalism in its actual functioning and ultimate development. The basic ideas of Positivism no longer arouse much interest save among historians, whereas the principal ideas of Marxism, for obvious reasons, are still an integral part of the political consciousness of our era. Yet on a scientific level, a satisfactory definition of the social order in Marxist terms is no more readily rendered than is one in Comtian terms.

The ambition of both men was to found a *science* of the *social totality*. Today sociology, like all disciplines that claim to be scientific, has become empirical, quantitative, and analytical. Modern societies know how to count, and if one may say so, they know how to count themselves. Nothing is more original. Montesquieu in his day believed that France's population was decreasing, and that only one tenth of the population of earlier days still remained. The editors of the article entitled 'Population' in the *Encyclopédie* sought to reassure the author of *The Spirit of Laws* with this fanciful argument:

Can we not presume as a consequence of these laws that the number of such human beings is determined strictly by the mutual necessity that exists between them and the world whose surface they cover? That the number could not diminish appreciably without altering the constitution of that world and consequently the harmony in which such beings must live with all other human beings in order to maintain the natural order? From these principles it follows that the population, in general, must have been constant and that it will remain so until the end.

The introduction of statistics – a fundamental chapter in the social science of our times – owes nothing or almost nothing to the great doctrines that hold first place in the history of ideas or in philosophy. Bureaucracies, for their own purposes, take a census of population, births, deaths, marriages and divorces, crimes, and suicides. Surveys of towns in Great Britain, investigations of working-class conditions in France, and Le Play's census of families are more closely related to what professors now call sociology than are those grandiose visions of the past and the future that positivists and the Marxists indulged in – and perhaps still do.

It was not until the middle of the twentieth century that governments had at their disposal the approximate figures for national product, and therefore for the first time were in a position to measure the wealth of nations, either as it changed between two dates or as it compared with others at a given moment. The procedures, now standard, of the opinion polls, with their questionnaires, interviews, and mechanical tabulation of results, have been perfected during the last thirty years. With the advent of these new statistical tools, sociology, already only one among several academic disciplines dedicated to the study of society, has been subdivided into specialities: industrial, urban, rural, economic sociology, etc. Far from embracing a social totality, sociology aims to be as analytical as it is empirical. By opinion sampling, professional sociologists predict approximately the outcome of elections. After the fact, they ascertain and explain the distribution of votes, and they analyse the motives of voting groups and sometimes of individuals. In these and other ways they deal routinely with the system of values or beliefs of a given social entity, more or less extensive, more or less aware of its own motives. But sociologists hesitate, on the basis of incomplete and imprecise research, to propound a theory about the social order. Such a theory would be imprudent if only because its object is in permanent change.

One might argue that economics and political science also have been split into specialized research disciplines, and that attempts to elaborate a theory of an economic or political order are neither unwarranted nor impossible. To counter this argument, and at the same time to define more precisely the meaning and scope of this work on the social order, we must analyse distinct and complementary technical, economic, and political concepts and then fix the place of the social concept among them.

Even though sociology has become analytical, empirical, and quantitative, it has not lost the sense of the *social*, nor, by the same token, of the whole or the totality. The favourite concepts of U.S. sociology, which are becoming those of world sociology (excluding Marxist-Leninist countries), apply to social man as such, whatever his activities might be, whatever organizations he may belong to – industrial corporation, scientific community, church, or political party. Every individual in a world society or in smaller groups has a certain status, possesses a legal authority or a *de facto* power, enjoys a certain prestige. He plays many roles because he has a family, practises a profession, belongs to a community. Each of these roles is partly determined in advance by collective obligations and prohibitions and is partly left to the discretion of the protagonist. Society is a sort of *commedia dell'-*

*arte* in which the actors have the right to improvise along prescribed lines. It is a strange theatre, like Leibniz's universe, which admits of no distinction between the stage and the pit, and in which everyone belongs at once to the cast and to the audience.

These innumerable actors would not constitute a society if most of them did not adhere, with more or less conviction, to the same values, if they did not behave as if they shared certain common objectives, if the environment itself did not limit their freedom of choice. The cast, which merges with the audience, does not know, in the final analysis, toward what end the theatre itself is evolving, but it does know that the performance will go on after it is gone. Each fragment of the play is ordained because the actors' roles are adapted the one to the other and because all of them are integrated into a system of institutions.

Since its subject matter is the social man – his status, roles, values, and systems – sociology remains indeed the science of society. Merchants, politicians, scholars, priests – all are equally representative of the *social man:* they all have *internalized* the obligations without which they could not maintain the place in one group or another that is their lot or has been imposed upon them. But precisely because each individual belongs to many groups and plays different roles in his family, profession, community, or church, the sociological synthesis is formal rather than substantive. The concepts that sociology elaborates are most abstract, most general; they could serve as a basis for the conceptualizations of other disciplines. But sociologists do not draw from this the conclusion that sociology is the supreme science of society or that its function is to subsume or to synthesize the other social sciences.

Anthropologists, who were the first to fashion and utilize some of the concepts which have become basic to sociology, such as notions of status and role-playing, were interested in societies very far removed from those that typify contemporary existence – societies made up of hundreds of thousands, not of millions or tens of millions; possessing only rudimentary tools, not fabulous modern machines; making only a feeble differentiation between social and individual activities, a differentiation that becomes increasingly pronounced as modern civilization progresses. Because of the very nature of the societies they study, anthropologists sacrifice neither of the twin purposes – *scientific* and *synthetic* – of the sociologists of the last century. But contemporary sociologists who are interested primarily in modern societies, and this means the majority of those who can be so labelled in the academic sense, neither could nor would want to take over the fields of economists, political scientists, or demographers. If they still have an ambition to synthesize, it seldom goes beyond an effort at conceptualization. From where, then, would the unity of sociology emanate? And what is meant by social order?

## *The Social Aspect*

The situation of a discipline that can be said to be the most general of all the social sciences while it seems devoid of unity or specific object seems paradoxical, yet it is profoundly logical. The birth of industrial civilization; the discord, glimpsed the day after the French Revolution, between society and state; the justifiable refusal to confound the science of production and trade with that of the social entity – all this facilitated a growing awareness of the social factor as such. But the social is assimilable neither to a specific activity of man, such as religion, art, or science, nor to a relatively limited segment of society, whether economic, political, or even technical or legal. All human activities have a social aspect: religion is not conceivable apart from the community of believers, nor is science conceivable apart from the republic of scholars. Similarly, the economic, political, or juridical system is a sector of the social system, even though the latter is not on the same level as the former. Similarly, the discipline that deals with the social system in its totality (or with social systems in their multiplicity) is not on the same level as that which deals with any particular segment.

These abstract remarks can be clarified with some deliberately simple analyses. Every human collectivity must solve its economic problems in order to survive. Everyone, whether as an individual or a member of a group, possesses only a limited store of resources, of time and labour. The disproportion between real desires and the means to satisfy them has existed as long as mankind, but one is not always aware of it; when long-established tradition limits desire, collectivities do not seek the most efficacious use of their tools or their working time, but content themselves with harvesting the fruits of the earth or producing a regular flow of the things they habitually consume. A creature filled with desires, capable of awareness and thought, man is no less essentially poor on that account, and hence the idea of economy defined in terms of poverty, or, if you will, of scarcity. The economic question *par excellence* is: how best to utilize the limited resources available to man?

Man, as he progresses toward fulfilment, is not satisfied with what nature in itself offers him. He begins to make tools, he cultivates the soil, he domesticates animals. Today he manufactures machines which take the place of the worker's hands and even of his brain. So-called economic activity, at the initial stage of production, includes a technical component, if we agree to call technical *the logical use of means, whether material or human, to achieve ends or create objects conceived in advance*. In current usage the term *technical* has both a narrow and a broader meaning: according to the first, the term designates all the equipment which, indispensable to factory workers, constitutes the environment of our daily lives. In this case, technology, perfected by science, is identified only with the tools and products of industrialization. Under the second, broader meaning, technology is not limited to technical objects, but relates to the whole process of *mechanization* – in other words, to the progressive transformation of human behaviour according to one rule alone, that of efficacy of thought and computation. In this usage, any rationalization of an activity with a view to manipulation or planning can be termed a technique. Brainwashing is a technique, derived from our knowledge of psychology, whose purpose is to manipulate individual psychic responses and to wrest from individuals words or deeds to which they would not voluntarily consent.

An economic regime which offers one of several possible solutions to the problem of scarcity comprises a technical component. Computations of productivity presuppose a technical analysis or an assessment of what engineers can accomplish with the assistance of available information and machines. But technical analyses, at least in a peacetime economy, are subordinated to economic calculations or estimates of productivity. Even with the aid of modern technology, one cannot do everything one would like to do nor, especially, do everything at once. Therefore, it is found best to assure maximum productivity from available resources, according to an order of preference which each person tends to establish for himself or which, directly or indirectly, partially or totally, the rulers establish for the collectivity as a whole.

An economic regime organized for production, trade, and distribution on the basis of scarcity implies, as a condition or consequence, a juridical order with fixed channels of command (a political order); but it remains specific and autonomous (like the discipline that governs it) since mankind, by the very fact of its human condition, faces eternal problems which throughout the centuries have received various imperfect solutions.

The political, like the economic, problem is also created by the human condition. It is based upon two facts historical experience proves are constants: the physical and intellectual inequality of individuals, and the need for discipline in the area that governs the activities or even the very existence of the collectivity – in other words, a distinction between those who command and those who obey (the same people might in turn command or obey, depending upon the time and the place). These two facts are interrelated without the one being the cause or the consequence of the other. Social inequality does not reflect the natural inequality of aptitudes. Aristotle wrote that among men some are destined to be masters and others slaves, but he added that many masters have the soul of a slave and many slaves the soul of a master. Vilfredo Pareto saw in the disparity between the hierarchy of privilege and that of ability one of the profound causes of revolution.

No collective activity exists without discipline but a collectivity does not necessarily possess a single chain of command. The authority of the leader can be limited to a single domain–hunting, war, religion. There is no lack of so-called archaic societies in which the custodians of peace, or guardians of the law, are not leaders of the hunt nor commanders-in-chief in time of war. Anthropologists have even noted the existence of societies that have no central control, that have never experienced the permanent concentration of power in the hands of one or several people.

As collectivities increase and as each becomes enclosed within itself, each claiming to be sovereign in relation to others with the same claim and consequently partially antagonistic, the power as the authority of a few over the many is bound to emerge and develop in terms of common interest. The authority indispensable to any collective activity crystallizes into power or becomes the state; the latter reserves to itself all questions that it designates as public, and, either by indifference, tradition, or deliberate will, leaves to the discretion of individuals questions that it concludes are private in nature. Thus a political regime is a way of organizing power, just as an economic regime is a way of organizing production and distribution. The former, which originates in the inequality of men in society and the plurality of sovereign collectivities, constitutes a solution to the problem of man's relation to man; the latter, which springs from the essential poverty of the species, constitutes the solution to the problem of man's relationship to nature.

Since both problems are present in all collectivities, and since the solution to both problems is a matter of interest to the entire collectivity one can understand why each of the two concepts has served at one time or another to designate the science of society. A study of the relationships of command develops into a study of power and its organization; it includes at the same time all of society as seen from a certain point of view, its internal order as well as the autonomy of the group in relation to other groups. Similarly, economics, as defined by Rousseau in his article in the *Encyclopédie*, having as its object the management of public as well as domestic affairs, presupposes a simultaneous regard for available means and purposeful ends; such an economy, viewed from a certain perspective, therefore necessitates consideration of all of social existence.

The social, as we have said, is not fixed at the same level as the political or the economic; it does not refer, at least at first glance, to a specific problem. One is tempted to define it as 'the problem of problems' in the sense that the social, however one defines it, is implicated in every human activity. Whether we employ the microscopic definition, *relations between individuals*, or the macroscopic *global society*, both the economic and the political regime envisioned presuppose a society. The action of economic subjects is social, just as an economic regime is an aspect of society. If sociology is a latecomer among the disciplines, the reason is not only tardy application of the scientific method to human reality. Recognition of the social dimension as indicative of all activities, whether material or intellectual, presupposes a differentiation of society itself that becomes more and more pronounced in modern civilization.

All of this points up the ambiguity in the notion of social order. Neither economics nor politics has a unique finality. According to circumstances, men direct their efforts toward a maximization of production or toward a lessening of social inequalities, toward a maximization of economic growth or toward raising the standard of living. Similarly, the efficacy or the legitimacy of power, the authority of the rulers, or the consent of the ruled may serve at different times and under different circumstances as the criteria for judging political regimes. But in any case, reference to the two problems, production and discipline, which are inseparable from the human condition in society, permits at least an approximate identification of those institutions that together constitute the economic or political order. All of these institutions are by definition social, since all of them are the result of cooperation among individuals and all exist within the context of a global system. In what, then, does the specificity of the social order consist?

The sociologist-philosophers of the last century did not confront this difficulty as we do; they believed in the existence of a fundamental and necessary social order. Comte foresaw the progressive achievement of an order that would express the eternal nature of man and society. Marx counted on the contradictions of capitalism to produce, dialectically, revolution and socialism, under which a social order, conforming to human calling, would develop. Modern sociology no longer grants an immanent necessity to development of a global society and no longer dreams of utopia; it oscillates between heeding the microscopic and bending its efforts toward the totality, but without assuming the possibility of combining the two.

Modern society, as we have said, involves an increasing differentiation between individual roles, intellectual activities, and social entities. This differentiation nurtures nostalgia for the lost dream of unity, a nostalgia felt alike by subject and object of sociology, by mankind generally and sociologists in particular. Thus the vain attempt to appease this nostalgia by some ideological system that will reduce the complexity of reality and herald a future more in keeping with man's desires and aspirations. But the observer who wishes to remain objective cannot depart in search of some such artificial simplification. Society cannot be reduced to a juxtaposition of the characteristic activities of the human spirit, or of those institutional systems that represent our response to the eternal problems of the species; the unification of society is not furthered by the fusion of these activities, of these systems, into some mysterious essence. Social unity is the provisional result of mutual relations among men, of their works and their systems. The social order which this work attempts to describe cannot be dissociated from the technical order, the economic order, the political order – although it should not be confused with any one of them. It is neither the effect nor the cause, neither the foundation nor the expression. Explicitly, it is the most general of these orders, since all human activity includes at least one social dimension. Concretely, it often seems more effect than cause, especially in modern societies which seem to have as their objective not a certain way of living together but the advancement of science, wealth and power. We still must ask the question: *What is the nature of relationships between individuals and institutions in the so-called modern and industrial societies that seem to have relatively definite objectives in each segment but lack a distinctive image of their own order?*

This provisional definition of the social still falls short of determining the purpose and plan of this work. Indeed, each system, whether economic, political, or religious, entails a social order; that is, it entails interpersonal relations of a determinate nature. Every measurable society, whether French, English, or American, and, a fortiori, whether Western or Soviet, entails a social order – that is, some sort of organization of multiple systems. Therefore it behoves us to identify those marks that truly distinguish the social order of modern civilization.

To prevent the investigation from becoming too scattered, we propose to keep to three fundamental themes.

Modern industrial societies are both egalitarian in aspiration and hierarchical in organization. They recognize the right of each individual to an equal dignity, to happiness, to citizenship, and, as a consequence, to an equitable share of the assets produced by society. But industrial societies also have as their objective the efficacy of the collective work effort, and this implies the subordination of all to the decisions of a few. In Part One, *The Dialectic of Equality*, we will deal with the issues of *equality* and *hierarchy*, as old as human society itself, and now re-established in their concrete manifestation by the unfathomable potentialities of science and technology.

In modern societies, as in all societies recorded by history, individuals belong to multiple groups, the principal ones still being the family and the working community. A technological civilization alters the relationships of these elementary systems, and in addition it evokes fresh aspirations even as it fulfils old ones. Just as each individual aspires to equality, he also aspires to *individuality*. He wants to be himself, not an anonymous and interchangeable cipher. But the very abundance that promises each person the possibility of realizing his individuality seems at the same time to carry with it the condition or consequence that he must submit to a pitiless mechanism of production and economic growth. This is the theme of Part Two, *The Contradictions of Socialization*.

Finally, the societies into which mankind is divided are more closely linked today than at any time in the past. Modern means of transportation and communication provide people with a kind of ubiquity as well as with information in unprecedented form and volume. The inequality of wealth in developed countries and in the so-called underdeveloped ones is not only a topic of passionate debate at the United Nations; it is a condition that is becoming familiar to the peoples themselves. The human species tends simultaneously towards both unity and division. From now on, technology makes the entire planet, not merely countries or continents, one intelligible field of history. All nations, or at least all those who purport to speak in the name of nations, aspire to the wealth and power industrialization alone offers. Yet never have the level and mode of the life of common men been as different as they are today; still close to primitive customs in one place, in another we are already transformed by vast changes of the age in which we are living, comparable only to the neolithic revolution which followed upon the cultivation of the soil and the breeding of cattle and paved the way for the first great human adventure of record. Part Three deals with *The Dialectic of Universality*.

Each of these three themes is dialectical in the sense that it is defined by the contradiction between the reality and the ideal, or between various aspects of reality and various ideals. The use of the term dialectic in these titles is not a mere concession to fashion: society of the industrial type is intelligible solely in its becoming. It has no fixed order: the only perceptible order is that of change. But change, in turn, cannot be reduced to progress toward a predetermined end, nor to an even evolution whose laws and results are known. Neither in science nor technology can the future be reckoned as a mere extension of the present, but rather it must be seen as a kaleidoscope of new creations and mutations, to a large degree unpredictable. Even if we presume to estimate not only the number but the knowledge and power of our descendants, we still could not say with certainty what the social order of tomorrow will be. Mankind's aspirations for equality, individuality, and unity were born long before the species possessed the means to satisfy them. No one knows if tomorrow men will be satisfied with what society has to offer; if they are not, no one knows how they will express their dissatisfaction.

History is not at an end. The societies of today are divided between spontaneous convictions, without which they would dissolve, and objective self-awareness, which has become inseparable from their very natures. They hesitate to define themselves by a single aim or ideal. They question the future and await a reply. But the future does not answer, or rather it tosses back to us, in another form, the questions we have put to it.

## Part One
# The Dialectic of Equality

Society is a hierarchy. All individuals are noble and
sacred; all beings (even animals) have rights. But
all beings are not equal, even though they are members
of a vast body and form part of an immense organism
that performs a divine task . . .

Human life would become impossible if man did not
endow himself with the right to subordinate animals to
his needs. It would scarcely be any more possible if the
world clung to the abstract notion that all men are at
birth equally entitled to wealth and social station.

ERNEST RENAN
'La Monarchie constitutionelle en France'

Modern society seems to conform to two imperatives: to produce as much as possible through mastery of the forces of nature and to treat its members as equals. In their relations with their environment, men gravitate towards collective power; in their relations with each other, they proclaim their determination to recognize each other as equal in worth.

There is a perceptible kinship of inspiration between Promethean ambition and egalitarian ideal. Conquest of the forces of nature rests upon science; scientific knowledge is theoretically accessible to everyone since it is the product of reason, which all men share. There is no basic inequality among individuals; all have a right to be citizens, to share the common good, to seek happiness. This message, broadcast in the eighteenth century by the products of a new era, has not yet exhausted its revolutionary potential.

But the egalitarian ideal is unequivocal. In every century it has been defined by negating some form of inequality. When Tocqueville compared post-revolutionary society with that of the Old Regime, he confused social equality and political equality in his notion of democracy. In his view, social equality stemmed from the elimination of the *estates*; political equality found expression in the right to vote and in the existence of representative institutions. But from the beginning of the last century the socialists refused to confine themselves to these two kinds of equality, which they said were merely formal.

Does not social equality logically imply at least a reduction of economic inequalities? And further, even supposing that a degree of economic inequality may be justified by an inequality of abilities and of services rendered to the community, must not equal opportunity be given to all? The first of these arguments leads to a demand for economic equality in the name of the equality of needs; the second to a protest against the transmission of social and economic inequalities from one generation to another. Carried to an extreme, the first argument would justify making income proportional to need; the second would require that all men be given an equal start in life, thus implying a social order strictly non-hereditary in character and devoid of any continuity. These diverse interpretations of the egalitarian ideal, although in certain respects incompatible, continue nonetheless to be present in the ideologies of modern civilization and in the consciousness of contemporary mankind. Depending on the country and the time, now one, now the other of these interpretations has predominated. Together they represent a continuing criticism of a social order that condemns itself because it invokes ideas that are ultimately contradictory and envisions a goal that is probably unattainable.

Although Promethean ambition and the egalitarian ideal share this common origin in rationalism, the will to produce as much and as efficiently as possible is, however, inherently alien to the concern for justice and to other humanitarian considerations. The rational organization of work increases the wealth that can be shared; it makes possible a higher standard of living for all and thus an eventual reduction of certain inequalities. However, it also requires efficiency in organization, which cannot be achieved without a hierarchy in which man has authority over man. Ideally this hierarchy would have to conform to a hierarchy of abilities. But, if there were a vast and evident gap between the least able and the most able (or skilled, or gifted), would the collective conscience accept such inequality?

The contradictions within the egalitarian ideal, together with the contradictions between that ideal and the other goals of the collectivity – productivity and the mastery of nature – have precluded any effective stabilization of modern societies. They are continually being unsettled by the progress of science and technology and by the dissatisfactions of men. Order in such societies is always provisional; it is not so much *in* process as it is *a* process. Therefore the best way to understand its direction is to focus our analysis on the most obvious inequalities, those which have been at stake in contemporary ideological disputes and historical conflicts.

These inequalities have been, so to speak, challenges hurled at societies themselves. The responses they have made enable us to identify the common characteristics as well as the specific dissimilarities of the social systems of our time. These challenges may be summarized in three words: *class, oligarchy,* and *race.* They denote the three principal kinds of inequality: (1) *socio-*

*economic inequality*, which depends on the part played by the individual in the productive process and in the distribution of income; (2) *socio-political inequality*, dependent on the part individuals play, separately or as members of a group, in the management of public affairs; and (2) *national* (or *racial*) *inequality*, as in the case of a sovereign state or a larger collectivity within which groups coexist that are differentiated by language, culture, or skin colour.

Is modern society being torn apart by the class struggle? Is it divided between the passive masses and an all-powerful elite? Or instead, thanks to economic progress, are classes tending to dissolve or coalesce? Is political power tending to become more widely diffused?

Pessimists and optimists, Marxist-Leninists and champions of Western democracy answer these questions differently. But, on the other hand, both camps would have to agree on one disconsolate fact: ethnic differences have proved to be the most difficult to reconcile with the ideal of equality.

# 1 Class Societies?

The interpretation of history in the light of the class struggle began well before Karl Marx. Eighteenth-century French historians and political theorists developed the thesis in the light of events leading up to the Revolution. The demands of the bourgeoisie were countered by vindications of the nobility and aristocracy based on claims of hereditary superiority. But the same demands provoked a defence and glorification of the rights of the people, so long trodden underfoot by the ruling classes. Before 1789 the conflict was three-sided. The exponents of royal absolutism, who invoked the continuity of kingly authority reaching back to Roman sovereignty, were opposed by exponents of the Germanic aristocracy, whose privileges were held to be as ancient as the royal authority and therefore equal to it in dignity. But the two camps joined to oppose those theorists who championed the people, oppressed for centuries but now growing aware of their own strength and of the long endured injustice.

After the Revolution, king and nobility were united in defeat and nostalgia. Comte de Gobineau took up the theory of the Germanic origin of the aristocracy to develop one of the leading racist conceptions of history. But others (Augustin Thierry, who preceded Auguste Comte as secretary to Henri de Saint-Simon, is one example) tended to recount the history of France in terms of class struggle. In the writings of Thierry the classes still appear as the heirs of two peoples, the victorious Franks and the Gallo-Romans who bowed to the law of the invaders. Another school (Guizot, author of *Histoire de la civilisation en Europe* (1828) and *Histoire de la civilisation en France* (1830), was the most famous of these) elaborated upon and in effect denigrated the simple idea of opposition of two races. Without denying the initial clash, they assigned particular roles to the Roman tradition, to the early liberties of the Franks, and to the educational activities of the Church in order to exalt the part played by the middle class as originator of municipal autonomy and of the representative principle – hence of civil liberty itself. Right up to the morrow of the defeat of 1870, the political debate waged by French historians centred on classes: their origin, their struggles, their role through the centuries. Marx was therefore entirely right when he wrote in his often quoted letter to J. Weydemeyer in March 1852:

As far as I am concerned, I cannot claim credit for discovering either the existence of classes or the struggles between them. Long before me bourgeois historians had traced the historical development of the class struggle, and bourgeois economists had laid bare the economic anatomy of classes. My contribution was to show (1) that the existence of classes is connected only with certain phases in the historical development of production; (2) that the class struggle leads directly to the dictatorship of the proletariat; and (3) that this dictatorship is merely a transitional stage leading to the elimination of all classes and the emergence of a classless society.

To understand the originality and historical significance of Marxist thought, it is helpful to place it in the context of its time. Franks and Gallo-Romans, bourgeoisie and nobility, middle class and workers (both urban and rural) represented the conflicting interests on which historians based their attempts to explain the evolution of European society. Seen from this point of view, the classes that had developed from the antagonism between the conquering minority and the subjugated masses had something not only of the orders of the *ancien régime* but also of the social and occupational categories, as modern sociology has distinguished.

European students of post-revolutionary society sought in the last analysis to answer a simple question: Were the classes in the industrial society basically similar to the orders of the *ancien régime* or were they essentially different? The Saint-Simonians accepted the second alternative; Karl Marx chose the first. The historical fortunes of Marxism are due in large measure to this choice which, however erroneous from a scientific point of view, has been politically rewarding.

The Saint-Simonians begin with an antithesis between two types of social organization:

> One aims at conquest, or theft on a national scale, while the other seeks to produce as much as possible. The first is necessarily dominated by the military, the second by industrialists. In modern society industrialists must take the place of the military. (Jurists and philosophers constitute an intermediate class in every regime.) An industrialist is someone who works to produce or to place within the reach of various members of society one or several material products to satisfy their physical needs or desires. . . . Industrialists as a whole work to produce or to make accessible to all members of society all the material means for satisfying their physical needs and desires. They comprise three large classes: agriculturalists, manufacturers, and merchants.[1]

These brief illustrations serve to bring out both the simplicity of the topics dealt with by the Saint-Simonians and the ambiguity of their thought and vocabulary. Their analysis of the existing social hierarchy continued to be dominated by the concept of the orders, or classes, of the *ancien régime:* the nobility and the military, theologians, philosophers, and jurists; the industrial class. Within the industrial class, which comprises all producers, there are three sub-classes that correspond to three areas of activity – agriculture, industry in the narrow sense, and commerce. Within each of these sub-classes a technical and bureaucratic hierarchy develops which, according to the Saint-Simonians, is necessary and hence unassailable and which is capped by financiers whose authority rests upon their competence. The Saint-Simonians were not unaware of the exploitation of the working masses by those who dominated industry, but they never believed that conflicts within the industrial class were the mainspring of historical change. They never accepted the thesis that the conflict between the proprietors and managers of industry and the proletariat could be resolved only through a bloody revolution.

Marx's originality lay in his interpretation of class struggle in terms of ownership of the means of production. The legal distinctions between the orders had disappeared, but in his view

1. Saint-Simon, *Textes choisies, Catéchisme des industriels*, 1st cahier, Alcan, Paris, p. 155.

there was still an inherent conflict between the privileged groups and the wretched masses. Within the industrial world, he saw alienation and hostility between the possessors of the means of production and the proletarians as more pronounced than it had been between nobles and peasants. Marx found it tempting to establish a kind of parallelism between the old antagonism (aristocracy *v.* bourgeoisie) and the new (bourgeoisie *v.* working class). From this sprang the Marxist notion of a fourth estate replacing the third.

If the two antagonisms are similar in nature, why would they not have the same origin? The aristocracy was a closed class whereas the bourgeoisie is legally open; one is born an aristocrat, but one becomes a member of the middle class. However, both classes possess the means of production – land in the case of one, machinery or financial resources in the case of the other. Both owe their power and their privileges to the place they hold in the process of production, to the ownership of those instrumentalities that are required for the creation of wealth. A higher class thus occupies a position that enables it to organize the work of the proletariat and to collect and divide the surplus value.

Under this concept an eschatological perspective opens. Throughout history, societies based on private ownership of the means of production have been torn by class antagonisms. But if private property is the ultimate source of classes, one has only to suppress the first in order to eliminate the second. Centring his interpretation on the conflict between industry's offspring, the proletariat, and the possessors of the means of production, and making this conflict the focus of his polemics, Marx offered a new theory of class antagonisms in pre-industrial societies and announced the disappearance of classes in the socialist regime that was to come. In contrast, the Saint-Simonians remarked upon the originality of industrial society as such, a society whose goal was production rather than conquest (or theft on a national scale). But Karl Marx concentrated on the inner contradictions of industrial society, which he believed would be divided into classes so long as capitalism continued to prevail, with its private ownership of the means of production and unrestricted competition.

Now, a century after the publication of *Capital*, what is the verdict of history? Has modern society evolved in the direction of a class society or of a society without classes?

## The Social Strata

Industrial society – whether of the capitalist or Soviet variety – is *differentiated* and *stratified*. The first of these terms suggests the multiplication of occupations that accompanies the multiplication of products. The second brings to mind the indisputable fact that the members of society belong to strata that are more or less clearly delimited and that lie one above another. These social strata form a hierarchy; however questionable the judgements of individuals or the results of scientific inquiry may be, there can be no question that, from the point of view of prestige, income, and power, those who belong to the liberal professions rank above industrial workers.

This inherent tendency of industrial society toward differentiation and stratification is no longer open to doubt. The percentage of wage earners in the total working force is increasing in the West, but this increase is hardly the same thing as the proletarianization which was predicted by Marx. The proportion of industrial or manual workers is not increasing. It either remains constant or decreases, depending on the growth of the so-called third sector, made up of those who perform services (all the occupations apart from agriculture and manufacturing). Depending on the nature of the regime and on geographical factors, the distribution of the working force among the three sectors varies at an identical level of development (as measured by production per capita). But these secondary variations do not conceal what Marx would have called the *tendential laws* of social development: a decrease in the percentage of manual workers, a rapid reduction of the primary sector (especially of agricultural labour), and an increase in the number of non-manual workers. The more production becomes rationalized, the greater will be the attention devoted to organization, exchanges, studies, research – the whole intellectual underpinning of industry and commerce – as well as to the general costs of production itself.

But another mechanism is operating at the same time: working hours are decreasing and real income is increasing because of the increase in productivity. And as the standard of living goes up, there is an increase in the proportion of individual income which is spent for luxuries or near-luxuries – or at least for such non-material things as services, leisure-time activities, and culture. As the wealth of the community increases and more resources become available for education, the community finds it to its interest to promote the intellectual development of an ever-increasing number of young people.

The ultimate prerequisite of this social transformation, it has now become evident, is neither planning, nor free enterprise, nor the foresight of capitalists, nor the demands of unions; it is the increase in productivity, in the value created per unit of working time. This is due to a twofold rationalization – that of tools or machinery on the one hand and of organization on the other. To be sure, the kind of economic regime, free enterprise or socialism, free market or planning, affects the character and pace of development. But, whatever its speed and however costly in human suffering, this essential twofold rationalization has been achieved during the last century only in a third of the world – the United States, Western Europe, the British dominions, Japan, and (in part, at least) Eastern Europe. Only for a privileged minority of mankind has scientific and technical progress made possible a demographic revolution (the prolongation of human life) and the social revolution which the tendential laws express.

The capitalistic society Marx described as being on the eve of its final overthrow bears little resemblance to Western industrial society as it stands at the beginning of the final third of the twentieth century. There is a more complex stratification, not a simple polarization of two opposing classes. There has been an increase in the standard of living of the masses, not a reduction to pauperism. Proletarianization has indeed taken place – if this term means the transformation of independent producers into wage-earners – but these wage earners are not poverty-stricken, nor have they been reduced to the uniform condition of an oppressed working class. Many distinctions are being restored among the mass of wage earners. It requires blindness or an excess of faith to discern Marx's prophetic picture in the reality of North America or Western Europe today:

> With a decrease in the number of capitalists, who usurp and monopolize all the benefits of this era of social evolution, there will come an increase in poverty, oppression, slavery, degradation, and exploitation. Also, however, there will come increasing resistance by an ever-growing, more disciplined working-class, organized and united by the very mechanism of capitalistic production. Monopoly will become a shackle because of the form of production which has grown and prospered under its auspices. The socialization of labour and the centralization of its material mainsprings will reach a point where they can no longer be contained within their capitalistic mould. This mould will shatter. The knell has already sounded for capitalistic property. The expropriators are now to be expropriated.[2]

Must it then be said that history has rendered its verdict, that it corroborates Saint-Simonism and refutes Marxism? Has the industrial class, after eliminating the military and the theologians, taken the dominant position? Has that class not become the whole of society, differentiated according to areas of economic activity, arranged hierarchically according to ability, but in no way torn apart by irreducible antagonisms? Such a conclusion would be premature.

## The Fact of Stratification

An analysis of the evident and essential fact of stratification may well begin with the industrial workers, who suggested to Marx his theory of classes. In every country there are among workers certain common ways of thinking and living, common attitudes related to the work they do and to their status in the factory and at home. A prime task of objective sociological study has been to determine the degree of homogeneity to be found within the stratum formed by industrial workers and the differences among them which result from their origin, the size of the industry, the nature of the work, etc. Apart from these basic studies there have developed four separate criteria for distinguishing the class stratum: (1) *The psychosocial cohesiveness of the stratum.* (How

2. *Capital*, Bk. I, ch. 32.

many workers live in the same way and have the same outlook toward society? How marked is this common feature?) (2) *Continuity from generation to generation.* (What is the degree of inequality at the start among children from different strata?)[3] (3) *The individual's awareness of belonging to a certain stratum* and the value he attaches to this affiliation. (Does the French worker, for example, regard his belonging to the working class as something higher than belonging to the French nation?) (4) *The self-awareness of the stratum* in relation to other strata and the recognition of a common task. On this last point Tocqueville as well as Marx can be cited. Tocqueville recalls for us the bourgeois who in the early days of the Revolution initially thought of himself as a member of the Third Estate and only later as an individual. Marx, in a well-known passage in *The 18th Brumaire of Louis Napoleon*, insists that despite their common condition, peasants do not constitute a class because they cannot achieve awareness of a common interest and fight for it on a national scale. Under his dictum a stratum becomes a class by achieving a political and, above all, a revolutionary awareness of itself.

Whichever of these four criteria one utilizes, it would hardly be legitimate to draw from the tendential laws of social evolution the conclusion that classes have disappeared. Under the criteria we have discussed, classes do exist more or less. The operation of the tendential laws weakens the reality of classes in many ways, but so long as social stratification exists (and it appears to be inseparable from industrial society), an interpretation in terms of classes will always be possible.

Class distinctions are weakened both by increasing heterogeneity within vast aggregations of men (e.g. industrial workers), which alone can properly be called classes, and by the homogeneity of a mode of living or consuming that is characteristic of the petty or middle bourgeoisie, whose ranks are being swelled by a growing number of families. In the mid 1960s, nearly half of all families in the United States had an annual income in excess of $6,000, which by any reckoning is well above the subsistence

3. Continuity in this sense is inversely related to ascending or descending mobility.

level. Even if relative inequality (as measured, for example, by the portion of the total income received by the top five per cent of the wealthiest taxpayers) has not been changed appreciably, the general increase in wealth has narrowed the gap between different modes of living. If the basic needs (food, clothing, shelter, and durable goods) are provided in an approximately similar way, what real difference is made by great fortunes or huge incomes, the latter partly recovered for public purposes through taxation?

Similarly, however imprecise statistics on social mobility may be, the trend is unquestionable. The higher school-leaving age for all children and the growing proportion of young people who attend secondary schools are certain indicators. The more society spends on educating its youth the less likely they are to remain confined to the environment from which they have sprung.

This weakening of class structure in the first two senses probably results in a comparable weakening in the other two. A person identifies himself all the more firmly with a special grouping if his personal welfare appears to be tied up with the welfare of that group. The possibility of bettering his own situation – or at least the increased opportunity to improve the prospects of his children – tends to loosen the ties that bind him to a huge socio-occupational stratum, even if this entails creating new ties to other groups which have a voluntary character or provide a political or ideological attraction. Thus when both the collective advancement of the strata and the perhaps even more rapid advancement of the individual appear possible within the framework of the existing regime, the vision of a deadly struggle in which one class is bound to win and the other to perish becomes less plausible and less attractive.

In short, most contemporary observers see social evolution as moving towards less heterogeneity between one stratum and another, hence towards less homogeneity within each stratum; towards less inequality in education, hence towards a greater degree of ascending social mobility; towards less solidarity within the strata, hence towards a decreasing penchant for an apocalyptic interpretation of the class struggle and the movement of history.

This second analysis confirms the first. In whatever sense the idea of class is understood, an industrial society does not tend toward the model of a *class* society. We must beware, however, of repeating Marx's mistake. It would be too easy to be satisfied with the tendential laws of social evolution. In fact, these laws, if correctly understood, reveal the gap between the egalitarian ideal and present-day realities in even the most advanced industrial societies.

## The Tendential Laws

The ideal of industrial society does not, of course, imply absolute equality of income. But, to judge by the virtually universal acceptance of the principle of a progressive income tax, there would appear to be a general desire to reduce economic inequalities, even when the upper range of incomes seems justified by ability or services performed. While conceding that inequality as such, even as reflected by the highest incomes, is not necessarily incompatible with the ideal of modern society, that ideal does condemn one form of inequality: the destitution of some at a time when the wealth of the community makes it possible to provide everyone with the minimum income required for what society regards as a decent standard of living. That ideal also calls in question the transmission of privileges, whether through the inheritance of wealth or through those advantages that children of the upper strata enjoy from the beginning. Now, it is a fact that destitution has not yet disappeared in the United States, which has the most fully developed industrial society. There is still great inequality of educational opportunity in Western Europe, where the percentage of children of industrial and agricultural workers in the universities is very low.

The racial heterogeneity of the American people is partly responsible for the existence of what has been called 'the other America' – the America of unemployed Negroes, of aged people deprived of security and essential services, of farmers whose holdings are too small to provide an adequate income, of industries and entire regions where the economic pace has slowed down or has been redirected by technological development in a way that produces endemic poverty. Remedies for some of these evils may be found in social legislation. But the sudden awareness of poverty in the midst of plenty is particularly interesting, because it illustrates the dialectic between the technological society and the egalitarian ideal.

In 1965 U.S. statisticians fixed $3,000 per person per year as the dividing line of poverty. As the general standard of living rises, they will tend to move this line upward. So long as poverty is defined not absolutely but in relation to a social minimum that increases with the increase in wealth, poverty is likely to be perpetuated in any regime where the distribution of income is determined by the output of work. From one point of view, poverty shocks the public because society is both wealthy and desirous of being egalitarian.

Moreover, there exists in the United States a form of absolute poverty – the poverty of black ghettoes, of young Negroes who are illiterate and who until recent years have been denied by racial prejudice effective access to all but the most menial employment. The existence of this conspicuous blight in an affluent society reveals a contradiction that must continually be overcome by social and economic reform. As the apparatus of production becomes increasingly rationalized, it requires workers who are more and more skilled. The accelerating development of technology, which rapidly makes entire occupations obsolete, requires retraining and thereby throws out of employment those workers who are least able to adapt themselves to some different and perhaps more highly skilled job. The very nature of technological society forces the weaker members to pay a disproportionate part of the cost of social progress. Can it be otherwise so long as wages are based on ability and not on need – and so long as society merely endeavours to alleviate the suffering of the victims?

This question would not be so sharp if personal abilities could be seen as the product of personal achievement. But do not most of those who hold the higher positions, which are the best paid and the most prestigious, hold them by virtue of birth in fortunate circumstances? The reference here is not to the more conspicuous forms of inheritance: of money (which taxation has reduced but has not eliminated) and of control of business enterprises (the

Ford and Rockefeller dynasties do exist and were not invented by the Communists). But even families of modest means seem to endow children of the upper strata with superior abilities to absorb the knowledge required by modern society. Sociologists have found that inequalities in education are not eliminated by merely opening the doors of secondary schools and universities to the children of the lower strata of society.

These inequalities have two main causes. The first is institutional in character. In most countries, such as the United States, Great Britain, and France, children belonging to the privileged groups have a better chance of entering the better schools which prepare them to continue later their studies in the universities. This educational inequality seems to be more marked in Great Britain, with its 'public schools', than in continental countries where, as in France, the best institutions are operated by the state and are free. But even in France the children of farmers or workers more often find their way into terminal institutions and technical schools than into the *lycées* (which correspond to the English 'grammar schools'). This kind of educational selection, which occurs when the student is between ten and twelve years old, lessens the likelihood that higher education will be available to the children of families in modest circumstances.

Institutional inequality of this kind is the most obvious, but perhaps not the most serious. Academic achievement reflects certain aptitudes which depend upon the total family environment of young children; it does not measure their natural aptitudes. Failure or success in school, then, depends in large part on social origin and family background. Thus, merely to put all children in the same schools at the outset of their education would not bring about an equal representation of the various social strata in the student population at the higher levels. Without special assistance many children from the lower strata could not overcome handicaps resulting from the disparity between the culture of the family and that of the university circles they seek to enter.

It may be objected that the rush of young people towards secondary education is something too recent (in Europe, at least) to permit any categorical judgement of the efficacy of institutional reforms alone. I do not deny this. But experience as well as reason supports one piece of evidence: the results of scholastic aptitude tests depend, and will continue to depend, on the family background of the student. Selection is thus made on the basis of the family's social impact on the child, not on the basis of what the accident of genetic inheritance has produced. In all probability the proportion of children who are mentally well endowed is the same in the strata of workers as in those of the middle class, although in the present state of our knowledge this cannot be either affirmed or denied categorically. But the proportion may not seem the same when it comes to selection for schooling, since family environment affects the development of aptitudes. To have equality at the start, a quasi-equality of living conditions in the different strata would be required. Inasmuch as the strata are distinct, however, such inequalities tend to persist more or less from one generation to the next.

At the present time the stability of these social strata is so marked that there is no cause for concern over the possible consequences of excessive mobility. But it should be remembered that movement upward in the social scale appears to be an unqualified good only if it does not bring with it a corresponding downward mobility – in other words, only if economic growth continues to increase the percentage of skilled occupations and makes it possible to accord a higher status to those who pursue these occupations. Moreover, if it is in the interest of society not to allow those who are highly gifted to be lost, it is at the same time a matter of indifference from society's point of view that among those of mediocre abilities, who probably form the greatest number, the children belonging to the upper strata have greater advantages than those of the lower strata. It is the intellectuals, and only incidentally the politicians, who are led by the ideal of equality to denounce these discrepancies and to propose radical measures for diminishing them – measures whose effectiveness is uncertain and, in any case, not immediate.

Finally, should we not keep in mind that the elimination of social chance would surrender the process of selection to genetic chance alone? Genetic chance is accepted today because it is, at least provisionally, uninfluenced by human decision. But if position in society were directly related to the aptitudes written upon the germ cells, another objection would arise: why not contend against natural inequalities? In Rousseau's words, why not strive toward equality with an energy that matches nature's opposition to it? Why not devote more attention to those who are less well endowed? Why not reward moral merit rather than ability or accomplishment? Then, some day, genetic chance might cease to be more sacred than social chance.

Let us put aside these reveries and, against the fanatical egalitarians, try to rid the concept of inheritance of pejorative connotations. How inhuman society would be if fortunate families and persons who had accomplished something were unable to pass anything of value on to their offspring! Giving opportunity to those who were born under adverse conditions should not entail destruction of the continuity necessary to safeguard human values which, however useless they may seem to be for technological efficiency, may turn out to be infinitely precious in a society changing faster than any mankind has ever known.

## The Revolutionary Outlook

Men's attitudes are not strictly determined by the objective situation. It is probable that social evolution will lead to a weakening not only of class consciousness but also of the revolutionary outlook that is part of this class consciousness. As the final third of the twentieth century begins, experience in most of the developed countries suggests that semi-peaceful competition among social groupings is gradually taking the place of the so-called deadly struggle in which one class was assumed to eliminate the other.

This general trend, however, gives no ground for a categorical prediction of the future. Consciousness and purpose are the human response to historical circumstances, and their manifestations in relation to class may not disappear merely because various strata of society are losing their cohesiveness and becoming like one another in their mode of living. In any case, such consciousness and purpose reside in a political party rather than in the class as a whole.

Moreover, observers sometimes confuse the ceaseless disagreements among social categories (trade associations, pressure groups, parties) with the Marxist class struggle. These differences are normal and essential in a free industrial society. Since technology requires a hierarchy, and since the social ideal demands a reduction of inequalities, a dialogue among groups, rather than among individuals, is the democratic way to resolve the antinomy. So long as the hope of equality is far from being realized, the disparity between lower and higher incomes remains great, the victims of progress are many, and relative wealth still means poverty for a great number. Reformist criticism, an active force in every democratic industrial society, may under certain circumstances pass once again into radical criticism, the kind incarnated in the proletariat and expressed theoretically in philosophy.

The choice between reformist criticism, which is always at work within Western society, and radical criticism, which the Marxist or Marxist-Leninist parties strive to keep alive, will depend upon future economic and social developments in the West. It will also depend on the dialogue between the West on one side and the Communist world and the Third World on the other.

The societies which call themselves socialist (and which by the outside world are called Soviet) have for the last twenty years confirmed Western reformers in their rejection of revolution. Marxism is a doctrine of collective salvation through the victory of the downtrodden (the proletariat) and the defeat of the proud and mighty (the owners of the means of production). Beyond revenge for the humble it promises freedom for everyone in a classless society. Monopolized by one state, however, the Communist ideal has been suspected of concealing a foreign nationalism behind a verbal universalism. It has failed to maintain the prestige of a message addressed to all of humanity, and despite dissociation of the Soviet bloc of states, it has not been able to regain its utopian innocence.

Moreover, the will to stage a revolution is at full strength only when it is directed towards an unknown future. The formula of Marxism-Leninism is in the process of being achieved in a number of countries; it is no longer the future but the present. Spatial distance is less important than temporal. Awaiting the final phase of Communism – 'to each according to his needs' – socialism, as it is being currently achieved, is not purged of the shortcomings which radical criticism denounced and still denounces. Exploitation and servitude have not miraculously disappeared along with private ownership of the means of production. So-called socialist society is no less differentiated and stratified than capitalistic society; it is merely differentiated and stratified in a different way.

## Soviet Stratification

In order to maintain the fiction that control of the means of production determines the relation of classes, official Soviet sociologists make a distinction between the working class, for whom the means of production have been collectivized, and the *Kolkhozians* (collective farmers), whose means of production are owned by cooperatives. To these two classes they add a stratum, the intelligentsia, that includes all the cadres of industry, commerce, and governmental administration. This theory is self-refuting. The intelligentsia is not identical with the working class even though it owns none of the means of production. As for the difference between the industrial workers and the Kolkhozians, it does not rest exclusively on the legal nature of property, whether state-owned or held cooperatively. This difference will be erased only when agricultural labour has been completely industrialized and the two worlds of city and countryside have become one.

Soviet theorists ought logically to adopt the ideas of the Saint-Simonians and include in the industrial class all workers, not excepting technicians, engineers, scientists, doctors, artists, government officials, etc. Indeed they may be headed in this direction, for they have introduced, along with the idea that classes need not be antagonistic to each other (an idea which is incompatible with the Marxist doctrine that if there are classes they are enemies), the concept of a state no longer 'of workers and peasants' but of 'the people as a whole'. Now in power, these Marxist-Leninists, former revolutionaries whose victory has turned them into defenders of the faith, have been rediscovering all by themselves the old conservative themes: the cult of national unity and the condemnation of individuals or groups who threaten to impair that unity.

To be sure, the Soviet society which the successors of the 1917 revolutionaries wish to preserve differs in many respects from Western society. Although differentiation among occupations, technical and administrative hierarchies, and inequalities of income are to be found, Soviet society does not know those enormous concentrations of wealth which private ownership of the means of production makes possible. There is nothing there corresponding to stocks and shares, capital gains, or speculative profits. However, the inequalities of income are almost comparable to the inequalities in wages and salaries in large business enterprises or governments of the West. In the interest of efficiency Soviet society may perhaps be led to restore some form of the profit system to create new incentives for the managerial personnel. Even so, in all probability the distribution of labour will not be the same in Eastern and Western Europe, even if the rate of development is the same. The Marxist-Leninist regimes have a primary concern with material production (according to Marx only manual labour is really labour), while Western regimes assign a larger part of the labour force to non-productive occupations – especially to distribution.

Whatever the actual disparities may be with respect to differentiation among occupations, social stratification, and inequalities of income, they are not of the essence of the matter. The fact that there are other forms of stratification does not provide an argument of sufficient weight to support the Soviet theorists in contrasting a classless society with a class society. We must consider again the four criteria by which we distinguished classes from strata in society: (1) *the degree of cohesiveness;* (2) *continuity from generation to generation;* (3) *the individual's feeling of belonging;* (4) *awareness of a common purpose.*

The first can be disposed of at once. Assuming the same rate of development, strata in Soviet society will not necessarily be either more or less homogeneous than those in Western societies. The planners will perhaps attempt to limit all consumers to the same kinds of goods and thereby try to reduce to a minimum disparities in standards of living. But so far their efforts have proved futile: a disparity of income in the ratio of 1:10 or 1:20 immediately results in a corresponding disparity in living standards.

The three other criteria pose some basic problems. The first may be formulated as follows: Does the technological and administrative hierarchy represent ability in a Soviet society? In a Western society is this same hierarchy the crystallization of differences based on inherited social status and only imperfectly rectified by the ascending mobility of the best-endowed children from the lower strata? It is difficult to give a categorical answer, since there has been no objective research of the kind which would make it possible to compare the continuity of social strata from one generation to another in both kinds of society.

During the years immediately following a revolution the new regime has no choice but to recruit from among the masses those young people who are to be given the advantage of secondary and higher education and who will thus come to occupy the more important administrative positions in the new regime. But one would have to know whether and to what extent this upward mobility, made necessary and inevitable by the revolution itself, diminishes as the regime becomes stabilized. Official statistics show that the higher strata of Soviet society – the intelligentsia, who represent fifteen to twenty per cent of the whole working force – are represented more than proportionally, in the neighbourhood of fifty per cent, among students receiving higher instruction. These figures are admittedly dubious, and in any event, it does appear that the percentage of children from working-class and peasant families admitted to the universities is higher in the Soviet countries than in the West – at least in Europe. But this point should be prudently interpreted in view of the uncertainty of both the figures and the statistical categories, and in the light of evidence that indicates that here, as elsewhere, the nature of man and society has produced the rapid re-establishment of an inequality in education. This results from the inevitable and desirable transmission to one's children of those incalculable spiritual advantages which a favourable cultural climate and a happy family bestow, and it apparently has not been offset by a regimentation of society that stops short of disbanding the family unit.

Beyond the Soviet intelligentsia there are at the very top of the social structure thousands of key officials, leaders in the higher echelons of the party, scientists, technicians, artists, and heads of corporations – the oligarchs of the Soviet regime, who correspond to the elite (ruling classes) of Western society. In which society do the oligarchs most often and completely owe their position to their own merit ? If we exclude the cases in which managers in the West are also owners of enterprises by inheritance, and these are becoming less and less typical, in both systems the rise towards the higher echelons of business, public administration, the army, science, or art, operates according to the same theoretical principles of merit (or ability). A scientific technological society dominated by an administrative hierarchy is theoretically a 'meritocracy'. That, at least is its goal. To some degree it must be its practice, since it is in the best material interest of such a society, as well as in the interest of justice, to assign the most important tasks, which are usually the most prestigious and best paid, to those who are the most competent. Neither Eastern nor Western society completely achieves the ideal of 'meritocracy' for the simple reason that neither has an infallible method of selection. Those with know-how are not always able to impart it and the most gifted for social promotion are not always the most worthy of great responsibility. It is axiomatic that war alone reveals a general's true worth; the equivalent of combat, that stern and almost infallible judge, does not always exist in more peaceful pursuits.

There is, however, more than a shade of difference between the two 'meritocracies'. Nonconformists fare better in the West; bureaucratic wire-pulling fares better in the East. A pluralistic society, by definition, offers more opportunities and above all a wider range of choice to the ambitious. The less society merges with the state the less is success dependent on the whim of those in power. In the West a man alone, with no other resources than his pen and his talent, is not condemned to silence by official repudiation. A citizen opposed to the 'establishment' is not thereby outlawed, and can still be heard.

But perhaps that which most clearly reveals the essential difference is the attitude toward class consciousness and purpose. Let us assume that a socio-occupational category becomes a class to the extent that its members are aware of belonging to it and think of themselves as forming a kind of unit as compared to other similarly unified categories. In Soviet society no class so defined (and this definition is suggested by the passage from Marx to which we have already referred) exists or can exist. The Kolkhozians think of themselves as Kolkhozians in contrast to the Kolkhoz general staff as well as to city dwellers in general or industrial workers in particular. Similarly the workers use the terms 'we' and 'they' in breaking down the socio-occupational category in which they belong. 'They' are the directors and the administration of the industrial establishment, as well as the functionaries of the state and other privileged people – 'the others' as distinguished from 'us workers'. But none of these 'we's', none of these strata, is in a position to express itself, to organize on a national scale and confront other strata. In the mid nineteenth century, according to Marx, the French peasants were incapable of becoming an organized class because they were so scattered and so immature politically. The Kolkhozians and the Russian workers are being made incapable of such organization by the Soviet regime itself, at least for as long as the party keeps its monopoly on ideology and communication and forbids the formation of any groups besides itself. In this sense it is true that in our era only *a class society is a free society*. Since every industrial society is stratified, conflicts between occupational organizations with some degree of class consciousness can be suppressed only by despotism.

It may be objected that as soon as the means of production have become the property of the state – of society as a whole – the reasons for the existence of classes with their antagonisms will have been eliminated. But this objection has no validity. The Kolkhozians have not been converted to the idea of collective ownership; the higher productivity achieved on the remaining individual plots of land is the best proof of it. To be sure, if the peasants accepted collective ownership, the regime could no longer be called in question in the same way, but the state's decisions on the distribution of revenue and subventions, on the amounts to be earmarked for investment and consumers' goods, would be open to challenge. In both East and West, the interests of the social strata may well be as opposed over a short term as they are interdependent in the longer run. While all the social strata profit ultimately from economic growth, they do not do so at the same time or to the same extent. When private ownership of the means of production has been done away with, the problems attendant on this condition remain, although the mechanics of allocating revenue are simplified. The basic issues can be stated simply: What part of the collective wealth should be assigned respectively to investment and to public consumption? What would be a fair scale of incomes? On which sector should the state concentrate its main efforts? These questions are now raised, debated, and resolved in the secrecy of the Kremlin. If social groups within the Soviet Union were allowed to organize, their representatives would be participating actively in the discussions and the dialogue probably would not be intrinsically different from that in the West. In no industrial society can conflicts of this nature be avoided; they can only be prevented from becoming open.

It is Marxism-Leninism which fosters the illusion, and, in part, the reality, of a basic difference between classes and their antagonisms. The revolutionary doctrine also attempts to confuse conflicts among social groups, unavoidable in a free industrial society, with the classic mortal struggle of class against class. It succeeds when it persuades those who represent the lower strata that private property involves exploitation of the majority and prevents any progressive improvement in the lot of all. Moreover, the doctrine permits Soviet leaders in good conscience to identify the class with the Party, the Party with the state, and the state with the Presidium (or Central Committee). It assures them there is no class antagonism when the Bolsheviks are in power, and that, in the limiting case of a socialist regime, contradictions cease to be contradictory.

Marxism-Leninism represents not a self-fulfilling prophecy but a self-verifying theory. Yet it cannot be said that the theory has finally moulded the world by transforming its own mistakes into truths through the agency of those who believe in it. Western society is coming less and less to resemble the class society pictured in the Marxist blueprint. And Marxist-Leninist society resembles less and less the ideal of a homogeneous, classless, and harmonious society. But, while the tendential laws of social evolution continue to thwart the Marxist-Leninist ideology here and there, they have not gone so far as to put an end to the double role of this ideology: the self-justification of the Soviet regime, and the corollary denunciation of Western regimes. So long as the ideological dialectic continues, the social order itself will remain ambiguous, now resembling one model and now another.

## The Underdeveloped Countries

The social order of the so-called underdeveloped countries is more nearly like that of the Marxist model (at least as depicted theoretically by Marxism-Leninism) than like that of the modern industrial state. There is a small and close-knit privileged stratum made up of landed proprietors and the leaders of industry, a clear separation between social and occupational groups, destitution among the exploited masses, who realize only vaguely that they are being exploited. The phenomena that impressed Marx during the first half of the nineteenth century, when he synthesized the socialist ideas of the era, can still be seen in one form or another in the countries of Asia and Latin America. The intellectuals of the Third World have borrowed from Marxism's basic arguments to justify their revolutionary intentions. They regard it as their duty to awaken a historical consciousness in landless agricultural labourers, and in industrial workers who have no other resource than the strength of their backs. In these countries, a more or less mythical proletariat may still be visible as the heart of the revolution for which philosophy provides a head. Some Western intellectuals, stripped of their messianic hope by the relative affluence of capitalism, look with nostalgia towards those distant lands which the modern world has already thrown into confusion but has so far failed to enrich.

But surely, from a rational point of view, to substitute antagonism between developed and underdeveloped countries for antagonism between bourgeoisie and proletariat is to refute not only the thesis of the pauperization of the working class but the whole theory of which this thesis forms but a part. The standard of living of the masses in the modern world is no longer determined by the kind of regime but by the level of development as measured in production per capita. A comparison between the living standard of the 'exploited' proletariat in the United States and that of the 'free' proletariat in the Soviet Union provides evidence of this. Nevertheless, it is commonplace for African, Asian, and Latin-American intellectuals to attempt to understand the world of today in terms of the concept of classes and class societies.

Because colonial empires were established by European powers, it is spiritually comforting for these intellectuals to attribute the poverty of their own people and the wealth of their former masters to capitalist exploitation. Since the United States has had scarcely any colonies, to make the indictment complete it is necessary to expand the ordinary meaning of exploitation to include not only the activities of large operating companies (without any seizure of sovereignty) but even foreign investments in local enterprises. Thus transferred to the international sphere, the class struggle – between the privileged have nations and the proletarian have-not nations – seems once again to require a new social order. This transference is logical only to the degree that humanity tends to constitute a single society. A new antinomy thus appears: Do not the European and American proletarians who benefit from the exploitation of the coloured masses have closer ties with their own countries than with their 'brothers' in Africa and Asia? The more society takes on a world-wide character, the more the proletarians become nationalized. Such is the penalty of unequal development.

The Soviet Union's message no longer stirs the mass of the workers in Western Europe and North America, for whom economic progress under a reformed capitalism has provided the expanding benefits of the welfare state, a steadily rising standard of living, relative security in employment, and the protection of free labour unions. In France and Italy, however, the parties which claim kinship with the Soviet Union are still powerful, either because of the heavy hand of the past, because men have not given up the hope of revolution, or because of the discrepancy between their ideal hopes and the actual gains achieved. If the Soviet Union's message still has some attraction, even in Europe, why should it be surprising that among Chinese and Cubans it seems to have regained its original freshness and irresistible eloquence?

The Soviet Union, by its own efforts, has risen to the highest or second highest rank in technology and military power. In view of its success as a socialist society, of what matter is the price that was paid – the deportation of the Kulaks, or the great purge, or the other crimes committed in the era of 'the cult of personality'? The new states are eager to forge their future, and they see the quickest route to modernity passing through the stage of collective greatness before culminating in material well-being.

These confused and profound sentiments are expressed easily enough in the language of the contemporary social sciences. The Bolsheviks thought they were establishing a regime to take the place of capitalism, but they discovered something quite different: a technique of progress for peoples who must or would skip the intermediate stages between a primitive economy and a modern industrial society. Whether identified with the proletariat or not, the Party performed the function of the entrepreneurs and did away with the former privileged classes who provided the means of accumulating capital and organizing skills. The revolution enlisted the masses and imposed forced savings, making a virtue of deprivation and overcoming inadequate techniques with the sheer weight of manpower. Why should the leaders of the Third World hesitate to justify what they were doing in terms of Marxist-Leninist theory, when so many Western reformers, filled with idealism, urged them in guarded language not to be hampered by liberal scruples but to subordinate everything to the urgent needs of progress?

Many governments of the new states prefer to call *building socialism* what appears to the Western observer as a strategy of development by planning under a one-party regime. Marxism-Leninism will continue to enlist recruits during the last third of this century. These proselytes will know little enough of Marx himself, and they are not likely to be capable of reconstituting

Communist unity on a global scale. On the contrary, the trend for all forms of communism is more or less nationalistic. But do gospels of salvation ever become widespread without schisms or heresy? The fragmentation of the universal church actually furthered the propagation of the faith. So all these frequently antagonistic parties will use the same words – class and class struggle, imperialism and socialism – and thus the doctrine of a class society will remain an integral part of the awareness that societies of the second half of the century will have of themselves. If it is a false awareness, a mythological one in certain respects, it is nonetheless effective. We need only to interpret the Marxist-Leninist ideology by the method which Marx himself taught us in order to understand how the combined expressions 'false awareness' and 'effective awareness' appear in their true light, in conformity with the experience of a century. Men have always created history in the name of ideas, but the history they have created has never faithfully reflected their ideas.

## The Immanent Laws

By means of technological progress and economic growth, an industrial society evolves spontaneously according to certain immanent laws. Its progress does not obliterate socio-professional distinctions nor a hierarchy of income, prestige, and authority. But it does narrow the gap between the various strata of society and blurs the boundaries between classes; it swells the ranks of the upper and middle classes and enables the majority of the population to satisfy its basic needs in an almost similar manner. Social unrest is a constant, but overt sustained violence tends to decrease. Conflicts are never eliminated but revolution seems anachronistic. The economic system, whether capitalistic or socialist, is consolidated by changes to both systems. Such are the tendencies viewed objectively. But the consciences of men are not determined thereby. The reaction to objective tendencies is influenced in each country by the stage of its development, its history, and by the peculiarities of its culture.

Democratic industrial societies, essentially lacking a common faith, whether religious or ideological, will continue to disappoint those who contrast them with the ideal image, an ideal which seems to recede just as one draws nearer. Equality in income or even affluence for all will be a mirage, an unattainable objective, for some time to come, for as one travels the road of progress the definition of one's goal changes.

Reality, too, is disappointing, perhaps even more so in the Soviet society, but the disappointment is not overtly expressed. Thanks to ideology, rulers identify themselves mystically with those whom they rule.

If the economic and social ideology of the Soviet system is a weapon against Western regimes in the Cold War, Western political ideology performs the same function against Marxist-Leninist states. Marxism-Leninism claims to unmask the class struggle concealed under the veil of democracy in the West while the Western regimes unmask the absolutism of totalitarianism concealed beneath the fiction of a society devoid of class antagonisms. Perhaps both will be arraigned by the spokesmen of the poor nations which, whatever system they adhere to, have still to discover the contradictions inherent in modern society, to say nothing of the disillusions of a never-attained affluence.

# 2   The Rulers and the Ruled

The Marxist theory of social classes was introduced during the transitional phase between the fall of the *ancien régime* and the rise of industrial society, when the privileged groups seemed to re-establish the equivalent of the legally suppressed orders. A more modern theory of the ruling class dates from the end of the last century, when Gaetano Mosca and Vilfredo Pareto subjected the practices of parliamentary democracy and the theories of socialist utopia to merciless criticism.

In one sense this modern theory represents a return to the primary sources of political thought. To the Greek philosophers there was no contrast so great as that between rulers and ruled – so few of the one, so many of the other. In the history of ideas, however, the concepts of 'political class', 'the elite', 'the ruling class', as defined and used by the two Italian sociologists, nonetheless constitute a new departure. They have served and continue to serve as weapons against ideologies of both the right and the left. Their neo-Machiavellianism attacks and unmasks with equal indifference all the parties in power and every established regime. The theory is damned east and west of the iron curtain; it follows an Italian tradition that takes its name from a political theorist who is both glorified and dishonoured. With their analysis devoid of illusions about social reality and their emphasis on the essential fact of the struggle for power, the neo-Machiavellians found easy targets in Italy and among the ideologues of bourgeois Europe in general. Italian parliamentarism of the last century mirrored the permanence of a political class based on the clandestine alliance between the elect, the great families, and the leaders of finance and industry. The slogans of popular sovreignty or of a classless society at once concealed and justified the effort of these privileged minorities to keep or gain control of the state.

Pareto did often refer to Marxism as if to take up the theory of the class struggle, only to turn the argument against the victorious socialists when they came to power. In fact he parted company with the Marxist doctrine of his day on one decisive point, namely the relation between society and state, social groups, and power elite. Marx held that the class struggle is both economic and political; the class that owns the means of production is thereby master of the state, either directly or through intermediaries. The neo-Machiavellians in developing their central theme of power of the few over the masses saw ownership of the means of production as only one among several possible bases for the rule of those whom Mosca calls 'the political class' and Pareto 'the elite'.

The Machiavellians contrast a twofold permanence (that of the leaders in any given collective activity and that of political power in a given regime) to the illusion of self-government and a stateless society. The idea of self-government is shared by democrats and socialists alike, although the latter see the necessity of postponing its realization until after the revolution. The notion of a society served by a pure and simple administration devoid of political personnel is shared by the Saint-Simonians and the Marxists, as well as by the technocrats of every country and sect.

Machiavellian criticism, according to Pareto's version of it, possesses features which supporters and opponents alike tend to confuse, although they are not bound together logically. The first is the affirmation of the *oligarchic fact* in the whole society as well as in every subsystem: always and everywhere the few possess power over their fellows out of all proportion to their numbers and usually to their deserts. Decisions affecting the lot of everyone are made by a small number of men – sometimes by only one. The second feature is the hypothesis that the few who command the many form a relatively coherent minority, intent above all on acquiring certain material and moral advantages. This minority imposes its will by force or guile, more often by a combination of both, the proportion depending on the nature of the regime. All ruling minorities justify their rule by a *formula* (Mosca) or by *derivations* (Pareto).

The oligarchical fact, together with the hypothesis of a single ruling class, lends itself to a cyclical interpretation of history as 'the graveyard of aristocracies'. The ruling class is weakened by high living or by death on the battlefields, or both; other minorities whose vigour is unimpaired, and who are near enough to the top to have hopes of reaching it, drive out those who hold power until their will to rule is sapped by their love of pleasure, their scepticism, or their humanitarianism. The formula may change, but not the underlying reality: the inevitable clash between a ruling minority and the passive, manipulated masses.

The oligarchical fact implies neither the hypothesis of *one* united ruling class, nor the cyclical interpretation of history, nor yet the negation of historical change. The neo-Machiavellians tend at times toward a common form of cynicism, but the doctrine itself, when properly understood, limits itself to stressing the contrasts between the *formula* (popular sovereignty, dictatorship of the proletariat) and the *reality* (representative government, the single-party system). It does not necessarily infer that these regimes are of equal worth or that the formulas are devoid of significance or influence.

Pareto applied his theory to expose the plutocratic make-up of the French and Italian parliamentary systems of his time. According to his analysis, both the Third Republic and the regime in Italy, dominated by descendants of the aristocracy joined with financiers and industrialists, provided paradises for speculators under the cover of democratic procedures and verbiage. This was bound to be temporary, however, since the excessive influence of the 'foxes' and the cowardice, blindness, or hypocrisy of the bourgeois made the coming of the 'lions' inevitable.

Similar arguments have been brought against Communist regimes. The millions of industrial workers who constitute the proletariat clearly do not rule. Between the omnipotence of the proletariat (the Soviet formula) and the impotence of the working class (the Soviet reality) there is a wider gulf than that between the fiction of popular sovereignty and the reality of plutocracy. The Italian fascists were able to cite Pareto in self-justification, and Pareto himself certainly would have found in the rise of Fascism, National Socialism, and Bolshevism a confirmation of his own prophecies – which does not, of course, imply the fulfilment of his desires. In each case the lions took over from the foxes and a new cycle began.

It is not our task here to choose between regimes and ideologies but rather to perceive behind the polemics of political debates the various forms assumed by oligarchy in typically industrialized societies. Neo-Machiavellian theory is confirmed by the everyday experience that demonstrates that the administration of things does not take the place of the government of people, although the one is every bit as important in the social order as the other. Government today must, as it always has, manage the external affairs of the collectivity, arbitrate conflicts between interest groups, establish rules according to which individuals may compete, maintain public order, and safeguard the interest of the nation. Those who govern make decisions affecting the lives of everyone (peace or war); a few make these decisions *in the name of all*. Every society develops a system which determines the method by which these few are chosen, and the way in which they exercise power.

The originality of industrial societies does not reside in the permanence of a political subsystem, but in the differentiation of the ruling hierarchies. In Western societies the same men do not control public administration and private enterprise; legislators and public officials are for the most part professional politicians. Scholars, artists, writers, professors, are all christened intellectuals and consider themselves dependent in their own activities solely upon the judgement of their peers; officials of trade unions do not obey the captains of industry; priests neither command nor obey the scholars or the political rulers. In short, the apparently characteristic order of Western industrial society consists of a dissociation of powers. Temporal authority is shared by business leaders, politicians, popular leaders, and military commanders; spiritual authority by theologians, intellectuals, and ideologues. The primary datum, then, is the plurality of ruling minorities, a plurality that permits objective comparisons of the various regimes.

## The Leading Roles

There are certain leading roles to be performed in any industrial society, and consequently the same kinds of men appear to perform them. According to Saint-Simonian doctrine, productive labour is the primordial activity; organized within the framework of an enterprise, it requires competent leaders from foreman to general manager and continuing through the various echelons of the technical or administrative bureaucracy. At the higher level of the state, regulations must be promulgated or decisions made from day to day, no matter how much weight is given to planning or to operation of the free market. In the Soviet Union, managers of enterprises and political administrators constitute a single corps. In the West, where most businesses are not the property of the state, business and government administrators are selected in a different manner and do not go through the same mill, although movement back and forth from private to public life is becoming more common even in countries still regarded as capitalistic.

Whatever distinctions may be made between public office and private career, however, men in both categories are forced to collaborate, just as public authority must intervene in some fashion to ensure the proper functioning of the economy. To be sure, there is a vast difference between the Soviet type of planning and the 'free enterprise' of American folklore, between absorption of the whole society by the Soviet state and the American devotion to semi-public organizations and private corporations. But these are merely two different modes of the same industrial order, modes which are not necessarily made similar by technological developments, but whose differences are lessened thereby.

No matter what form the regime takes, industrial society requires the same kind of scientific, technological, and administrative abilities, but not always the same political skills – although *some* political competence is necessary. In other words, industrialists have not become rulers, and public administration has not eliminated politics. But the inclusion of political competence in the social order is fundamentally different in East and West; the Soviet Union's single party occupies the first place in society itself, whereas in the West political parties are limited to a strictly political role.

Both the Communist single party and the multiple parties of the West are indispensable organs of what sociologists call the political subsystem. Government personnel are chosen and replaced by means of this subsystem. The single party is essential to the formula of Soviet legitimacy; the Communist Party, as the embodiment of the proletariat, has not only the right but the duty to exercise absolute power in order to further socialism. Multiple parties are engaged in peaceful competition for power in accordance with the formula of democratic legitimacy based on the process of free elections. Western parties – at least those which abide by the rules of the democratic game – are not 'total' organizations. Their activity is limited and secondary, except at election time. In no case do they constitute a hierarchy paralleling that of the official administration; they have no formal representatives in business, in most regional and municipal administrative bureaucracies, or in the armed forces; they do not dominate the labour unions.

A multiple-party state limits the influence of the political on the social order; the one-party state (where the state and single party are practically one) places the stamp of the political upon the entire social order. It does not suppress the political or governmental function but rather tends to confuse it with the administrative function by suppressing the neutrality of the latter.

Even in a single-party system, there are still some lineaments of categories that are clearly separate in the West. There are political personnel (in the narrow sense of the term), high officials, labour leaders, and managers of industrial plants who have been trained in scientific or technological discipline. Others have no speciality save politics, which is the art of forging a career in the party or of making decisions on a level that makes even the professional specialist nothing more than an amateur. But these categories, each of them geared to some definite function, are socially more or less merged. The party acknowledges neither the independence of unions nor that of civil or military technical experts. Even a half century after the seizure of power, the hierarchy of political commissars has not disappeared from the Soviet Army.

Moreover, the party covets first place in the spiritual world. Atheistic propaganda against the churches has lost its virulence and the Soviet Union concedes that religion is a private matter, but Marxism-Leninism, which represents a dogmatic denial of all forms of transcendence, is a concern of the state. The arts and literature must follow the dictates of the party and be placed in the service of the revolutionary cause, which by definition is identical with the very cause of humanity.

If we agree to define *theologians* as the interpreters of traditional faith, *scholars* as those who have mastered one or other of the positive disciplines, and *ideologists* as those who elaborate political or historical doctrine, then one might say that the Soviet hierarchy of values places ideologists at the top and theologians at the bottom. Scholars occupy a middle position; they are crowned with prestige and are recipients of innumerable privileges, but are still deprived of final authority, both temporal and spiritual. Ultimate value judgements are made by the ideologists who are also the leaders of the masses, the men who head the party apparatus.

Thus the Western social order, characterized by dissociation of the ruling minorities, stands in contrast to the social order in the Soviet Union, China, and the people's democracies, where all such groups are unified in the single-party system. The West frequently appears to be threatened by the consequences of this dissociation, by the loss of a collective will in a given country and of leadership conscious of its ends. On the other hand, the Soviet countries seem to sacrifice group autonomy and intellectual freedom to a concern for unified power. Since Westerners and Soviets both claim to be democratic, their scientific conflicts, which mirror their ideological disagreement, are fought, so to speak, on reverse fronts. One line of attack on the West attempts to demonstrate that the pluralism of the strategic minorities is but an illusion and one minority is really behind the curtain, the master of the game. Partisans of the Soviet system who follow this line are constrained to attempt to demonstrate that the omnipotence of the single party sanctions true freedom. How much truth resides in the Marxist and the neo-Machiavellian charges against Western pluralism? How much truth resides in the self-justification of the single-party regimes?

## The Distribution of Power

Let us now go over the evidence again. Power is unequally distributed among individuals in all collectivities, partial or global. Even when they freely elect their representatives, most individuals do not feel that they have real influence over the course of events or the conduct of diplomacy. In a complex society no regime can promise all its members effective participation in ultimate decision-making and rarely do they give any assurances of such participation. It is probably not misleading to assert that even in the United States only a few thousand people have any *direct* influence on the conduct of foreign affairs.

The issue raised by both Marxists and neo-Machiavellian polemics can be summed up in these questions: Is the dissociation of ruling minorities genuine? Does a minority overtly or clandestinely dominate all other minorities so that pluralism is only fiction, as is true competition between parties? Marxist-Leninist propaganda denounces political monopolists; C. Wright Mills equated this with a power elite; the disciples of Mosca and Pareto discerned the persistence of a ruling class behind the veil of democracy. Attacks of this kind are difficult to refute because they oscillate between banality and paradox, advance facts that are accurate but draw false conclusions from them.

Regimes of the Western type become stable when the representatives of the different minorities accept almost unanimously the regime itself and agree upon the rules of the game. If we presume that a portion of the ruling minorities, the leaders of the masses in unions or political parties, say, and the intellectuals or ideologists are hostile to the regime, its defenders will tend towards solidarity in the face of common danger and unite against those who, once in power, would set up a radically different system and thereby remove the heads of the erstwhile regime. (Historical experience, of course, proves that privileged groups have not always been able to unite against an absolute enemy.) When the ruling minorities all rally to the existing order, and refuse to cooperate with those who are not of their group, Marxists and neo-Machiavellians would find it easy to demonstrate that the categories really constitute a single group with a single purpose. As soon as 'the essential' is at issue it is enough for the demonstration to give an appropriate definition of 'the essential'. For example, the Marxist will say that only the complete nationalization of the means of production is essential. From that he will deduce that all ruling categories are in agreement when the essential is at stake and that the pluralism is a fiction.

Any state, having its own institutions and values, has at its disposal only a very narrow range of choices in foreign policy. Even when parties of sharply conflicting domestic views alternate in power, diplomacy is rarely subject to radical alteration. Under these circumstances it is easy to invoke this consistency to support the idea of monopolistic political influence or of some mysterious, all-powerful ruling class.

However, there are many tests to demonstrate that dissociation of groups within the power structure is not an empty fiction. Empirical studies show that while business leaders do have effective influence in Western democracies they are merely one of many pressure groups shaping government policy. Depending on which capitalist country one is talking about, and on the policy at issue, this influence varies in importance. In the case of foreign policy, dissociation would be fictional if diplomatic decisions were dictated by bankers or heads of private corporations. But here again, empirical study has dispelled mythology. Even colonialism, which Marxism-Leninism cites as proof of the omnipotence of monopolistic capitalism, has been imposed on the reluctant capitalists by political leaders as often as the reverse has taken place. The present-day diplomacy of the United States is far more concerned with preventing the expansion of Communism, a matter of international power politics, than with saving the investments of U.S. corporations.

Speaking more generally, the sources of power appear to be separated rather than joined at all levels, in small cities as well as in central governments. The same men do not have all the prestige simultaneously nor do they exert influence simultaneously in all domains. This does not mean that the notables of the community, the leaders of the nation – high officials, legislators, business leaders, journalists, presidential advisers – pay no attention to one another. They have to know each other, and they have to co-operate. But the hierarchy that characterizes each segment of social activity is not so clear-cut in the so-called Establishment created by all the leaders of the various categories when they are taken together. In their relationships they come together more or less as equals, and the prevailing mode of intercourse is one of discussion and dialogue.

Is it proper, then, to lump together as the ruling class all the leaders of the various groups, clustering around the politicians who are directly linked with the principle of legitimacy? This is a matter of semantics. What matters is not to ascribe to this ruling class a coherence and a continuity handed down from generation to generation which it does not possess. It is in fact a wide-open class, in accordance with the basic principles of today's democratic order. No one occupies a definitive place in it permanently. The electoral process exposes today's victor to the inconstancy of fortune and offers the vanquished an opportunity for revenge. Aside from politics, many are given the chance to climb to an establishment into which they were not born – by the trade unions, the business community, the universities, the military, the church, the intellectual community, and the research laboratories.

Actually, the agencies through which individuals join the Western social order are more often threatened by the absence of *one* ruling class than by the existence of any approximation of absolute power; it is more threatened by the division of parties and the conflict of ideas than by the conspiracies of monopolists. The early theoreticians of industrial society feared the consequences of lost spiritual unity; what could be the basis of any *consensus* if, as a consequence of the weakening of the religions of salvation, the members of society no longer believed in the same God and no longer acknowledged the sovereignty of the same modes of thought? The industrial societies of today are even further removed from spiritual unity than they were a century ago when these fears were first voiced. They have not split up, but during the period between the two world wars the danger of such a disintegration at times appeared imminent. In any case, as the example of the new countries often demonstrates, what renders the order of pluralistic societies precarious, when the old oligarchies are broken up by industrialization, is not the fact of oligarchy, nor the inadequacy of democracy, but the dissociation of the ruling minorities and their quarrels. The process of modernization must create an order acceptable to the majority as well as to the privileged few; this requires a continuous dialogue among interest groups, political parties, and ideologies to further the establishment of an effective authority based on a common purpose.

As for the self-justification of single-party systems, there is a germ of truth in the arguments made on their behalf. A career is open to talent, at least during the first phase following the revolution. The party provides the sole framework within which ruling groups can find a place; once the old upper strata has disappeared, jobs seem to be distributed on the basis of personal merit. Income, housing, automobiles belong to the administrative office held; they are not the private prerequisite of the jobholder; and disfavour, whether warranted or not, strips the individual of these advantages. Moreover, it is argued that the militants bring a special dedication to their party work, and the workers have a special sense of participating in their particular enterprise. An open, less hereditary ruling class, plus mobilization of the masses into various specialized groups for purposes of production and political action – these two themes with many variations form the basis of the case for a regime in which the bulk of the population plays no part, either in the selection of the group in power or the replacement of one group by another.

Whatever validity may be attributed to these arguments, the fact remains that the order of Soviet societies is clearly authoritarian and hierarchical on principle, acting in accord with the official ideology by the will of the rulers, not because of the pressure of technical-administrative requirements or other abstract necessity. The Communist Party, organized along the lines of democratic centralism, is subject to the authority of a very small group. The rank and file Party members, the ordinary citizens, have no share in the struggles which, in the privacy of the Kremlin, involve only the small minority who establish the dogma, make the important administrative decisions, manage the affairs of the Soviet Union, and promote the Communist cause throughout the world. Such a regime might perhaps be justified on grounds of the social utility of the concentration of power but it cannot without paradox be justified by the democratic ideal.

The order of industrial society, then, assumes forms both oligarchical and hierarchical. In one, leaders of the multiple hierarchies are engaged in a constant dialogue and the political subsystem is relatively separate from other subsystems. In the other, the political subsystem, organized as a single party, imposes a supreme, temporal, and spiritual authority over all the leaders of all other hierarchies; all of society thereby becomes political since administration, government, society and the state are merged.

## The Inequalities of Success

The controlling idea of the preceding analysis is simple and almost self-evident. Every activity inevitably entails an inequality in terms of success. The people in any society, especially a society that tends to be as competitive as those of the West, make value judgements about each other's accomplishments. In this sense, the more a society is imbued with a competitive spirit, the more it admits of inequality among individuals. Western society takes a sporting attitude toward equality: Let everyone begin at the same starting line and may the best man win. Each of the numerous roles to be played in such a society allows for various degrees of excellence. Furthermore, some of these rules imply the power of one man over another. An industrial enterprise may presuppose effective coordination of the activity of hundreds or thousands of workers. At each level one individual gives orders to other individuals and makes decisions which affect the lot of his fellowmen. Do these value systems and power hierarchies merge at the top? Do the same people simultaneously enjoy the advantages of each of these two apparently distinct hierarchies? In the final analysis this is the question that the concept of a ruling class raises. Are all the privileged people of a political system unified in their manipulation of the masses, in their maintenance of the existing order, and in the exploitation – for their own profit – of the power, *de facto* or *de jure*, at their disposal?

The Marxist-Leninists deny the existence of democratic dissociation of the ruling minorities and claim that the 'monopolists' are the true masters. Defenders of Western democracy reply that the omnipotence of a strategic minority (that of the managers of large corporations) exists only in the imagination of the Soviet spokesmen who persist in discovering elsewhere what they are accustomed to finding at home. In the Communist countries the unity of dogma, party, state, and society is proclaimed with pride by the various people who are its beneficiaries. They justify spiritual unity by the truth of their ideology and contend that class antagonisms are bound to disappear with common ownership of the means of production. They justify temporal unity by the non-transmission of privileges from one generation to another and by the vastness of the party's historic mission. As for the neo-Machiavellians, they deny that the conflict between the two ideal types – dissociation or unity among the ruling minorities at the top – is of real moment. The iron law of oligarchy, the effective exercise of political power by the few, the impotence of nearly everyone to influence the course of events, the pride of the mighty, and the resignation of the humble – these characteristics, common to all industrial societies, strike them as all-important. By the same token, they view the differences in political arrangements among societies as insignificant.

We have attempted to stress not only that which is common to the two ideal types of society but also the ways in which they differ. Their common basis is a certain democratic notion (in Tocqueville's sense of the term). No modern society any longer maintains a legally constituted aristocracy. In Western Europe, the United States, the Communist countries, and Japan, there is no law that prevents the child of a worker or peasant from rising to the highest position in the social order. Thirty years ago newspapers in France published a picture of the brother of the President of the Republic who was still living on the family farm and using a horse-drawn plough; today he would drive a tractor and would be significantly less different in dress, manner, and outlook from the brother who had achieved political eminence. It is still true, however, that legally open elites are not necessarily really open. Societies of the Soviet type may reduce inequalities at birth, in conformity with the aspirations of our time, but they offset this by granting to the party the monopoly of political action, setting up their ideology as the highest truth, and subjecting artists, writers, sometimes even certain scientists, to the authority of the ideologists. The party, at one with the state, reconstitutes the temporal and spiritual unity which was the hallmark of aristocracy.

By contrast, it is easy to point up the originality of the Western regimes. To be sure, the electoral process does not always or in every circumstance guarantee that the people, the 'common man', will have an effective influence. Let us suppose that the right of suffrage is limited to only a fraction of the population, that all the candidates come from a small area and, conscious of their place of origin, are determined to safeguard their rights. The legislature might be a rival of the king; it might limit the king's power and favour the gradual establishment of a constitutional form of government; but in spite of all this it would still not express the wishes of the humble. Even the introduction of universal suffrage does not guarantee that the governed will effectively influence the rulers. When land owners and factory owners, the present day 'feudal lords', control locally all the reins of power, representative institutions serve as an instrument of social conservatism.

This condition can no longer be found in the developed countries. The rural social structure cannot resist the modernization of farming methods. Even when farmers, the small or great landowners, or large corporations, with the help of salaried employees, exploit the land, the personal ties which used to subordinate the many to the few tend to become loosened. With increasing diversity of the roles to be played, accompanied by impersonality of individual relationships, the electoral process no longer furthers the manipulation of the masses by those in power; rather, it becomes a challenge of sorts launched against the powerful, who themselves are divided into groups, each of which hopes to maintain the existing order. The way these groups triumph over their rivals is to obtain the most votes, which requires some response to the needs and demands of the voters.

As society becomes more and more modernized, the dissociation of the ruling minorities results in the increasing effectiveness of the electoral process. Pressure groups, intellectuals, and ideologists represent numbers, ideas, diverse levels of society, and contradictory claims. They exert a direct or indirect influence on the politicians and the rulers. The leaders of some categories at least are themselves obliged to heed the complaints and the demands of those whom they represent. Indirectly, by means of social pluralism and competing political parties, industrial society is nearing the democratic ideal. This is not to say that the people govern or that they have a 'general will' of their own apart from the incessant exchanges between individuals and groups; but free discussion between the controlling majority and its opposition, between labour unions and pressure groups, between intellectuals and those in power – despite the iron law of oligarchy – assures the ruled those guarantees which they may reasonably expect and gives the rulers little opportunity to misunderstand the profound desires of the masses.

In the countries of the Third World the conditions necessary for the implementation of Western methods are seldom fulfilled. Competition in elections between political parties or candidates for political power sometimes works to the advantage of plutocratic conservatism, propping up the old ruling classes who are incapable of modernizing the economy; at other times it merely results in a permanent instability. Dissolution of the political entity itself is not uncommon when each of the parties represents not a social but rather an ethnic or regional group. The single-party system steers clear of these reefs, or seems to. It is an oligarchical system, but it may be a modernizing one if it becomes an agency of action, able to impose discipline and inspire its militants with faith, and to enlist the masses and communicate to them the impetus that emanates from power. But the prerequisites for the application of Soviet methods also are seldom realized. Hostility to the Soviet Union or to China and the revulsion of intellectuals and militants against the merciless tactics of Marxism-Leninism have turned many South American and African countries away from the notion of using the Soviet Union as a model, even though they have found the Western model also unacceptable. Thus, most of the regimes in the new countries that call themselves socialist or democratic or both are neither socialist nor democratic in the sense that these words are used in the Soviet Union and in the West.

It is in the nature of these ambiguous regimes that they do not tolerate the dissociation and open discussion characteristic of the West, nor do they attain the temporal and spiritual unity in which the Soviets pride themselves – not without some pangs of conscience. The freedom of a functioning pluralism is denied them because of the heterogeneity resulting from the coexistence of traditional and modern segments of social life and because of the lack of cultural unity. Totalitarian unity is forbidden them by the resistance of both the old and the new elites. Consequently, intermediary formulas take different forms, depending on a variety of circumstances. In one place a charismatic leader, surrounded by henchmen, holds on to supreme power but fails to suppress at a lower level the rival parties, religions, provinces, and ideas (Indonesia). In another, the army seizes the state and liquidates a corrupt monarchy (Egypt) or political parties and parliament (Burma), thus transforming itself into a political agency that creates a modernizing oligarchic regime, more authoritarian than totalitarian, without an official ideology and therefore without spiritual unity.

It should be possible on the basis of these examples to outline a typology of political regimes. But what concerns us here is their social infrastructure. The essential element in industrial society is the substitution of many hierarchies for a single one (or just a few). Ancient empires consisted of a mass of agricultural workers at the base – a mass from whom were collected the necessary taxes for the maintenance of the upper classes – and, at the top, the king, the nobles, warriors, and priests. Situated between the mass and the elite, merchants and artisans usually became rich only by supplying goods (because of their skill and shrewdness) to the privileged few. In theory, the industrial order eliminates priests from formal participation in public affairs and subjects the military to the state, that is, to the civil authority; professional soldiers are no longer aristocrats but civil servants. Modernization of the Third World dissociates the age-old society of the villages which retained many of the characteristics of feudal regimes. It makes available many increasingly specialized careers. Inevitably the state is divided, if it is not actively fought over, by the old elite and the new (graduates of universities, engineers, technologists, lawyers), by civil and military modernizers, and by intellectuals who draw more or less inspiration and actual support from one or two of the ideologies that are spreading throughout the world. The more modern a society becomes, the more numerous are the opportunities for the ambitious to gain advancement outside politics. But while politics remains virtually the only road to prestigious positions, the despotism of a single party devoid of ideology will probably seem the only solution to the group in power; the opposition may conclude that the normal way to acquire power is by assassination.

## The Contradictory Solutions

Is the antinomy of pluralist dissociation and partisan and ideological unity a historical accident? Will it still have any significance twenty or thirty years from now? By the beginning of the next century, will our quarrels be judged as anachronistic, as ludicrous as those of the Montagues and the Capulets or the Guelphs and the Ghibellines? I always hesitate to answer such questions. I believe less than most in the predictability of the future. However, if I must choose, I would hardly hesitate: the two ideal types of social order which, if we are to believe the evidence, will be transformed over the next decades, represent two contradictory solutions, intelligible in their very contradiction, to the immanent problems in industrial civilization.

Let us immediately dispose of the overly simple ideology by which each regime justifies itself and condemns its rival. The Marxist-Leninists proclaim that they have done away with class warfare and that the state represents all the people. The Western democracies reply that they, and they alone, safeguard the people's freedoms and that single-party totalitarian despotism, useful perhaps, if not necessary, during the early phase of industrialization, has no further *raison d'être* once mass consumption has been achieved. Each regime continues to predict the death of the other though, under the doctrine of coexistence, it claims it does not entertain any desire to implement the demise.

The Soviet regimes are precarious, if not artificial, because they attempt to establish a unitary authority, at once temporal and spiritual, whereas the secularization of society and thought would leave only scientific propositions on the one hand (limited therefore to facts, concepts, and regularities) and opinions and beliefs on the other. To proclaim a historico-political ideology the official truth is to depart from the principles of rationalism by which the Marxist-Leninists set great store. The state would manage to impose this ideology by force, for a while. But the effect of such an ideology would be constantly weakened by a scepticism which the police could repress but whose spread it could not prevent. Similarly, on the temporal level, the regime is torn by an ineluctable dilemma: if it respects its own constitution, which is democratic-liberal, the factions within the party will, little by little, come to resemble the parties of liberal democracy; the alternative requires the party to remain committed to what Lenin called democratic centralism, which in fact is the quasi-discretionary authority of the controlling group. Under this dispensation only the members of the Presidium or, perhaps, the Central Committee can take part in the competition for power; stress therefore is placed on the inherent contradictions between ideology and reality, between the democratic formula and the actual despotism. The aspirations of the intellectuals will encounter the resistance of the leaders, who will be anxious to prevent open criticism of the very foundations of the regime. A secular society that preaches the primacy of science and claims to be democratic cannot attain definitive stability within a single-party totalitarian system because the system controverts the very ideas it invokes.

Western societies, highlighted by the dissociation of ruling minorities and by permanent debate among them, are more faithful to their ideas, but they have no sense of security regarding their future. They are beset not by a contradiction between practice and the ideology they invoke but by an internal conflict that is inherent in their practice. Political parties must take the lead and at the same time take every precaution to respect the law;

dissatisfaction, the source of progress, must not erupt into violence. Western regimes are never entirely successful in hitting upon a definitive compromise between the resistance of the conservatives and the impatience of the radical utopians. The social order always seems unjust to those who subscribe to the egalitarian ideal, whether that ideal is interpreted as requiring equality of opportunity at the start or the lessening of existing socio-economic inequalities. *A fortiori* the order will appear unjust whenever public opinion is sharply divided over application of the various interpretations and hesitates over the familiar slogans. 'from each according to his ability'; 'to each according to his needs'; 'equality of opportunity for all'.

The internal contradictions in the Soviet regime and in Western systems are different in kind. On the Soviet side they have moral as well as social significance. Those in the West are strictly social. The Soviet regimes are their own critics; they can escape condemnation by their own ideas only by professing to be provisional. After the establishment of socialism, the single party, its historic mission accomplished, will disappear. Pluralistic Western regimes admit their imperfections; the iron law of oligarchy and the changing demands of technology do not permit them completely to realize their ideal of self-government or of equality of opportunity or rank. They are less threatened by these contradictions than by the possible instability of governments subject to ceaseless criticism and made inefficient by the pressures of partisan rivalry.

Does Soviet society, which imposes a bureaucratic hierarchy on all collective action and ultimately on global society itself, present a picture of the dominant future order? If so, it must be assumed that the ruling minority will continue to justify its monopoly of power by the proletariat's mystical assignment of authority to the party, or the people's assignment of authority to the state. When necessary, it might obtain a striking confirmation of this assignment by carefully manipulated elections, but it will not expose itself to the risks of competition. Why should those in the know submit to the judgement of those who are not? Is not the political notion of democracy, of a government created by the people, in fundamental contradiction with the very essence of a scientific society?

Those who pursue this vision display their own contradiction by the manner of their attack upon pluralism. As idealists, they reproach those who define democracy as a dissociation of ruling minorities and competing political parties for subscribing to elitist prejudices. The realists deride the electoral and representative ritual while observing with pride or consternation the advent of a technocratic era.

## The Institutional Interpretation

Let us return to the present. Now and for the foreseeable future of two or three decades, the only institutional interpretation of democracy, in the political sense of the term, is one based on competition, election, and debates. Such an interpretation will permit the continuation of inequality of power among individuals and variations in the influence of the leaders. Such a society, devoid of a closed and permanent oligarchy, agitated by constant rivalry and debate between pressure groups, is not inherently susceptible to complete manipulation by a conspiracy of 'monopolists'. Of course, public opinion is moulded and distorted by the media of communication – press, radio, and television – some of which are owned or controlled by special interest groups. But the dispersal of these rival groups makes it impossible for any one of them to portray a world too remote from reality or to impose a policy that would obviously run counter to the spontaneous aspirations of the nation. The interrelationship between public opinion and those who control the means of communication is such that the very question of ascertaining which of these calls the tune seems senseless to me.

Development of the technocratic idea of rule by a scientific/technological elite is wholly unlikely. Both in the Soviet regime and in the West the rulers are amateurs in matters of science, strategy, or economics. If they can be called professionals, their training is in the art of human relations, and their abilities are those required to forge a career in politics or statecraft. In all likelihood American politicians would fare badly in the arena of the Kremlin, because tactics adapted to competition in the Bolshevik style hardly resemble those which ensure success in the Congress (and the inverse is true). But different though they might be, the rulers of both regimes have a specific talent, even though scientifically trained men are more numerous in the Kremlin than in the Capitol.

The time has not yet come – if it ever will – when machines will make human decision-making unnecessary. Strategic decisions, clarified by theoretical studies, remain adventurous – judgements made by one group in relation to others for the purpose of gaining ends or achieving values. Some economic decisions involve a dimension which cannot be reduced to calculations of maximization or optimization; they impose sacrifices upon some and offer advantages to others. There is no machine, for example, that can rationally determine what portion of our resources should be devoted to cosmic exploration. There is no machine that can decide, without risk of error, who are the most deserving or the most competent to command.

But once the technocratic illusion is dispelled, once the necessity of a truly permanent political power is recognized – a contested, arbitral power, exercised by a few in the name of all – the ineluctable question arises: Will a society in which large enterprises employ computers, as today they use duplicating machines, grant an effective role to amateur rulers and permit the ruled to entertain hopes of understanding their lot and exerting some influence on it?

The optimists meet this implicit issue by stressing the importance of raising the intellectual level of the many. Industrial society tends to employ fewer and fewer illiterates; therefore, for reasons of self-interest, if not of humanitarianism, it attempts to reduce their number. It needs, even in the lower categories, workers who have attended secondary school for at least a few years. As working hours decrease, as the working week is reduced, as entry into professional life is delayed, and the retirement age is advanced, a larger number of ordinary people have an added opportunity to continue their education. Thus there is opportunity for better-educated men to become more aware of the social context and entertain the legitimate ambition of attaining the status of participants rather than submitting passively to a destiny forged by others.

We shall refrain from describing as utopian this vision of a society whose increasing complexity will still be rendered intelligible to the ordinary man. But we shall also avoid any complacent illusions. Even in countries where the standard of living is highest and where the proportion of national income devoted to training the young is greatest, the majority of workers are incapable of understanding how their industries function, and most citizens have at best only a partial understanding of the diplomatic and economic problems which their rulers must face. Only a minority of citizens take an active interest in public affairs. The distinction between active and passive citizens – not in the sense it had of voters and non-voters during the French Revolution, but in a specifically sociological sense – shows no signs of being at the point of disappearing.

What proportion of the population would have the *genetic* ability to reach the intellectual level necessary for understanding a social order constantly in the process of transformation because of scientific progress? How many individuals, given the occupations to which most of them are destined, could reach this level and remain there during the course of their lives? We cannot answer such questions with any certainty. As far as one can judge, only a minority, which probably does not exceed ten to twenty per cent, has been granted by genetic chance the intellectual aptitudes which would make higher learning easy for them. Another minority, victim of the same chance, will forever be incapable of such studies. The majority, fifty to seventy per cent, those with average talents, will rise more or less, depending upon family background and the opportunities society offers. This majority of the average makes intellectual progress, but the superior minority progresses still more and, in all probability, much faster. And society is becoming ever more complex as the masses become more educated. At present, of these two processes, the first is the more rapid; the minority capable of rational discussion grows larger, but the gap between this minority and the rest of society is not becoming narrower.

On the other hand, we have not yet reached the stage when only mathematicians, physicists, and engineers will be capable of ruling a scientific society. Important strategic or economic decisions can and must be made by cultivated men, who are not necessarily technicians and perhaps cannot be. The President of the United States does not need to understand the mechanism of the thermonuclear bomb or of an electronic calculator to understand the respective advantages of one system of weapons over another. That the decision of a single man may entail such consequences makes the observer shudder. But would it be more reassuring if the decision were made by a technician or a technique?

The administration of any complex enterprise requires the services of experts, experts who possess special knowledge lacked by the man in final authority; so it is that whoever rules an industrial nation must be able to consult specialists and heed their counsel. He will never himself be expert in all the areas that concern him; whatever his early training, most of the time he will be called upon to act as a cultivated man of wide understanding and broad interests, rather than as a scientist with a great depth of knowledge in a single field. I am one who rejoices in the fact that society is not and cannot be ruled by scientists.

# 3  Racism and Nationalism

For nearly two thousand years, Christianity has acknowledged that every person has an immortal soul. Democracy grants to each individual the dignity of citizenship and gives substance to that dignity by the right of suffrage and equality before the law. Democracy today is not satisfied with merely formal, legalistic equality; it attempts to reduce socio-economic inequalities, to abolish them from the start.

At the same time, modern civilization is permeated with a competitive spirit and committed to a hierarchical organization. Whether administrative or technical, some form of hierarchy is indispensable for the efficient operation of any collective enterprise in which thousands or tens of thousands of workers are involved. Competition is inevitable where social position is not conferred by heredity. Usually there are more applicants than there are jobs when the more prestigious and well-remunerated positions in contemporary society are open to competition.

This combination of hierarchy and competition, which is characteristic of industrial societies regardless of their regime, can take many forms. Determinants are the opportunity for ascending mobility; the persistence of deference (or its absence) which the privileged minorities traditionally inspired; and the rate of economic growth which raises the standard of living for all, even without substantial reform in the distribution of income. Barring some catastrophe, technological progress, which is indispensable to increased productivity, will enable the developed countries to continue to shorten working hours while increasing the worker's income. Most families will probably be able to satisfy their basic needs, and to provide an environment in which the children of the common people will be less disadvantaged in society than they are today. But the intellectual disparity between the elite and the masses will not necessarily be lessened; some groups will continue to feel shut off from the higher culture by the very nature of the work they do. Most of these will feel that they are unable to influence the decisions made by 'the others' – the rich, the economic monopolists, the politicians, the strategic minorities, in Soviet societies, the controlling Communist Party. The 'common man' vaguely imagines all these forces as remote, strange, and all-powerful. The multiplication of intermediate echelons in the economic and social pyramid does not suffice to suppress the image of the dichotomy 'they' and 'we', those who command and those who obey, an image usually consonant with the experience of the worker in industry and entirely believable in the eyes of the citizen confronting that fearsome protector, the Leviathan.

So far we have examined the dialectics of equality within a political collectivity established in a prescribed territory and subject to a central authority. We have presumed this society to be homogeneous, or at least we have assumed no other kind of heterogeneity save that of social strata. On this hypothesis, it has seemed probable that the demand for equality would be individual rather than collective. The various strata would not confront each other as ultimate enemies, the freedom of one entailing complete victory over the other.

In this perspective, Marxism is essentially the doctrine that teaches one stratum, that of industrial workers, that they can expect nothing from reforms achieved under a system based on private ownership of the means of production. The industrial worker becomes a proletarian, in the special ideal sense that Marx gave the word, when he identifies himself with no group save the proletariat, thinks of himself exclusively as a proletarian, and can conceive of no future consonant with his desires save through the triumph of the proletariat. Let us generalize about the case of the proletariat, and state that the social strata that are, or believe themselves to be, unjustly treated conceive of their liberation either in individual or collective terms. Either the entire class will be 'liberated' by a revolution, or else it will be freed when the individuals who constitute it no longer consider themselves oppressed and foresee an opportunity for their own advancement or for that of their children.

Social evolution in Western industrial societies has entailed both 'collective liberation' via universal suffrage and the strengthening of unions, and 'individual liberation' through broadening educational opportunities and social legislation. 'Liberation' of the disadvantaged strata by means of 'individual' achievement obviously necessitates 'collective' measures, but these do not entail the overthrow of the established regime or recourse to violence.

At this juncture let us turn our attention to the 'polyethnic' society, to use a current expression. Any society is polyethnic which includes groups that differ in culture, language, past history, or colour of the skin – groups more or less conscious of their singularity, or whose singularity is more or less clearly perceived by the majority of the population. The sense of belonging to a historic cultural group is currently expressed as *national sentiment*; Westerners speak of *tribal consciousness* to designate this same sense of belonging in reference to Africans or other groups more or less clearly marked by their use of language. The adjectives *racial* and *racist* are ordinarily used when the colour of the skin is different, and they take on particular point among those who exclude, despise, or detest a group so identified and insist that their enemy is essentially different or evil; wickedness cannot be rooted out if it is implanted in the blood. Finally, use of the vague term *ethnic* has become a way of avoiding both the terms *national* and *racial*, the first of which seems to call for a political awareness or intention, while the second presumes a biological origin.

The demand for equality which is concerned with socio-professional stratification may also reflect the existence of a *hierarchy of ethnic groups*, a hierarchy which the group at the bottom of the scale calls *discrimination*. Historically the hierarchy of races has emerged quite as spontaneously as that of individuals or of the socio-professional strata. In any given activity, public opinion establishes a distinction between the best and the less good; so a collectivity spontaneously confers a specific value upon each professional activity and places the professor above the mechanic (without, however, all the strata of society necessarily being in agreement on these values). Within a political society, ethnic or national minorities are rarely placed on a footing of equality. In nineteenth-century Belgium, the Walloons were the superior ethnic group, and so only French was recognized as the official language, despite the bitter protests of the Flemish people. Similarly the British in Canada enjoyed superior status, as did to a certain extent the so-called WASP (white Anglo-Saxon Protestant) in the United States.

A national claim is called *nationalist* when an ethnic group, through those who speak in its name, aims at total independence, the right to constitute itself a sovereign state. When ethnic groups protest against the inequalities of which they consider themselves victims, but do not strive for separation, we speak of the problems of *national minorities*.

National demands in Europe have been associated with both democratic ideology and industrial modernization. The principle invoked in the condemnation of the orders, or estates, in the French Revolution logically involved the equality of ethnic groups. If a worker is worth as much as his boss, if his voice should carry as much weight as his employer's, why would a Fleming be worth less than a Walloon, or a Czech less than an Austrian? Historically, the logical implication was not accepted more readily in one case than in the other. That ethnic group which is actually superior socially regarded its own superiority as legitimate and based this superiority on its nature, its essence, and its past – so, in the eighteenth century, did the aristocracy behave in the face of the rising tides of revolution.

Advent of the industrial era aroused the interest of the masses in demands based on nationality. So long as most of them lived according to their own local custom in village communities, the language of the state and even the person of the sovereign mattered less than civil peace and the quality of administration. But when schooling becomes open to everyone, when a changing social order replaces a stable one and personal advancement becomes a normal ambition, all men begin to take an interest in the nationality of the state. Even those who have no clear awareness of politics as such, or of unity of the state as the supreme consideration, are affected in their personal lives by the consequences of the sovereign's nationality. Members of minorities who are treated as inferiors have less chance of succeeding in their private careers, and at the same time may be excluded from any participation in government. As society and the state draw closer, national claims or claims to statehood inevitably become social, and social claims become national.

During the final third of the twentieth century, ethnic conflicts over social, political, or racial dominance – in turn or simultaneously – appear to be more likely than the continuation of the class struggle in the Marxist sense.

## The Ethnic Subgroups

Every state, even one supposedly homogeneous, contains subgroups to which the individual is aware of belonging without rejecting a simultaneous adherence to the national culture and the state. Germany still contains *Länder*, each of which has a dialect and traditions different from those of other parts of Germany; these differences might perhaps seem insignificant to the superficial observer, but they are often cherished with great fervour. In France, the Bretons and the Basques are more conscious of their ethnic roots today than they were half a century ago. The Bretons have become aware at the same time of their underdevelopment and of the disadvantages of their geographical position; this material concern seems to increase the drive for spiritual identity, reflected in the attempt to preserve their Celtic language by insisting that it be taught in their elementary schools. In Great Britain the national feeling of the Welsh and the Scots is increasing rather than diminishing. The French-speaking inhabitants of the Jura region protest their inclusion in the canton of Bern. Throughout all of Europe a reaction, still mild, is building up against the cultural uniformity which the modern state tends to impose through administrative centralization. Only rarely do these ethnic demands assume a violent form or take on a political or racial character. The Welsh and the Scots are obtaining as much administrative and cultural autonomy as they want; they have access to the higher state posts without having to circumvent any special set of obstacles, and they have their share, perhaps more than their share, of the most envied positions. The Basques and the Bretons, even if they think they are unjustly treated and deprived of a fair share of the collective wealth, do not dream of an independent state. It is within France itself that they put forward their demands – to rise, collectively or individually, in the social scale and to preserve their own language.

At the other extreme, the demands brought by the Algerians against France in the world context of the 1950s inevitably assumed a national character. It was not that the Algerian population was ethnically homogeneous or that such homogeneity was reflected in language, custom, or even religion; even so the gap between the Algerian masses and the French minority in Algeria was too great to be bridged by the formula of integration – that is, by giving theoretically equal opportunities for personal advancement to French and Algerian youth.

In France proper, the opportunities for the son of a worker and the son of a bourgeois are not actually equal, but the inequality is tolerable and tolerated because there is a common language and an awareness of national unity forged by the centuries of common history. In Algeria the inequality of opportunity remained great, regardless of legislation; it was proportional, so to speak, to the social and cultural gap between the privileged group and those who had long been disadvantaged.

The prevailing culture in the French schools would have remained always foreign to the Algerian Muslims, Arabs, or Berbers, even to those converted to Christianity. Although in a sense democratic, the system of tests and competitive examinations is bound to reinforce social inequalities which are rooted in the ethnic difference. It is an irony of history, but an intelligible one, that Algerians who had received a French education headed the nationalist movement, just as it was those about to become French who were the ones who wished most to remain Algerian. This is readily explained; they understood that they were the victims of an inferior status imposed upon them by the French minority, and they had everything to gain by establishing a state in which they would become part of the ruling group by virtue of the removal of French competitors with comparable training.

Is it inevitable that a situation like that in Algeria should result in the establishment of an independent state governed by an elite drawn from the underdeveloped masses, while the former rulers, forced to choose between emigration or minority status, should almost all choose emigration? In Rhodesia and in South Africa, the white minority is convinced, and probably correctly so, that the democratic process of universal suffrage, if initiated, would more or less rapidly give the reins of power to the elected majority, in other words, to the blacks. They also believe, and probably correctly, that they could not survive as a white minority in a state governed by Negroes, at least in the present state of native development.

The French in Algeria, forced to choose between individual equality (*integration*) and collective equality (*independence*), came around at the last minute in favour of individual equality but within the framework of a 'France from Dunkerque to Tamanrasset', a framework in which the underdeveloped masses would have been the minority. As long as they were trying to safeguard their domination within the Algerian framework they denied 'Arabs' the right to vote, just as the whites of Rhodesia and South Africa deny the ballot to Negroes. These African whites cannot resort to integration within a larger framework where the present ethnic majority could be reduced to the status of a minority. They feel that they are fighting with their backs to the wall, and this is true; to accept individual equality of blacks and whites would entail consequences which most whites would regard as intolerable. (I am not judging; I merely record.)

Between the integration of ethnic groups by honest application of legal and social equality, and the enforced separation of such groups, as has been undertaken in South Africa under the doctrine of apartheid, there is a middle course for federal or unitary states that contain distinct ethnic groups – as demonstrated by Belgium on the one hand and Canada on the other.

In Belgium, two linguistic communities have seen a gradual inversion of the hierarchy – a process brought about by democratization and the sheer weight of numbers. A century ago the Flemish bourgeoisie had largely become Gallicized; they seldom used the Flemish tongue except to address those whom they called '*les gens du peuple*' (the people). The demand for linguistic equality was inspired by Flemish intellectuals, but it sprang from the desires and needs of the people and was in essence popular. Even today most men speak only one language; if they have to learn another in order to get an education, they are at a disadvantage with those whose cultural language is the mother tongue. These practical considerations are reinforced by the self-esteem of the group. So the Flemish ethnic group has sought and obtained equality for itself, for its culture and language.

The Flemish constitute the majority of the country, but they know that French is more widely used in the world than Flemish and therefore is more useful. In regions where there is a mixture of both, French tends to win out over Flemish; hence the attempt to map out once and for all the boundary between two linguistic communities. On one side of the boundary, instruction would always be given in Flemish, on the other in French. The Flemish community is no longer willing to risk a gradual spread of the Walloon community's language. Equality would require that law come to the aid of the weakest; the law would thus compensate for the greater attraction of a language spoken by several tens of millions against that of one used only by a limited group.

At this point the Walloons, in turn, make claims. Having become a minority in a unitary state, they no longer accept unreservedly the rule of the majority. They insist that their representatives should have a veto of sorts over decisions made by the representatives of the other community. They rebel against the requirement that their children learn Flemish, although the fact that Flemish children must learn French seems entirely natural to them. Is this illogical? Is it a departure from the principle of equality? Certainly. But as a practical matter this attitude is not unreasonable. A knowledge of Flemish is of no use in the world outside. The Walloons want their children to learn one or two foreign languages, but why Flemish, when English, German, Spanish, or Russian would be far more useful?

The French-speaking Canadians, unlike the Walloons, have never constituted the dominant ethnic group. Abandoned by the then leaders of France (apart from the Church) soon after the Treaty of Paris, they numbered some 70,000 in 1763. Today they exceed five million in Canada itself, concentrated for the most part in the province of Quebec, where they form a dominant local majority (more than eighty per cent). For a century now, Canada has been a federal state, and the French-speaking Canadians enjoy an extensive autonomy; the flag of the province of Quebec preserves the fleur-de-lis of ancient France. The language of the primary and secondary schools and the universities is French. Nevertheless the so-called national or nationalistic aspirations are not appeased.

The complaints are many. The number of French Canadians holding higher posts in the federal government at Ottawa is by no means in proportion to their percentage of the population. When a British-Canadian director of some federal administrative agency answers that he would gladly employ French Canadians if he could find any qualified candidate, this brutal announcement produces a tempest of indignation in Quebec. In the province of Quebec itself the principal industries are owned by the British or Americans. English-speaking Canadians do not willingly take the trouble to learn French (sometimes they do not even identify the so-called dialect spoken by their compatriots with French as it is spoken in France); they regard it as normal and necessary that the French Canadians learn English. And finally, the French Canadians feel, most of the time justly, that Canadians of the other ethnic group look down their noses at them and fail to treat them as equals. Some take the extreme view that Ottawa is not their capital and that federal officials are foreign to them. The extreme nationalists will regard themselves as free only when Quebec becomes a completely independent state. If Gabon is entitled to independence, why not Quebec?

For our purposes we do not need to ask what will be the destiny of this island of a French-speaking province within a North America which is English-speaking all the way to the boundary of Mexico. What we are interested in is the mechanism of nationalist claims in an industrial and democratic society. A minority community regarded as inferior for historical reasons – most usually, military defeat or differing cultural patterns – wants *recognition*. It may be satisfied for a while with an autonomy (a kind of defensive nationalism) which ensures it against forced assimilation. In a second stage, however, as this minority becomes urbanized and developed (in the sense that the term 'development' has acquired in our time), it is no longer resigned to surrendering the direction of the state to the members of the dominant community. In the case of Quebec, within the province itself, the nationalist majority takes measures to impose 'Frenchification' on 'foreign'-owned businesses. On the federal level it demands an increased proportion of the national revenue and of government jobs. The ultimate goal is envisioned differently by different groups. A faction among the intellectuals – the professional people who are most aware of the disdain or indifference of their English-speaking compatriots, and also those most seriously challenged by individual competition – goes so far as to demand complete independence. The masses, concerned for their standard of living and unable to estimate the economic and social consequences of independence, do not support the extremists with the same fervour. Those French Canadians who have been successful in the English-speaking community and have won *personal* recognition regard those who cry for independence as troublemakers; refusing at first to take them seriously, they end up treating them with fierce hostility. The politicians support a 'moderate nationalism' and, depending on the winds of popular sentiment, opt for either a 'revolution for independence' or 'constitutional reform'.

Comparable problems of 'national minorities' and equality of language' are arising or are bound to arise in Asia and Africa. India and Ceylon have been involved in difficult negotiations over the Tamil minority who live in Ceylon. In southern India the Dravidian population does not accept Hindi as the national language. Riots over language have broken out in connection with the establishment of boundaries between various states in the federal republic of India, since inclusion in a state entails official linguistic consequences. The issues are not different in kind from those identified in the European and North American experiences cited above.

Racial conflict, or what passes for such, can be explained by a similar mechanism. But this is inherently more difficult to settle even if one accepts, in the abstract, the theses of biologists that are the most incompatible with racist concepts. The case of the United States is the best known and the most typical; no society embraces more wholeheartedly the democratic gospel of human equality and none has experienced greater difficulty with the conflict between egalitarian principles and the feelings of people aroused by the existence of a coloured minority. The population of the United States is less ethnically homogeneous than that of any other Western power, and the different ethnic groups form strata of sorts, superimposed on the general social stratification. Most of these groups, having arrived in the country at different times, have become more or less rapidly integrated into American society. The term 'integrated' here does not mean that the members of an ethnic group – Irish, Italian, Polish, German, Jewish are among the most conspicuous in the United States – have lost all awareness of their original community, which was at once linguistic, national and religious; indeed they are not blind to the fact that the members of one such community (Protestants of British origin) tend to consider themselves superior by virtue of their generally longer tenure and still hold a large share of the better positions. The integration of a minority ethnic group is basically achieved whenever its members accept and conform to the rules laid down by society as a whole, or by the state.

These various racial groups on the whole have accepted the principle of advancement through individual competition, and thanks to the combination of universal suffrage, public education, steady economic growth, and their own genius for organization for self-protection and advancement within the pluralist society, they have acquired a sense of belonging. They think of themselves as entirely American, completely loyal to 'the American way of life', entirely faithful to the republic.

This does not mean that the manifestations of heterogeneity have disappeared. Studies in political sociology, particularly those dealing with elections, are of special interest in the United States because they reveal the contrary effects that ethnic origin, religious affiliation, and social position frequently have on the way people vote. The WASP – white Anglo-Saxon Protestant – still has a better chance of becoming the head of some large enterprise than a Polish Catholic or even an Irish Catholic. But there are many roads to advancement. The standard of living, even for those at the bottom of the scale, is satisfactory for many and is buttressed by realistic hopes for advancement. First-generation immigrants compare their lot with what they remember of conditions in 'the old country' rather than with that of the American upper classes. The second generation has gone to school in America and has adopted the credo of its new country. From each ethnic group an elite arises to guide the others and give them hope of rising, in turn. Violent reactions against the established order or against the hierarchy come less from the newest immigrants than from older, more established groups who feel their position or their values threatened by the late-comers.

In the case of the Negroes, the mechanism of *integration* that has worked for other minorities has not yet proved adaptable, even though they have been in the country from the very beginning. The alternative, *separation*, has been condemned by the U.S. Supreme Court, in a highly significant reversal of the previous interpretation of the U.S. Constitution which had permitted racial segregation – for example, in theoretically equal schools – as not incompatible with the principle of equality. *Equal access to separate but equal facilities* – such was the formula under which the states with large Negro populations kept the races effectively apart after slavery was abolished in the course of the Civil War. Such separation within a single collectivity in practice reduces the ethnic group which provides the occasion for it to the status of 'untouchables'. The choice, as the Supreme Court came to recognize, is one-sided, and the implication of inferiority is inescapable.

The difficulties involved in integration for American Negroes include all those we have noted for all ethnic groups – or, to speak more generally, all disadvantaged groups that belong to a system which operates primarily on the basis of individual advancement. Children of the ethnic group or class regarded as inferior have a special handicap to overcome; they do not begin at the same starting line as their competitors. The Negro minority, some twenty million people, is underdeveloped in comparison with most other ethnic groups. The percentage of illiteracy and poverty is greater and that of college graduates and individuals practising a well-paid profession or trade is lower than in the other ethnic groups (except the much smaller groups of Mexicans and Puerto Ricans). This underdevelopment has a tendency to perpetuate itself; the schools attended by Negro children are often inferior; the poverty of families in the 'black ghettoes' that are now to be found in all the major cities creates a depressed total environment. Under the Supreme Court's anti-segregation precedent, the laws of the United States have been revised to forbid virtually all forms of public or private discrimination or segregation. But legal equality is not enough when the members of an ethnic group labour under such great environmental disadvantages in a system of individual competition.

The government is now more or less committed to a combination of *legal measures* (universal extension of the right to vote, abolition of the more obvious forms of segregation, integrated schools, etc.) and *social measures* (slum clearance, better schools, welfare services, etc.) especially tailored to the needs of the Negro minority. These, presumably, will gradually reduce the gap between the progress of the Negro ethnic group and that of other groups. Will the goal of integration then be reached, or at least will the United States come close to reaching it? Let us frankly admit that we do not know.

A *social* minority is integrated when those of its members who have been personally successful have no feeling of having betrayed their class and are accepted by others in terms of the role they play, without regard to their origin. A *national* minority is integrated when those of its members who serve the state are neither condemned by members of their own ethnic group nor held in suspicion by members of the majority group. Finally, the integration of a *racial* minority which bears distinctive physical traits, such as colour of the skin, presupposes the disappearance or marked reduction of what sociologists and psychologists call prejudice, the bitter emotion that is manifest in stereotypes of disparagement still current – the portrayal of the Negro or the Jew or the member of other conspicuous minorities as an inferior being, depraved, dangerous, and odious. Under these circumstances, individual advancement becomes a symbol of group advancement to the degree that individuals, while still identified by their race, are not thereby reduced to inferior status – that is, when those in the majority approve of them and demonstrate that they no longer feel it necessary to set them apart from their ethnic group. (How often has a Jew heard from some non-Jew who wished him well words spoken with no idea of giving offence: 'But you're not like other Jews'?)

In comparing the case of the Negro with that of the Negro, I have already implicitly subscribed to a sociological interpretation. The sociologist, indeed, is tempted to see only a difference in degree between the integration of the Negro and that of other ethnic groups such as Italians, Poles, or Ukranians. Many causes, however, strictly social in nature, come into play in the case of the dark-skinned minority. Despite their long residence, American Negroes are further removed from the upper classes than were the ethnic groups that came as recent immigrants. Descendants of slaves, they are still marked, especially but not exclusively in the South, by the memories they and society as a whole have preserved of the circumstances attendant upon their arrival in America. A part of that heritage was almost a century of 'second-class citizenship' under legal segregation that followed the end of slavery and continues *de facto* in some degree today. Under those circumstances, the Negro elite is only beginning to provide leadership comparable to that of other ethnic groups. Their university graduates, while fewer proportionately, are nonetheless numerous in an absolute sense; there are more doctors, lawyers, teachers, and other individuals who have received a higher education among the twenty million Negro Americans than there are among all the Negroes of Africa – ten times as many. But these individual successes have not yet brought about a fundamental change in the attitude of many Southern whites towards desegregation nor have they prevented the establishment in the great cities of separate neighbourhoods for the Negroes who have migrated north and west in increasing numbers. In these slums the breakdown of family life is marked and virtually condemns a majority of the young to poverty and delinquency. This segregation is not legal but, for economic reasons, it exists nonetheless. The value of land and houses is generally *presumed* to decrease when Negroes move into a neighbourhood – a fact which, true or not, symbolizes a moral resistance to integration.

Apart from psychosocial factors, does this resistance stem from purely biological causes? Is it proper to differentiate between ethnic groups whose language, culture, or tradition sets them apart and to differentiate between those which are identified by the shape of the skull or the colour of the skin? Aptitudes of an intellectual order are conditioned by genetic inheritance, but, whereas environment does not change the genetically determined colour of the eyes or the hair, intellectual abilities may blossom or wither depending on the family situation and the early school influence. Intellectual potential, as it is revealed by school and university competition, is the result of a complex of genetic-environmental qualities; it is impossible, in any concrete case, to assign a relative importance to one or the other of these factors. The fact that children from the upper strata are proportionately more successful does not prove that the frequency of genes which condition intellectual capacity varies from one social stratum to another. Experiments performed to prove the thesis of genetic equality – that the proportion of superior, average, and low IQ's in a random sampling of Negro and white children is the same – are not entirely conclusive, but the results tend to support the thesis of equality.

Huge collections of human beings are habitually spoken of as races and are characterized by physical traits; cranial measurement is no longer as fashionable as it once was and classification according to the colour of the skin is not very meaningful, but we still deal in physical characteristics of race. In these broad terms there is no reason to ascribe any genetic superiority to one over the other. White people have dominated history during the last few centuries because they have initiated a technological revolution comparable in impact and significance to the Neolithic revolution of agriculture and husbandry. Perhaps the coloured profile will catch up in the coming decades or centuries. In any case, the present advancement of Europeans and Americans cannot be said to prove that a greater number of men of white skin possess genes denoting intellectual capacity necessary to a technological civilization.

Depending on circumstances, the genetic explanation is accepted with complacency or rejected with indignation. In athletic competitions, Negroes in the United States usually win dashes and jumping events. Since no scale of values has been established between dashes and long-distance races, there is no pejorative connotation to the widespread opinion that Negroes are better endowed by nature for the former than for the latter (an assertion, incidentally, that has in no way been proved). As for intellectual aptitudes, however, the repudiation of racism leads us to reject the hypothesis that there is an unequal frequency of them among various human groups: to do otherwise would be to imply a theory of racial inequality.

In no case is such a hypothesis proved, whether one is dealing with social classes or with great populations which share certain physical characteristics. Historical appraisal of the contributions made by white, yellow, and red peoples also shows the hypothesis to be very improbable. The fear of a deterioration of the genetic inheritance, based on the theory that families in which genes conducive to intellectual aptitudes are most frequent have fewer offspring than others, was widespread at the end of the last century; it is less so today because of the scientific uncertainties involved.

A population must live in isolation and be forced into endogamy by social conditions imposed from without in order for selection to be operative so that certain genes, and with them certain aptitudes, eventually acquire an unusual frequency. The Jews are not a race; the Ashkenazim and the Sephardic Jews are genetically distinct, but each of these groups may be different from the surrounding population solely because of centuries of endogamy.

In the present state of our knowledge there is nothing that identifies a mixture of races with a genetic deterioration. Indeed, many biologists hold the opposite view. Urbanization and increasing social mobility should attenuate the tendency to marry within restricted groups and thus reduce the risk of hereditary transmission of defects due to recessive characteristics. Moreover, most Negroes in the United States have 'white blood' in their veins, and many whites have 'black blood'.

However, the biological case against racism, overwhelming though it may be, does not support the assumption that integration of Negroes will be achieved in the same way as the integration of other U.S. ethnic groups. Anti-Semitism, which at first suggests a natural analogy between historically defined and racially defined ethnic groups, in fact provides a somewhat less optimistic view. Social prejudice, supported by the pseudoscience of semi-intellectuals, transformed into a supposed 'race' an originally religious community which through enforced segregation gradually became a quasi-total society despite its total lack of political form. This culminated in the madness Hitler unleashed against the Jews, who were relatively numerous in Germany (about 800,000) and who for a century had played an outstanding role in that country's cultural and economic life. It is not our task here to determine the number of Germans who tended towards anti-Semitism, nor to analyse the circumstances which enabled the majority to accept the poisonous doctrine. What does concern us is the psychosocial mechanism by which any identifiable group might become the object of hatred.

As social beings men think in an *essentialist* way. Every ethnic or social group has its own global image or stereotype of other ethnic groups. Inevitably this stereotype is defined by an ensemble of traits which may be flattering or odious. When a group accused of deicide has lived in ghettoes, the population that surrounds it might react violently when that group leaves its segregated quarters and tends to become 'integrated'. In the eyes of traditionalists such a group symbolizes modern civilization – the decline of noble virtues, the worship of money, the international mobility of personal property. Georges Bernanos, loyal to the values of the old regime, never understood the connection between the anti-Semitism of his master, Edouard Drumont, whom he admired to the end of his life, and the anti-Semitism of Hitler, whom he detested. For a later generation of disturbed Germans the Jews symbolized plutocracy, democracy, capitalism, defeat, the Weimar Republic, socialism. All the Hitlerites needed to do was to translate into a racist philosophy this *essentialist* way of thinking; they then imposed this interpretation of a hideous stereotype upon a civilized nation.

Before 1933 the stereotype of the Jew was kept alive in the unconscious mind of the masses. Many socio-professional groups (doctors, lawyers, small businessmen) were, or believed they were, victims of the competition of 'foreigners'. The humiliation of defeat in the First World War, compounded by economic dislocations and the privations of unemployment, was conducive to seeking and finding a scapegoat. Armed with scraps of outmoded anthropology, the Hitlerites attempted to establish scientific justification for their decision to exclude the Jews from the collectivity. The later decision to exterminate them as a 'final solution' seems to stem from psychopathology and involves a kind of macabre logic: If the Jews are harmful animals, why allow them to live?

Extreme racist philosophy is the final manifestation of essentialist thought, but every national stereotype involves some degree of essentialism. Even the opponents of colonialism and anti-Semitism often follow the same road themselves, without realizing it, when they direct against those they condemn the very mode of thought used by those they criticize. Jean-Paul Sartre's portrayal of the anti-Semite is no different in kind from the anti-Semite's image of the Jew, although the language is different, Sartre speaking of an essential *will* or intuition, not of a *nature*. When Sartre likens the execution of the Rosenbergs to ritual murder, he is thinking and writing in the manner of the anti-Semites; another French writer does the same when he states that Americans have a mental age of thirteen.

Essentialist thinking has a double aspect: it assigns to *all* members of a socio-ethnic, historical, or racial group certain characteristics which one does indeed encounter more or less frequently among some of its members. It explains these traits not in terms of social circumstance or of life situations but in terms of the nature of the group itself. When the group is regarded as good, its positive traits are held to be characteristic; when the group is regarded as bad, only negative traits are cited in building the stereotype. If individual members of the group demonstrate in practice that they do not deserve contempt, they are regarded as exceptions; they are atypical.

The essentialism of opponents of colonialism, racism, or anti-Semitism usually stops halfway. The anti-anti-Semites do not assert that anti-Semites are dedicated to their degrading and disgraceful hostility because of their genetic inheritance or inner nature; they do yield, however, to the tendency to regard *all* colonials, *all* anti-Semites, and *all* southern whites as *essentially* defined by contempt for the natives, hatred of the Jews, or their insistence on segregation. The portrait they draw of these types is just as coherent, just as comprehensive, as the stereotypes of the Jew, the native, or the Negro held by their opponents. In this view an anti-Semite must be totally anti-Semitic, although there are many kinds and degrees of anti-Semitism; for example, unfavourable judgements made against Jews may be little different from similar judgements made in ignorance about other religious, political, or social groups. The same critic who rightly explains the behaviour of the native in terms of the total colonial situation may be unwilling to explain the behaviour of an individual colonialist in terms of the same situation, to which he may have been heir and which he had not desired.

The persistence of social stereotypes and the propensity to essentialist thinking acquire if not a new significance at least a different impact when the distinguishing feature of the ethnic groups is the colour of the skin. Those in favour of social integration may turn out to be no less resistant in private to mixed marriages between Negroes and whites than are the segregationists. To justify their distaste, parents are not lacking in reasonable arguments; 'things being the way they are', a white woman who marries a Negro will find doors closed to her, and her children will be penalized. Even if all whites could be psychoanalysed and freed from the stereotype of the Negro as an intellectually inferior creature, endowed with extraordinary sexual prowess, and thereby be freed of their psychic objections to the idea of 'racial mixture', I doubt whether this would suffice to ensure 'integration' in the sense that we have used the term. How can the vicious circle be broken? Recognition is denied because the ethnic majority is backward, and underdevelopment persists because of the denial; racial mixture is frowned upon because of the adverse situation those with mixed blood must face, and the situation is caused by disapproval of racial mixture. Even though the majority of Negroes *consciously* desire integration, not separation, in reality many of them want separation as well as integration.[1] Integration is important as a symbol of equality, but separation is more comfortable because Negroes and whites, although they have long lived in the same culture, remain different, not because of genetic inheritance but because they have been conditioned by their environment as different social beings.

A collectivity within which the hierarchical order does not endanger civil peace and political unity has as its basis the primacy of a reference group. In modern societies the state itself, inseparable from the nation, possesses this primacy. When the subgroups are too alien to one another they cannot unite by giving their first loyalty to the same model community. The Negro problem in the United States is tragic because Negroes and whites, despite their theoretical loyalty to Americanism and its values, have remained socially so alien they may perhaps be tempted to formalize their separation at the very moment they achieve the right and the ability to become united.

Leftist intellectuals readily attribute to the ruling minority responsibility for the attitudes they condemn, particularly racism and nationalism. But scientific studies as well as historical experience refute the myth of innocent masses and guilty elite. Tolerance, the acceptance of the *other* as different but not inferior, is observed more frequently as one goes up the social and intellectual scale. Many rulers, it is true, have cynically exploited mass prejudices (if one should call anti-Semitism, for example, prejudice); but prejudices exist just the same. In the beginning, the leaders of the Bolshevik Party were less anti-Semitic than the rank and file, although Stalin later decimated the Jewish intelligentsia on his own initiative. It is well known that the small settlers in Algeria were the most hostile to integration, and the same is true of the lower-class whites in the south of the United States; for it is the little man who loses his only claim to superiority when the inequality of ethnic groups is blotted out.

Perhaps people are more prone to a feeling of collective self-esteem whenever they have less personal reason for claiming distinction of any sort. In every country there are millions who in

1. Many Jews have reacted similarly to the denial of recognition by choosing separation: Zionism is an expression of this. The myth of a continuity between the kingdom of David and modern Israel developed later.

a half-dreamlike way share in the lives of the important people of the great world. When they are young they sometimes dream of being admitted to the magic circle; then, resigned or drained of ambition, they substitute for the dream a sense of identification with the glory of their idols or with the greatness of their country. When a national team wins an athletic victory or a scientist or writer brings honour to his country with a Nobel prize, the triumph of the few becomes a source of pride for the many.

Must we conclude that in the last analysis the insurmountable obstacle to equality is the very nature of social man? Modern society, as we have said, is competitive; it claims that roles are distributed according to merit. In spite of or perhaps because of the egalitarian ideal which it proclaims, it incites individuals and groups continually to compare themselves with others and to assess their own place in the hierarchy of values. How could envy and self-seeking demands fail to result from such incessant comparisons?

Whenever classes, in the age-old sense of the term, lose their consistency, when the material circumstances of life become more identical for an increasing fraction of the population, everyone tries to become part of a distinctive group at a higher level in the scale and to give visible proof of his rise. The search for status, to use the stock phrase, is a sign of vague discontent, of a need to find some sort of external reassurance, a certain unmistakable emblem of success.

In societies that are sufficiently developed and homogeneous there are two factors which help to lessen the inevitable conflicts of individual competition: the almost universal rise in the standard of living brought about by economic progress, and the variety of forms that success may take. But these factors do not immediately affect conflicts between ethnic groups, races, and nations. Quite the contrary; never has the inequality among peoples been so great, and never have these peoples been so conscious of this inequality. Within nations themselves, as well as on the international stage, ethnic disputes, which are national at one extreme and racial at the other, seem certain to become more threatening during the next few years.

The quest for social prestige within an ethnically homogeneous society is perhaps inconsistent with the ideal of equality. It is the psychosocial counterpart of that ideal, and it becomes all the more inevitable since economic progress and mobility tend to erase former class distinctions. The more external conditions resemble each other in a competitive society, the more small groups will multiply; these hope to be recognized as possessing some merit or good not shared by the rest. Not everyone can belong to the small group of innovators; hobnobbing with princes will always be limited to a minority; illustrious ancestors cannot be bought. Snobbery is an innocent, sometimes ridiculous, sometimes brilliant, form of the desire for distinction and prestige.

One must admire the irony of history. It was the French aristocrats, threatened by the bourgeoisie, who were the first to conceive of racist theories for their own self-protection. Two centuries later these theories served to justify the bloodiest drama of modern times. As for those European aristocrats who found no new basis for pride, they had to find satisfaction in snobbery, which they themselves enjoy and which they occasionally proffer to others. Will snobbery be the last incarnation of racism for the rich, or must it be said that racism is the snobbery of the poor?

We shall content ourselves with saying that the social order will achieve peace when the desire for distinction and prestige finds expression in nothing more harmful than snobbery.

## Part Two

# The Contradictions of Socialization

It is certain that at all levels of the social hierarchy, the average well-being has increased, although not always at the most equitable rate. The malaise from which we suffer is therefore not due to any increase in the number or intensity of the objective causes of our sufferings. It attests not a greater economic misery but an alarming moral misery.

ÉMILE DURKHEIM
*Le Suicide*

In Part One we employed the adjective *social* in the sense in which it is used in the current phrase *the social problem*. During the past century socialism was characterized by the desire to institute reforms which, going beyond the traditionally political, would affect the social organization of the community; it aimed at eliminating injustices or at restoring the *consensus*. In Part Two we shall use the adjective *social* in the sense suggested by the *socialization* or *socio-industrial order*.

Up to this point we have surveyed the following conflicts: *economic* conflicts between classes, *political* conflicts between ruling minorities and the masses, *political* and *economic* conflicts between the ethnic groups of various nationalities or races. Our analyses lead us to the conclusion that when the stake is strictly economic conflicts tend to decrease in intensity, but that the tension between the egalitarian ideal of industrial society and the technical and political hierarchy has not been resolved. At the same time, inequalities between ethnic groups tend to increase even though people at all social levels can share in the general well-being.

Tension between reality and the ideal is not a pathological phenomenon; it is the normal consequence of a civilization in which men assume full responsibility for organizing institutions and processes according to their conception of justice. To raise the standard of living may be seen as no more than a necessary condition for the appeasement of conflicts, but to protest against all individual or collective inequities, as well as those that are excessive or patently unjustifiable, constitutes the motivating force of historical flux. The risk of violence arises even in developed countries when economic progress ceases or when a political regime is threatened.

If we turn our attention to global society we are, so to speak, absorbed in the individuals who people it, already formed by and for it. In the following chapters we shall consider the primary mechanisms of the socialization process.

At first glance these mechanisms seem to remain what they have been throughout the ages. The social order derives from the biological nature of man, however diverse the social expressions of this nature might be. The family is the initial environment to which the child owes his first experiences and from which he receives an indelible impression. Even in its simplest form the family represents a complex ensemble. It is determined simultaneously by internal relationships between parents, between parents and children, among the children, and by external relationships with the surrounding community and its critical aspects of socialization: schools, churches, mass communication media. Have the tools of modern technocracy altered the mechanisms of socialization?

There is nothing to indicate that socialization is any more coercive than it has been in the past. Social classes began to arouse indignation not from the moment of their origin but from the moment when they should no longer have existed, from the day when an ideal which condemned them began to be spread abroad. Similarly, there is nothing novel in the fact that men are socialized, shaped by the characteristic culture of one collectivity among the many. What is novel is the loss of certain illusions: no human person can exist prior to or outside the process of socialization. Also new is the desire to create persons, not interchangeable individuals in an undifferentiated mass or robots in the service of monstrous bureaucracies. No one has underlined more forcefully than Émile Durkheim the twin aspects of the modern conscience: the socialization of individual conscience and the ideal of personal autonomy, which define modern civilization (or at least that part of civilization that remains faithful to liberal inspiration).

Therefore we arrive at the second theme of this study. Industrial civilization, as we were saying, consists of a hierarchical order and of an egalitarian ideal. Within certain limits it succeeds in reconciling the one with the other. At the same time we would say industrial civilization subjects individuals to a strict discipline in their work and to the influence of a public opinion that is diffuse, unwieldy, and elusive, expressed through the constant pressures of the communications media; and yet it claims to have a philosophy of freedom, a philosophy of personality.

This ambiguity, like that of the social classes and the elite, has been at the centre of social philosophy, or sociology, for a century and a half. It was implicit in Marxist thought, especially in the ambiguous concept of *alienation* as well as in the Durkheimian concept of *anomy*. Critics of contemporary civilization fear that the individual is either losing his personality in the crowd or his identity in solitude, that he is passively submissive to an alien order or, for want of self-discipline, given to every kind of temptation.

These fears seem contradictory, but sociologists, while critical of modern civilization, have all pointed to the common origin of apparently conflicting phenomena. Division of labour in industry can result in the mutilation of every individual. It might also remove the individual, as a cog in a huge machine, from the authority of internalized norms.

The problems we will deal with in Part Two are less easily delimited than those discussed in Part One. Class struggle, the elite and the masses, nationalism and racism – these topics crop up in the daily press. They intimate the stakes involved in political battles; every regime includes an ideology which relates to these terms. Our task is to discover the reality behind the illusions and the rationalizations. *Alienation, anomy, the masses* – these concepts are apprehended with precision only by intellectuals, even though these notions define some of the ills which affect the common man. They constitute the themes of a study which has more to do with the human character of industrial civilization than with the economico-political system; more to do with its culture than with the status of property or the conduct of public affairs.

Our task becomes more difficult. How can one disentangle the tendencies of industrial civilization when the conditions of life change so much from one human group to another because of the natural environment or the historical past? To be sure, societies acquire the same technical infrastructure as they become more modernized. But the social aspects of industrial civilization are influenced in many ways; they are not determined solely by technology.

More often than in the preceding section, we will observe the multiplicity of trends, but we will refrain from forecasting the ultimate victory of one over another. In the developed societies, where national production and the income of most families increase from year to year, the average man's life, divided between work and non-work, tends to be comfortable and secure, apart from periods of internal crisis or war. Does such a life have meaning in work? Ought one to fear the enslavement of all to some impersonal power as a consequence of the indifference of the individual to what goes on outside the narrow sphere of his own particular life? Or, on the contrary, is man possessed of an obsessive concern for others, for their opinion? Does mankind represent an ant-hill colony or a free community? Is man lost among the masses or is he an autonomous individual?

Perhaps these questions cannot be answered. Science gives to an increasing number of individuals a freedom of choice that was hitherto inconceivable. Who can foresee the use to which these individuals, or humanity itself, will put the freedom they will acquire?

# 4 The Family, the School, and the Masses

In the second volume of *Democracy in America*, Alexis de Tocqueville devotes a chapter to the effects of equality on the family. The following are the principal ideas of that famous analysis:

> At the same time as power escapes the aristocracy, one notes the disappearance of what it possessed of conventionality, austerity and legality in paternal impact and a kind of equality established in the home. I do not know if, all things considered, society is the loser because of this change, but I am inclined to believe that the individual gains from it. I believe that as customs and laws become more democratic, the relationship between father and son becomes more tender and more intimate; rules and authority are less in evidence, confidence and mutual affection are often greater, and it seems that family ties are strengthened while bonds with society are loosened. . . . An analogous revolution modifies the mutual relationships of children. . . . What I have just said about filial love or paternal tenderness is also true of all those deep feelings which arise spontaneously from nature itself. . . . Democracy loosens social bonds but it tightens the bonds of blood. It brings members of a family closer together at the same time as it separates citizens from one another.[1]

The contrast between 'social bonds' and 'natural feelings' arises from a timeworn philosophy. *Natural* feelings always are manifest as *socialized*, in some way or other. With the human species an initial phase in the evolution of life begins. Men and societies transform themselves because of the preservation of what has been acquired, and these changes do not spring from genetic mutations, although humanity also changes genetically, influenced by mutations and natural selection. Socialized man is naturally historic. The family in the democratic era is not to the

1. Vol. II. Bk 3, ch. 8.

family of the aristocratic era what nature is to society, but rather what one social type is to another.

Or, to put it differently, the ideas of Tocqueville have lost nothing of their relevancy to the present. Reduced to their essentials, they can be summarized by two propositions: on the one hand, the tendency towards equality within the family, between father and children, among the children; on the other, the strengthening of emotional ties among members of the family. These two propositions pose the problem which still seems to us today to be at the heart of what can be called the sociology of the family: the family as an institution has lost most of its functions. Some observers hasten to conclude from this that the family is in a state of decline, on the point of disintegrating, and they find in countless statistics arguments to support this thesis. But does not the family, created and preserved by decisions freely made in a civilization that claims to place the rights of the individual above all else, impart to feelings 'a vigour and a tenderness which it did not formerly possess'?[2]

## The Family Pattern

The characteristic features of the family in the most representative areas of modern civilization, that is to say, among middle-class city dwellers, are agreed upon almost unanimously by most observers. Normally, in its simplest form, the family consists of two generations rather than three – parents and children; the presence of grandparents is no longer common and is usually due to economic pressures rather than to the wishes of those involved. The age at which children leave their parents varies from country to country and from class to class, if going to boarding school is tantamount to leaving home. A number of circumstances actually determine the choice between becoming a boarder or remaining a day student. There is the de luxe boarding school reserved for the exclusive use of the upper classes, as exemplified by the 'public' schools of Great Britain or the private ones in the United States. On the other hand, sons and daughters of the working or lower middle classes usually live with their parents as long as they are

2. ibid.

attending elementary or secondary schools. However, the parents' place of residence in the country or in very small towns occasionally causes people of modest means, in France for example, to choose boarding school for their children. In Germany and in the Anglo-Saxon countries university students almost never live with their families, whereas in French middle-class milieus they live at home.

More and more rarely does the family serve an economic function. There exist, to be sure, even in the most progressive countries, business or agricultural sectors where the family unit is not entirely separated from the unit of production. If the age-old identification of place of work with place of residence has not entirely disappeared from the European and American country-side, it is already anachronistic; mechanization has made such inroads on farming and the crafts that family working units are becoming increasingly rare. This rationalization of both tools and management does not condemn private enterprise as such; but it does create that physical and especially moral separation between one's business and one's family that is typical of life in the city.

Stripped of its economic function, the family risks being deprived of its religious or even of its social sanction. Based upon the free decision of two people, it exists precariously since such decisions are revocable. The conception of marriage which springs from individualist concepts carries with it the notion of the legitimacy of divorce; the parties reserve the right to revoke the decision they have made. Having freely chosen one another, they can admit without undue embarrassment that they were mistaken. To be sure, in the West the Catholic Church continues to forbid the practice, and nations like Italy, where the Church remains a state within a state, do not officially recognize divorce. Elsewhere, while the marriage ceremony in a church or synagogue remains the custom, it is strictly a private affair, as is religion itself. Here the state permits the dissolution of marriages which the Church has blessed and proclaimed indissoluble; the law does not refute the logical consequences of the philosophy implicit in the modern conscience.

This philosophy is contrary to that held by some rightist

European parties, which picture global society as a natural hierarchy, patterned after the image of the family. The sovereign issues orders as a father would and the father, in turn, represents a sovereign in the eyes of his wife and children. Modern society is, as we know, as spontaneously hierarchical in fact as it is egalitarian in ideal. Japan has demonstrated by deeds that even the values and models of behaviour ascribed to hierarchies of feudal origin were in no way incompatible with modernization. There, both family and society have for a long time preserved a structure that is authoritarian and, especially, communal – in spite of an industrialization which was not originally accompanied by democratization in Tocqueville's sense of the word. Since 1945 Japan, too, seems to have been affected by the egalitarian movement, but even after a lost war and an American occupation it has not on that account disavowed its cultural heritage. In any event, in Western countries, the individualism condemned by counterrevolutionaries has pervaded the family; natural hierarchy, continuity from generation to generation, the authority of tradition – these characteristic features of order as conceived by conservatives in Europe tend to become obliterated here as they have disappeared in society as a whole. The theorists who surrounded Pétain at Vichy substituted the slogan *family, work, fatherland* for the motto *liberty, equality, fraternity.* But the family they dreamed of could no more have been recreated than could the industrial worker be returned to the plough.

The egalitarian idea, the principle of individual freedom, challenges those two marks of merit which many an illustrious philosopher, from Aristotle to Auguste Comte, deemed natural: the superiority of the masculine sex and that conferred by age. Adolescents, it is said, do not refuse to listen to the advice of an elder but they no longer obey the orders of the old. Women demand *true*, not theoretical equality. Just as American Negroes believe that separation is incompatible with equality, so women no longer accept a division of labour which would deprive them of full and complete participation in professional and civic affairs. They are no longer willing to devote themselves, as if this were their natural destiny, to the care of household and children.

A French writer (André Gide), born in the last third of the past century, wrote: 'Family, I abhor you.' Before 1914, militant members of revolutionary parties were often hostile to marriage on principle. They affected *companions*, not *wives*, as if so to protest against bourgeois customs or to symbolize the strictly personal nature of the union of two beings. An elderly lady who served as my translator in Moscow once reminded me, with an indulgent smile for her youthful follies, that she too, before the revolution, had refused the ceremony of marriage. There no longer is any question of such a refusal in the Soviet Union or Eastern European countries: revolutionaries get married these days, ideologists praise the virtues of the family and denounce divorce as unworthy of a good Communist.

This turnabout lends itself to ironic comments. Revolutionaries in power restore certain of the institutions which they had condemned when their goal was to destroy the established regime. The saying of a Bolshevik has often been cited: '*their Westminster*', and even works of art are condemned as belonging to the detested universe. After the victory, anarchists and builders, temporarily united by the crisis, draw apart, and the builders inevitably win out. They distinguish between politico-economic institutions which one party, having achieved rule, can abolish, and those which have their origin in the biological nature of man and whose particular form, part of a culture, has slowly developed during the course of time.

The family ceases to belong to the parties of the right when it is infused with a democratic spirit, in harmony with Tocqueville's prophecy which we mentioned at the beginning of the chapter. It no longer provides the basis for a social hierarchy any more than it borrows from that hierarchy the principle of its own cohesion. Aside from these obvious thoughts, certain real problems emerge.

The first is concerned with the facts themselves. To what extent has the egalitarian trend already won out? The family, hierarchical and authoritarian, still exists in all Western nations, even the most developed ones, more or less frequently depending upon the nation, the social class, and religious affiliations. Such families are to be found more frequently in rural areas than in large cities, among Catholics more than among Protestants. However, even in Germany, where the old-type family had remained exemplary in the higher echelons of society, it has been shattered or weakened by war.

Sociological studies enable one to follow such changes, but analyses conducted by the classic methods of interviews and questionnaires are likely to touch only the surface of such commonplace but mysterious phenomena. The questions asked do not lead to a profound understanding of the relations between husband and wife, between parent and child. The following are examples of questions used in one such study to determine whether the family structure is authoritarian or democratic: 'As you were growing up, let's say when you were about sixteen, how much influence do you remember having in family decisions affecting yourself?' or: 'At around the same time, if a decision were made that you didn't like, did you feel *free* to complain, did you feel uneasy about complaining, or did you feel it better not to complain?' The latitude within these two types, as defined by the answers to questions such as these, allows for great diversity.[3]

In the second place, the egalitarian idea does not have a single or definite meaning when it refers to relations between the sexes or between generations – that is to say, relations between individuals different by *nature*, incumbents of positions whose roles are *inevitably* different. The Spanish philosopher Ortega y Gasset, in one of his last books, delivered himself of a cheerful polemic against Simone de Beauvoir's *The Second Sex*. He did not hesitate to make use in scarcely modified form of classic arguments:

Because, in fact, this inwardness that we discover in the feminine body and which we shall call 'woman' presents itself to us from the outset as a form of humanity inferior to the masculine. This is the second primary characteristic in the appearance of the She. In a time like ours in which, though to a diminishing degree, we suffer under the tyrannical myth of 'equality', a time in which we everywhere find the mania of believing that things are better when they are equal, the foregoing statement will irritate many people. But irritation is no guarantee of perspicacity. In the presence of Women we men immediately divine a creature who, on the level of 'humanness' has a vital station somewhat

3. Glen H. Elder Jr, 'Family Structure and Educational Attainment: a Cross-National Analysis', in *American Sociological Review*, Vol. 30, No. 1, American Sociological Association, February 1965, pp. 81–96

lower than ours. No other being has this twofold condition – being human, and being less so than a man is. This duality is the source of the unparalleled delight that woman is for the masculine man. The aforesaid equalitarian mania has recently resulted in an attempt to minimize what is one of the fundamental facts in human destiny – the fact of sexual duality. . .

Mademoiselle de Beauvoir thinks that to consist in 'reference to another' is incompatible with the idea of person, which is rooted in 'freedom towards oneself'. But it is not clear why there must be such incompatibility between being free and consisting in reference to another human being. After all, the amount of reference to woman which constitutes the human male is by no means small. But the human male consists pre-eminently in reference to his profession.[4]

Ortega y Gasset defines femininity by a relationship to the body different from that which characterizes the male sex; women are the weak sex. 'This patent characteristic of weakness is the basis of woman's inferior vital rank. But, as it could not but be, this inferiority is the source and origin of the peculiar value that woman possesses in reference to man. For by virtue of it, woman makes us happy and *is happy herself, is happy in the feeling that she is weak*.'[5]

The foregoing, of course, has to do with an ideology of femininity bound up with its social context. But the Spanish philosopher, who extended Dilthey's philosophy, also wrote that man has a history, not a nature. He would have readily acknowledged that woman, as he defined her, is not 'a product of nature but an invention of history', just as is art. This philosophy counters the dominant notions of our era. It would certainly not be acceptable to all the members of the second sex – but then neither is the philosophy of Simone de Beauvoir. From given biological data which science has not yet modified and from endlessly changing social circumstances, women will choose, within certain limits, their method of fulfilment. It is not desirable that all cultures should adopt the same models or that they should acknowledge an equal value in all models.

It would be absurd to believe that men and women, choosing

4. *Man and People*, W. W. Norton & Co., Inc., New York, 1957 pp. 131–2.
5. ibid. p. 135.

freely, would necessarily settle upon the same kind of existence. It would be equally absurd to extrapolate the continuation of certain tendencies and to misinterpret the causes which might lead to a reverse trend. It is probable that the juridical or social barriers which exclude women from certain professions will tend to be lowered. Women will not tolerate easily exclusion from certain activities, whether by law or by custom. It does not follow, however, that in the foreseeable future all women will wish to practise a trade or that most occupations or positions considered socially superior will cease being, for the most part, the preserve of men.

The percentage of girls who want to take up the same studies as boys increases with the spread of modern civilization's values, particularly those which U.S. sociologists call achievement values: values linked to intellectual training, to competence, to the capacity to produce or create. Similarly, the percentage of married women who work outside the home is high; it will remain so, and, at least during the next decades, it will go even higher. This trend is obviously less pronounced when the children are very young. In 1964, in the United States and Great Britain, the percentage of working wives increased to fourty-four per cent for women between the ages of forty-five and fifty-four, thirty-one per cent for women between twenty-five and thirty-four. The proportion is slightly less in the United States than in Great Britain for women around the age of forty. It is predicted that by 1975 these percentages will have increased considerably.

It is possible that with a continuing rise in the curve of affluence a second income might not be as coveted as it is now in many families. Today the available purchasing power seems inadequate for the normal needs of most households. The desire for emancipation – because emancipation is not yet an accomplished fact – is coupled with impatience for things that economic progress has not yet provided out of a single worker's income. These two motivating forces will perhaps subside in the years to come.

One hesitates also to express general theories about 'the education of children' or 'the autonomy of the young'. In certain countries – Sweden, for example – girls and boys are handled exactly alike and enjoy the same freedoms. Among contemporary middle-class Europeans and Americans, the rearing of girls is extraordinarily *liberal* compared to what it was a hundred years ago, or even fifty. The *trend* is also obvious again. But it would be deceptive to imagine that the Nordic pattern is the inevitable result of an evolution common to all the nations of modern civilization. During their first years of family life and at school, children will not be subject everywhere to the same kinds of authority. French parents readily judge American children to be badly brought up, whereas American ethnologists and sociologists think the discipline still in force in most French schools is often cruel. Perhaps the autonomy of adolescents, which is readily expressed in an ideology of 'the young', has deep roots in the structure of contemporary society. It is less bound to cultural traditions than is initial education since cultural traditions are the more imperious for being the less conscious. On one side and on the other, prudence demands that we recognize the persistence of diversity among classes and nations and the evidence of tendential laws.

Thus we come to the decisive problem. Does the family, stripped of its economic function and its social sanctity, preserve its cohesion solely because of enfeebled traditions? If it is to become fully individualistic and egalitarian, is it on the road to disintegration? Has it lost its human significance and its social role? Some observers intimate this. Personally, I am inclined to an opposite view. A family of the democratic age, to use an expression of Tocqueville's, governed by individual ethics, whose nucleus was formed by a marriage in which the principals themselves took the initiative – such a family unquestionably is exposed to the dangers of dissolution. Of 10,000 couples in 1960, the annual number of divorces in France was twenty-eight, in Germany thirty-four, in the United States ninety-one.[6] These national averages conceal enormous variations between regions: in the Paris area, eighteen divorces for every 100 marriages, in Lozère (a poor farming *département*) two for every 100. In the United States one out of five marriages is dissolved by divorce. It has not been shown that European countries might not some day

6. The figures for the three countries were in 1937: twenty-seven, thirty-three and eighty-six respectively. The growth rate is therefore slight.

catch up with the Americans in this area. The divorce rate is not an indication solely of a country's degree of development.

It is useless to deny the frequently deplorable consequences of divorce, particularly for the children. The high rate of divorce in the United States, particularly among Negroes, is in the last analysis a symptom of *anomy*, to refer again to Durkheim's concept, which we shall analyse later. But divorce is also the price to be paid for the victory of freedom of choice, for responsibility placed in the hands of individuals themselves. The efforts or sacrifices which this joint accomplishment entails, in the absence of external obligations, explain the number of failures and desertions. This number also is indicative of the magnitude of moral or affective expectations.

One expects so much more from private life because it differs from other forms of sociability. In one's trade one may feel very replaceable but one remains the most irreplaceable of beings for one's nearest and dearest. Never has the contrast between professional and home life been so sharp – between the anonymity of one and the intimacy of the other. Never have the intervening groups between one and the other been so threatened. Villages dwindle. Reconstitution of equivalent communities in cities or in suburbs is a constant theme for discussion, an objective of urban renewal, of city planners; but it is still in the developmental stage. Local neighbourhood relationships, friendly or not, have lost their immediate significance, their affective richness. Only in his own home does each person seek compensation for the cold efficiency of work; there he no longer has the feeling of being alone among a host of solitary beings. Perhaps the contradictory opinions about the family in contemporary society spring from this: the family is created by decisions that individuals must make and remake, and such individuals demand more from society than did their ancestors.

Tocqueville contrasted the democratic family, as he observed it, with the authoritarian and hierarchical aristocratic or middle-class family. A French historian, Philippe Ariès, searched further back in the past; he traced the development of the family whose model was created, between commoners and nobility, by the bourgeoisie. He perceived first and foremost in the roots of the modern family, during the seventeenth and eighteenth centuries, the attention lavished upon children and their education:

The care lavished on children inspired new feelings, a fresh affection which seventeenth-century portraiture expressed so forcefully and happily: the modern feeling for the family. Parents were no longer content merely to bring children into the world, to help establish some while disregarding others. The morality of the times impelled them to give to all their children, not just to the eldest son, an equal preparation for life, and by the close of the eighteenth century, this included daughters...

The family and the school together removed the child from adult society. The school enveloped the formerly unrestricted childhood in an increasingly severe system of discipline which, in the eighteenth and nineteenth centuries, resulted in complete confinement at boarding school. The solicitude of the family, the church, moralists and guardians thus deprived the child of the freedom he once enjoyed in the company of adults.... But this rigour denoted a sentiment different from the erstwhile indifference: it was the expression of an obsessive love that was to dominate society from the eighteenth century on.[7]

An awareness of population problems and a self-imposed reduction of the birthrate were indications of this new mentality. Another indication was the strength of the bonds of affection within the family. Ariès notes:

The modern family has withdrawn from community life not only its children but a large portion of the time and concern of its adults as well. This denotes the family's need for intimacy and for identity: members of the family are united by common feelings, habits and ways of life. They despise the promiscuities imposed by an earlier sociability. It is conceivable that this moral bond was at bottom a middle-class phenomenon: the great nobles and the common people, at either extremity of the social ladder, preserved for a longer time the traditional proprieties and were more insensitive to the pressures of proximity. The lower classes have maintained almost to our day their taste for living side by side.[8]

The same historian links family sentiments with class feelings. There was a time, he recalls, when extremes of living conditions were accepted without protest or distaste.

7. *L'enfance et la vie familiale sous, l'ancien régime*, Plon, Paris, 1960, p. 464.
8. ibid., p. 465.

Men or women of quality, dressed in all their finery, felt no embarrassment in visiting wretches in prison, in hospitals, or in the streets, who were almost naked in their rags. The juxtaposition of these extremes no more humiliated the one than the other.[9]

But there came a time when

the bourgeoisie would no longer put up with jostling crowds or contact with the common folk. The bourgeoisie broke off contact; it retired from that vast polymorphic society to reconstitute itself as a separate entity, in a homogeneous milieu, among fenced-in families, in homes designed for intimacy, in new sections of the city, protected from contamination. The juxtaposition of inequities, which had once seemed natural, became intolerable to the bourgeoisie: the distaste of the rich preceded the shame of the poor. The new society assured to each a way of life, a reserved space where it was understood that dominant traits were to be respected, that one should conform to a conventional model, an ideal type, and not stray from it, on pain of excommunication.[10]

In certain respects such a description, influenced by the characteristics peculiar to French culture, is still valid for modern societies. The physical separation of social classes by a certain mode of life, the crowding together of families of similar status in the same neighbourhood, each withdrawn and self-sufficient – who has not witnessed this, from Jerusalem in the state of Israel to Paris or New York? The segregation of the Negroes in the northern cities of the United States is but an extreme form of this kind of social segregation which has accompanied the development of modern society since the seventeenth century in Europe and has blossomed in the last century.

In our time it is possible to observe, particularly in the cities of the Third World, a survival of earlier mixed conditions in certain parts of town, the typically bourgeois forms of nineteenth-century segregation, alongside the current forms of this segregation, as modified by the growth of middle and lower middle classes. But economic progress has in no instance suppressed the division of urban space according to the lines of demarcation between the social strata. It has perhaps made it even more distinct; it has diminished the relative importance of the so-called common

9. ibid. p. 466.
10. ibid.

people's milieu which maintained a tradition of side-by-side living. As everyone's income increases, new families in turn adopt the middle-class way. The concern for conformity is nowhere as widespread as in the United States, where the middle-class way of life is that of the majority; there was no American Old Regime to provide a formal consistency to the social distinctions of the last century, which still survive to some extent in Europe.

Those who deplore the disintegration of the family only see one side of the story, and a narrow one at that. To be sure, adolescents enjoy a good deal of independence even before they start to earn their own living; they choose their mates, and the girls, too, benefit by this freedom. The less a family resembles a collective entity or institution that persists throughout generations the more fragile it becomes. But it often gains in loving cohesion what it loses in stability. More than ever, to cite Tönnies' famous antithesis, it represents the community (*Gemeinschaft*) that survives in a civilization which is dominated by the life principle of society (*Gesellschaft*). More than ever the bourgeois pattern remains peremptory and tends to spread: penchant for privacy, concern for the education of children, awareness of social distinctions (expressed by strivings for individual status rather than by class consciousness).

In the first chapter we examined educational inequality, a phase of the dialectic of equality. The origin of that inequality lies in the continuity of the family and in the bond between family and class feeling. In France, Ariès writes, seventeenth-century charity schools 'founded for the poor also attracted the sons of the rich'.[11] But, from the eighteenth century on, middle-class families withdrew their children from the system that provided primary education for the common people.

This kind of educational segregation accentuates social and physical segregation and neither has yet been overcome in any modern society. It is the family as much as the nation that transmits the explicit and implicit norms of social class. Thus the exponents of tradition fear disintegration of the family, and the champions of social justice may view the persistence of it as an insurmountable obstacle to equality at the starting line.

11. ibid.

*The Education Explosion*

France, like Britain and Germany, is currently experiencing a social change that has been called an 'educational explosion'. The number of students attending French secondary schools was 100,000 in 1850; by 1910 it was 200,000. Whereas this represented an increase of 100 per cent in sixty years, the total population remained almost stationary during the same period. The figure for 1930 was 350,000, but by 1951 it had climbed to 1,204,000. By 1961 even this total had more than doubled (2,524,000). A bit less than twice this figure (4,650,000) is expected by 1970.

The figures for instructional personnel in higher education are no less revealing. The number of teachers had doubled in the course of a century, from 1840 to 1951. This number doubled again in the nine years between 1951 and 1960, and for a third time between 1960 and 1963. The total number was but 2,707 in 1946; it exceeded 15,000 in 1963 and will reach the 50,000 mark by 1985. In 1912 those who received the *baccalauréat* constituted less than one per cent of that generation; today the recipients of the degree constitute fifteen per cent of their generation. The percentage is expected to rise to thirty per cent by 1985. In 1960, twenty-eight out of every 100 youths aged seventeen were still attending school. The figure will be about forty by 1970.

The problems created by this influx of students in the secondary schools and universities do not concern us here. But the relationship between the qualifications imparted to the young and the jobs they will have to fill, a relationship as yet ill-explored, affects the stability and organization of society as a whole. The time is past when the bourgeoisie, as portrayed in literature, saw budding revolutionaries in all the gifted children of poor families who did well in their studies. Those of the right as well as of the left accept the principles of free access on the basis of talent to secondary schools and colleges. They also agree, at least theoretically, that the best graduates of secondary schools or colleges should be admitted to universities regardless of social origin.

The countries of Western Europe – France, Italy, Germany, Great Britain – suffer at the moment from a shortage at the middle and top levels of academic achievement. They could use more university graduates and Ph.D.s than they have. Only two per cent of the total population of France today have a college diploma; according to present predictions this figure will rise to eight per cent in 1985. It is quite likely that some of these graduates will in the future fill jobs of a kind they now consider beneath them.

On the basis of our present knowledge, it is difficult to make any longer-range projection. How can one forecast, decades in advance, the division of labour among the various occupations and trades or the kind of training necessary for each of them? Perhaps education increasingly will be regarded as something valuable in itself to which everyone is automatically entitled as the prerequisite of personal self-fulfilment, and in that sense divorced from the training that may be required for occupational skills. It is at least conceivable that many men will learn for learning's sake, not just in order to wangle a parchment or to obtain a more remunerative position.

For the present, however, the social order continues to be more pedestrian in this regard. A person's career seems to be, and apparently will continue to be, largely determined by the kind of education he received early in life. If social status is dependent on the possession of a degree, if educational success is to a large extent determined by family environment, even in an increasingly mobile and intellectually oriented society the family will retain an importance which some are inclined to deny it. Although the evidence hardly warrants categorical statements, it seems probable to me that the close relationship between socialization through the agency of the family and socialization through the agency of the school (the term as used here includes all levels through the university) will persist in the foreseeable future.

In France and Great Britain a kind of *de facto* segregation appears very early in the schools, affecting all children of ten to twelve years and over. Only a small number of children from working-class or peasant families are admitted to the type of schools that would give them a real chance of reaching the university level. The fact that secondary education is free in France has not accelerated the so-called process of 'democratization': there has been only a limited increase in the percentage of working-class and peasant youths receiving a classical education proceeding to the college level. The real revolution consists in the realization by the parents themselves of the importance of schooling for the future of their children. In France this dates back less than twenty years; it is still too early to observe its effects.

The French figures for the social origin of students are significant, and they are not very different from English or German figures. In 1961–2, out of 1,000 working people the number of students in the category of salaried farm workers was 1.4; workers 1.9; service personnel 1.7; farmers 3.9; white-collar workers 6.8; industrialists, including artisans and shopkeepers, 18; middle range non-manual categories 25.4. The figure for the liberal professions was 79.3; among heads of industry 106. The probability of attaining a higher education among 100 children born twenty years previously is 0.7 for salaried farm workers, 1.4 for labourers, 2.4 for service personnel, 3.9 for farmers, 9.5 for white-collar workers, 29.6 for small shopkeepers, 58.5 for the upper echelons and the liberal professions. Salaried farm workers, labourers, service personnel, and farmers represent about sixty per cent of the population; they provide about twelve per cent of the students. The higher categories, the liberal professions and heads of industry, represent approximately five per cent of the total manpower and about one-third of the students are coming from this category. If one adds to these two categories the middle-range white-collar group about fifty per cent of the students come from less than ten per cent (about eight per cent) of the population.

The causes of 'this educational inequality' are essentially the same in all countries, although the consequences vary. The causes are first and foremost institutional. In France the quality of secondary schools, for the most part state-supported, varies according to the importance of the surrounding area. A secondary school in a small city is not as good as a large Parisian *lycée*. Workers, artisans, and peasants automatically send their children to a technical or 'general' school from which few real students emerge. In England the entrance examinations for grammar schools determine the scholastic careers of most children, and here success or failure depend upon family environment as much as upon aptitude. Teaching methods and the manner of selection (examinations and competition) add their impact to that arising from the nature of the institution itself. Instructors are not always aware of the fact that they are lecturing to children who live in a cultural context far removed from that of the school and its masters. Most examinations measure acquired knowledge, such as mastery of the language, which is absorbed almost unconsciously in the course of daily life, and thus individual aptitudes are inevitably intertwined with the varying process of socialization of the family. Social or financial limitations must then be added to institutional and pedagogical causes of inequality; American research has demonstrated that the proportion of young people of equal scholastic merit who go to the best secondary schools or, in a later phase, attend college varies according to the parents' social level and financial means.

These three causal agents exercise a powerful impact, but it would not be impossible to apply reforms that would sensibly reduce, if not eliminate, their effect. Elementary and secondary schools cannot all be of like quality, but the premature segregation that prevails in Continental European and British schools is not inevitable. The manner of selection, rooted as it is in tradition, could be modified by quite a different type of entrance examination, one which would permit a better – or less bad – differentiation between native aptitudes and such capabilities as are evidently the consequence of family and environmental influence. Having said all this, is it possible to counterbalance the influence of the family on scholarly achievement? The number of brothers and sisters, living conditions, the transmission of culture by the parents themselves, the varying degrees of importance attached to studies by children who accept the values of their environment, family socialization – all these will remain, for as long as one can foresee, the principal factors which, together with inherited aptitudes, will determine the school and university careers of the young.

These traditional educational inequalities, borne out by French and European statistics, are very much greater than the irreducible inequities implied by the fact of family continuity. But, according to reliable statistics, even in the Soviet Union about fifty per cent of the students come from less than twenty per cent of the population. And, in the United States, with its universal free education, statistics, however imperfect, bring to light the same phenomenon of inequality, although it is of a different nature in some respects. To begin with, the changes illustrated by the figures relating to France – the prolongation of schooling, the increase in the percentages of students of every age group – began earlier in the United States and are more marked than in Europe. In 1900 about 6.4 per cent of the seventeen year-olds finished high school, in 1939–40 this percentage rose to 50 per cent, in 1960 to 65 per cent, and in 1970 it will be 70 per cent. Similarly, the percentage of the eighteen- to twenty-one-year-olds enrolled in institutions of higher learning (colleges), which was 4 per cent in 1900, rose to 15 per cent in 1940 and approximately 35 per cent in 1965. In 1960, 17 per cent of a given age obtained a B.A., compared with 7 per cent in 1938 and 2.2 per cent in 1910; 3.4 per cent received an M.A., compared with 0.9 per cent in 1938 and 0.15 per cent in 1910. Lastly, 0.43 per cent received a Ph.D., compared with 0.13 per cent in 1938 and 0.02 per cent in 1910. From the evidence, it is plain that the offspring of the lower classes have a greatly increased chance to pursue their studies to the university level.

Nonetheless, inequalities persist. They result primarily from the tremendous diversity of secondary schools, caused either by the quality of the teaching or the social prestige attached to the kind of diploma obtained. A certain correlation, although not so pronounced as in Europe, still exists between a student's social origin and his scholastic achievement. World-wide statistics, though approximate and inexact, give an idea of the figures for various categories (out of 100 upper- or upper-middle-class boys, 85 per cent enrolled in college in 1960, and of 100 girls, 75 per cent enrolled). These percentages decrease to 60 and 38 respectively for the lower middle class, to 38 and 18 for the lower, and to 6 and 2 for the lower lower class. But in 1940 the percentage for the lower middle class was 20 (without differentiating between boys and girls) as compared with 60 and 38 twenty years later. If we accept scholastic achievement as a valid measurement of aptitude, we can divide the population of young people into four quarters according to intellectual capacity: the upper and upper middle classes would account for 20 per cent of the top quartile, the lower middle class 40 per cent, and the lower classes 40 per cent. All those of the first group, that is, those who belong to a privileged social group, would finish high school; only two out of twenty would not go to college, three out of twenty would not finish college, and fifteen out of twenty would go on to the end of four years of higher education. Of the forty of the second group, nineteen would finish four years of higher education, and of the forty of the third group, eleven would finish.

The formula for educational equality, that is to say, the substitution of purely genetic chance for the combination of both genetic and social chance, is an abstraction, not an ideal. No one has yet suggested taking children away from their parents in order to guarantee equality from the very beginning. Moreover, it would be necessary to take them away the very day of their birth, since the psychoanalysts now teach us that the very first years forever fix each individual's psychic destiny.

Nobody knows the precise percentage of individuals in a given population capable of achieving without extraordinary effort the level of the *baccalauréat*, licentiate, or doctorate (in the United States, high school diploma, B.A., M.A., and Ph.D.). Nor does anyone know what portion of its resources each of the national groups will set aside for the training of its youth. The strictness of selection will be in proportion to the volume of resources available, as is already the case in the Soviet Union and Japan. In Japan there are three times as many candidates as there are places available in the universities. For one place in any one of the three leading institutions (Tokyo, Kyōto, Hitosubashi) there are several dozen applicants.

It is not important for us to predict how far this trend will go in the next fifty or a hundred years. It tends towards a greater homogeneity of social classes, increased educational facilities for everyone, and therefore towards a lessening of the gap between the socio-professional categories in the total population and the place of these same categories in the student population. This gap concerns us in so fár as it confirms that continuing heterogeneity of modern society which many observers, impressed by certain economic changes, are inclined to overlook.

Even an ethnically homogeneous modern society nonetheless remains socially heterogeneous. This heterogeneity is responsible for educational inequality; or, rather, the one is the expression of the other, since scholastic opportunities could be equalized only if the process of socialization in the family did not create differences among children which cannot be charged to their inherited aptitudes. We cannot doubt the evidence regarding the inequality of aptitudes, but neither can we doubt that inequality of achievement shows a marked correlation to social determinants that include the family environment.

This heterogeneity, inseparable from the process of socialization of the family, is not a temporary phenomenon. Children will always be advantaged or disadvantaged by the mark left upon them by their very early experiences. To be sure, these experiences are not all determined by the occupation or social rank of parents; the wealthiest families sometimes create a neurotic atmosphere. But, aside from financial difficulties, the social level remains an important factor in success or failure in school and university.

Such being the case, modern society cannot be said to be responding to a single trend moving towards more similar living conditions, increased class mobility, and greater equality at the starting line. Two opposing trends are present at the same time. One tends towards a reduction of economic inequalities, increasing educational opportunities for all, a growing demand by all parents for intellectual training for their children, and a general widening of the social horizons of working-class families. But there is a counter trend: socialization of the family continues to leave its imprint on each individual; competition will be open to larger and larger numbers of children. But it will also be sharper, as upper-class parents become even more emphatic in urging their children to take their studies seriously in order to avoid slipping back into a lower level of the hierarchy.

These two opposing tendencies have long been foreseen by philosophers of history. A society dominated by the scientific spirit needs a certain degree of mobility, but not a mobility pushed to the extreme. It must assure to the greatest number the intellectual training reserved for a minority in traditional societies. Such a society has every reason not to permit exceptionally gifted individuals to be wasted, no matter what their social origins; but apart from this, it matters little where those who reach the university level come from. The efforts of middle- and upper-middle-class families to prevent their children from becoming *déclassé* and thereby losing the advantages of their birth are perhaps in contradiction with abstract notions of justice, but they result from the spontaneous operation of the basic mechanisms of society. In short, socialization by the family and socialization by the school will remain linked to each other, and the heterogeneity of social classes, so far as intellectual or cultural development is concerned, will be maintained.

### The Age Groups

One might contend that we have neglected two other factors of socialization which cast doubt on the preceding analyses. At school, not only do the study courses and the teacher–pupil relationships impose norms or patterns of conduct on an individual but so do relations among students themselves. Within the family, relations with members of the same age group might be no less important than parent–child relations. Moreover, modern means of communication, radio or television, reach into all homes; how then could the young fail to be influenced by the messages that come to them from all over the world and are part of their daily lives?

There is no question of the importance of age groupings. For every child, socialization through contemporaries is an integral part of the same process that is effected by the school; in every institution a subtle relationship takes place not only between teachers and pupils but also among pupils. The nature of the one helps to establish that of the other.

Sociological studies, especially those which have been conducted by sociologists with an ethnological bent, reveal the extreme diversity of pedagogical methods employed from country to country, as well as considerable variations within a country. Perhaps, viewing the matter as a whole, one would be tempted to say that the *liberal tendency* is advancing. By liberal tendency I mean a number of particular things: the teacher's awareness of those characteristics peculiar to children of different ages which results in the effort to take into consideration the specific needs of the young, to make discipline as intelligible as possible, to dispel confusion between the teacher and the superego, sometimes even to stimulate pupils from their tenth or eleventh year to organize themselves and to create, so to speak, their own society. But although apprenticeship for democracy at school through the spontaneous organization of students, with the full accord of the teaching staff, is frequent in the United States and more frequent still in Sweden, there is scarcely any sign of it yet either in Germany or France or, so far as I know, in the Soviet countries. 'The new education' has probably diminished the authoritarian nature of traditional practices, but it has not generally or profoundly transformed it.

There are groupings according to age in all countries, but their modes of behaviour vary considerably from country to country according to social class and, within each class, according to the attitude toward adults. The intermittently erupting bands of adolescents in revolt against society make for good newspaper copy, but in most cases as these bands become more notorious the more eccentric their actions become and the smaller the minority of youths whose interest they arouse. It could be that our society reflects a rather general tendency: an awareness of adolescence by the adolescents themselves, an arm's length view of the society into which one is about to enter – a society that is somewhat suspect, to which the young feel alien. If this is true, it might be an anticipatory reaction of sorts to the anonymous rationality and the strict discipline of the occupation that awaits. Like the family, the sociability of age groups is complementary to the sociability of work because it is fashioned along different lines.

These inevitably commonplace statements interest us less than the conclusions suggested by them, which have as their themes social homogeneity or heterogeneity. Although one forgets in the stadium the social origin of athletes and although seats of learning, from primary school to university, assemble youth from all social levels, it remains true that most of those who are grouped by age, especially if they are at all organized, in most cases come from the same social stratum. In so far as family and school together make for cultural diversity, the influence of the age groups tends to work in the same direction.

The media of communication – radio, television, newspapers, phonograph records – are means which, according to some, tend to transform populations into think-alike masses, to render them indistinguishable one from another. Since this term 'masses' has entered into current usage and implies a certain image of modern society, perhaps it might be useful to distinguish its several meanings.

Newspapers and political parties use the term, first in a natural sense, merely to designate the largest number. Communist leaders freely use the term 'masses' where British labour unions refer to the 'rank and file'. People on vacation become masses because they number in the millions; and one speaks of the masses of American tourists in Europe. This meaning does not concern us.

Quite different is the meaning attached to the word by Ortega y Gasset in his well-known book *The Revolt of the Masses*. The mass is contrasted to the elite as mediocrity is to quality.

The division of society into masses and elite minorities is not a division of men into classes, and such a division cannot be likened to a hierarchical scale divided into higher and lower classes. It is obvious that one will find in the upper classes, if they have really become superior, a larger number of men who will adopt the 'great medium' than in the lower classes, which are usually made of colourless individuals without quality. But in the last analysis, one might find masses and an authentic minority in every social class.[12]

We shall also set aside this meaning of the word as formulated by an aristocratic critic of modern society.

The text which we have just cited points up an almost inevitable ambiguity: except in rare cases, certain purely intellectual qualities cannot be acquired save by members of a socially superior milieu. These attributes are indispensable to the performance of certain social functions. In fact, these functions are effectively performed only by members of the highest social levels. In this respect there are, or so it seems to me, far fewer changes than the Spanish philosopher suggests. The novelty is this: politically,

12. Editions Stock, Paris, 1961, pp. 54–5.

those who govern, in representative democracy and one-party regimes alike, address themselves to the average man and use language and arguments adapted to the presumably lowest level of their public. Language comprehensible to all becomes the language of propaganda, sometimes that of parliaments; it is not the language of experts, of public servants, or scholars. The aristocrat denounces the lowering of the elite to the level of the masses, the democrat denounces the manipulation of the masses by the elite. Both emphasize certain aspects of modern society, but the latter seems to me closer to the essential: whether in science or in art, the elite draws away from the masses – to their good or detriment. One could argue about this endlessly. In any case, if the intellectual elite pays court to the man in the street – the common man – it is not constrained to do so because the mediocre revolt, but because of its own mediocrity, its own demagoguery.

Between the neutral and pejorative senses of the word, two meanings intervene, one psychological, the other sociological. The word 'masses' is sometimes used as an equivalent for crowds, in the sense that Gustave Le Bon gave to the word 'crowd'. (In German, crowd psychology was translated as Psychologie der Massen.) It is more accurate to make a distinction between crowds and masses. Crowd psychology has as its theme the behaviour of men in a group, side by side in a street demonstration, a stadium, or a parliamentary assembly. Emotionality, intellectual mediocrity, the crowd's propensity towards violence and irresponsibility – these are commonplace ideas. Every society has experienced the phenomena of crowds. What is new is this: scholars, utilizing what they have learned from Pavlov and Freud, have constructed a theory from which was developed a technique of manipulation.

Thus we arrive at the final meaning of the word. The notion, a rather vague one, bound up with the notion of masses, is one of non-differentiation, of a loss of social structure. But, in actuality, the techniques of psycho-political manipulation are painstakingly adapted to the specificities of social groups. At first glance, the very idea of 'massification', the tendency of the entire population toward homogeneity, is surprising. Are radio and television about to erase those cultural distinctions bound up with differences between social classes? On this point we must again be cautious about drawing conclusions. The widespread use of television has been in effect for only one generation in the United States, and for less than that in Europe. The uses to which it will be put remain uncertain. The following remarks are therefore provisional and hazardous.

The thesis concerning the trend toward cultural homogeneity seems to me to contain an element of truth; cultural patterns, inseparable from small communities and farm life, are pushed back by the diffusion of patterns which originate in urban civilization. Communications media such as radio and television contribute mightily to the opening up of isolated family and village social structures. Similarly, the specific culture of the workers' aristocracy of the last century cannot resist the combined impact of intellectualization of the trades on the one hand, and of radio and television on the other. The workers' aristocracy is henceforth not so much an elite born of manual skill and concrete experience, as a semi-intellectual elite. The television technician belongs rather to the engineer's world than to that of the day labourer. Having risen in his professional activity, he will participate in the culture of the upper classes, transmitted to him by the media of communication in a more or less degraded form; he will not be tempted to create his own culture. Communication between the social classes has become too easy (even though the distance between them may remain great) for the maintenance or reconstitution of an authentically popular proletarian and peasant culture.

Having accepted this element of truth, the thesis that the new communications media have primarily social and cultural influence seems to me at this time more false than true. Radio and television as instruments of socialization are not powerful enough to win out over that of the family and the school. A number of uncertainties persist. What is the influence on children of the images presented by television? Does it distract young Americans from studying or reading? It would be ridiculous to presume to give answers to all such questions that would be valid for every class today and for all countries tomorrow.

But I believe we can affirm that the movie-radio-television culture, in which apparently the whole population participates, does not imply that youth is becoming more and more homogeneous, that erudite culture has been suppressed, or that 'massification' – the disappearance of the highest aptitudes and values – is inevitable. Radio, movies, and television are, in turn, giving evidence of an increasing diversity; different programmes are available for intellectual elites and the people at large. Even when the programme is of ordinary quality – which is often the case – it does not follow that listeners hear it in the same way or that viewers see the same thing. For a long time children's books have ignored social distinctions, but this fact does not prevent young workers and bourgeois, each dreaming about the same exploits, the same heroes, from living in distant worlds. Whatever the relations between so-called mass culture and so-called learned culture, the one conveyed by pictures, the other by writings, the inequities of intellectual training and the differences in way of life and work which result from them persist in large measure: the distance between the reader of *Le Monde* and the reader of *Courrier du Cœur*, between the reader of the *New York Times* and the reader of the *New York Daily News*, may not be the same as that which existed a century ago between the common man (who did not know how to read) and the bourgeois; but it has not disappeared, and perhaps it has not lessened. In the United States, mass circulation magazines and television networks count their audiences in multiples of millions, and so a certain type of communication reaches individuals in every segment of life. But the *New York Times* still has only a few hundred thousand readers.

It is through economic progress that the trend toward a certain form of social homogeneity is visible. A growing percentage of families has the necessary income to adapt to the bourgeois style of life. Statistical studies show the extent to which in any given country, but to a lesser degree in Western countries, extra money is spent in almost identical fashion. At a given income level, it is possible to predict with a fair degree of accuracy the percentage of families that will purchase a refrigerator, a car, or a camera. This uniformity of modes of consumption includes as yet only a segment of the population, more or less extensive depending upon the achieved stage of development. But mainly the uniformity of certain modes of consumption (food, clothing, even housing) does not yet entail uniformity in value systems. Occupation and educational background will serve to maintain a distance between the social classes. To repeat: the more society is 'intellectualized' and made 'scientific', the greater the impact of intellectual inequalities.

## Family v. Society

We began this chapter with a quotation from Tocqueville. We should like to terminate it with another passage from the same book, *Democracy in America*, by the same author:

> I see an immense crowd of equal and similar men ceaselessly milling about in order to acquire for themselves those vulgar little pleasures with which they satisfy their souls. Each one when viewed separately is like a stranger to the density of all the others; his children and his personal friends constitute all of humanity for him; as for being a part of his fellow-citizens, he is next to them and does not see them; he touches them and does not feel them; he exists in himself alone, and for himself, and though he still has a family one may say that he no longer has a country.[13]

Indifference to the city, withdrawal into private, that is to say, family life – such will be the destiny of most men in a democratic society where 'each individual is weak and isolated, and society is alert, provident, and powerful'. Although these passages are often cited as proof of the author's exceptional lucidity, modern society, as we have lived in it for the past half century and as we observe it today, does not bear out this dream or nightmare. It is not true that 'violence is rare, cruelty almost unknown'; it is not true that 'talent is becoming rarer', although it is true that 'intelligence is becoming more widespread'. Unfortunately, it is not true that 'all the bonds of race, class and homeland are slackening, and the great bond of humanity is becoming tighter'.[14] Our century is that of the welfare state; but it is also the century of Stalin and Hitler, of revolutions and wars, of genocides.

Tocqueville imagined what Aldous Huxley called the 'brave

13. Op. cit., Vol. II, Bk 4, ch. 6.
14. ibid., ch. 8.

new world' – a social order quite conceivable, which intellectual aristocrats, nostalgic for liberalism, denounce with ironic indignation during the intervals between two carnages.

In what way was Tocqueville mistaken? He was not mistaken, apparently, about the close-knit democratic family, which allowed great latitude for individual choice, and which was held together by bonds of affection and made stronger by the fact of no longer owing anything to other institutions. Nor was he mistaken about the importance which modern society accords to the ideal of equality, or about the extension of public services and social laws. Tyrannies are, as he has said, in a sense guardians. Even authoritarian regimes rule in the interest of the ruled, or a sizeable fraction thereof.

The first and most serious error is to have believed that 'all the bonds of race, class and homeland are slackening', and that 'the great bond of humanity is becoming tighter'. The error is interesting; it is, one might say, the exact counterpart of Marx's error. The latter fixed his attention on nascent industrialization, the struggle between proprietors and employees, the reorganization of classes based upon equality of income, and the place occupied by each group in the process of production. He misjudged the consequences of economic progress, the general enrichment from which the workers would in turn profit. Tocqueville did not ignore the industrialization process, although it is not highlighted in any of his books. It is in contrast to aristocratic society that he sets off the originality of modern society. In the latter he discerned certain trends, the growth of the bourgeoisie for example, but he did not understand precisely the accompanying mechanisms for raising the standard of living for all, for the diffusion of well-being – that is to say, the mechanisms of technical and economic progress. But above all he did not understand the dialectics of equality; he did not foresee that as soon as a kind of equality was obtained, fresh demands would spring up. Juridical equality is nothing without economic and social equality. But the latter remains impossible, even in a society that is ethnically homogeneous. This inequality, which would be compatible with the ideal of modern society if it were strictly individual in character, if it were attributable solely to inequality of aptitudes, seems always to be collective in its social, national, or racial origins. Moreover, the bonds of nation, race, and sometimes even class, far from slackening, have tended to become strengthened. Nationalism and racism emerge automatically from a democratic civilization that destroys closed communities, makes of each individual a member of a group, and encourages each group to compare its condition with that of other groups.

One response to the trend of modern society is the withdrawal within himself of each individual 'who still has a family but not a country'. But the history of our century becomes unintelligible if one does not also perceive the opposite trend. Under certain stresses the same individuals who in normal times apparently enjoy the pleasures of home, television, a car, weekends in the country, suddenly behave wildly. They see themselves only as Frenchmen, or proletarians, or whites. War, crisis, foreign despotism, revolt of a scorned ethnic minority, tear them loose from their habits, and we see them quite ready to die for a cause: agitators of a party, soldiers of their country, heroic and cruel, forgetful of themselves, but also of the rights of others. Tocqueville did not deny that 'democratic governments could become violent and cruel during moments of great ferment and danger', but he added at once: 'such crises are rare and temporary'. And a little further on: 'I do not fear that they will encounter tyrants in their leaders, but rather mentors.'[15] Having learned from experience, we fear tyrants more than mentors.

Tocqueville's second error is to have exaggerated greatly both the *equality* and *uniformity* of conditions. The formula for equality is only valid, not without some reservations, for a fraction of the bourgeois segments of the population; it is applicable only to the economic aspects of life. Businessmen and professors, buying the same foods, indistinguishable by their attire, driving the same kind of cars, perhaps share the same human condition: possibly both buy refrigerators, television sets, and washing machines with the same frequency. But they are still not *alike*, nor will they become alike. A technical or scientific society entails a differentiation and a hierarchy neither one of which is on the verge of disappearing: a differentiation of values and a hierarchy of

15. ibid.

intellectual levels. The homogeneity of ways of life is superficial as long as intellectual and moral heterogeneity persist, and with them the desire to differentiate, to practise all sorts of snobbery, even that of racism.

One might counter perhaps by maintaining that the media of communication are spreading the uniformity that Tocqueville had foreseen long ago. I personally believe that nothing of the kind is true, or at least that the risk is less one of *uniformity* than of *conformity*. This risk has existed ever since each individual, enclosed in his inevitably specialized occupation, came to apprehend the world solely from the slanted and fragmented news gleaned from newspapers, radio or television sets – all subject to governmental or private regulation. The distance between the scholar and the man in the street, despite the latter's progress, is just as great today as it was before. What is novel is that millions of men have acquired a partial understanding of global society and national problems, which optimists hail as a stepping-stone along the path of true participation, while pessimists see in it only enslavement to a prefabricated public opinion manufactured by the ruling elite – public or private, according to ideological taste.

Neither side lacks arguments in its favour. If I had to choose, I would align myself with the optimists, but not without hesitation or anguish. Hitler and Stalin, a cultivated people mobilized by a demagogue of diabolical genius, millions of totally free men, acclaiming from afar a cruel tyrant – these experiences in our own century bring home to us the power which Caesars or factions wield to mobilize crowds, sometimes even before these crowds have been uprooted by some historic storm. Perhaps television is less favourable to such events than radio because it may reveal the lies of these people if not their set purpose. A third man might henceforth be interposed between the state and its people: the foreigner, speaking for an adverse regime whose message can always penetrate barriers and fog. In the long run even totalitarian propaganda exhausts itself. Its militants tire of building a new city; withdrawal to private life gradually subdues partisan exaltation.

Oscillation between political fanaticism and the indifference of the petty bourgeois is not equivalent to the conflict between conformity and personality. If conformity is called the individual's submission to his group, then we may speak of the bohemian's conformity as well as Babbitt's. Perhaps there is no conformity more rigorous than that of literary coteries. Avant-garde movements are justly considered intolerant. They are numerous enough to reassure those who fear uniformity, but they remind us opportunely of a banal truth: minds capable of facing the disapproval of their peers, whether conservative or revolutionary, are few in any society.

# 5 The Socio-Industrial Order

Of all of Lenin's books, *The State and Revolution*, written in exile just before the seizure of power in 1917, is the most utopian. It is also the book which exerted the least influence upon Marxist philosophy and the course of events. It provides evidence of the possible conjunction in Lenin's mind of an acute realism with a set of almost childish illusions: action sometimes means forgetting the dream. Running a socialist society, Lenin wrote, would be simplified to the point where anyone would be able to exercise the necessary administrative functions and the workers themselves would take turns supervising the activities of employees of the state.

How much more perceptive were the Saint-Simonians and the Positivists, the first theorists of the last century! Auguste Comte wrote:

> There can no more be an army without officers than one without soldiers. This elementary notion is just as pertinent to the industrial order as to the military. Although it has not yet been possible to systematize modern industry, the spontaneous division which has gradually developed between entrepreneurs and workers is certainly the germinal element necessary to its eventual organization. No large-scale operation would be possible if each participant had also to be an administrator, or if management were vaguely entrusted to an inert, irresponsible community. Modern industry obviously tends to increase continually the size of enterprises, with each increase immediately giving rise to greater expansion. This natural tendency, when properly regulated by a moral authority, far from being unfavourable to the proletariat, alone will permit the systematization of material life.[1]

The allusion is to a hierarchy which is immanent and indispensable to industrial enterprise, which itself is continually

1. *Système de politique positive*, Vol. I, 1851.

expanding, and Auguste Comte's analysis of this decisive point holds true today. His comparison of the industrial order with the military order may at first seem surprising, but another quotation, taken from a writing of Comte's youth, complements and corrects the analogy:

This is the place to observe, in reference to the people, the fundamental and favourable difference that exists between their present-day coordination with their industrial leaders, and their former subjection to military leaders. This difference will make apparent one of the most important and fortunate contrasts between old and new systems. Under the old system, people were *regimented* in relation to their leaders; under the new, they are *united* with them. The military leaders exercised the power to *command* whereas today industrial leaders provide only *leadership*. In the first case the people were *subjects;* in the second *members*. Such in effect is the remarkable characteristic of industrial combines that those who are involved in them are in reality all collaborators, all associates, from the common unskilled labourer to the richest worker and the most enlightened engineer.[2]

These two texts combined seem to me to pose the central problem of the socio-industrial order. The typical business enterprise in modern society has thousands of labourers and employees. If these workers obey the heads of business and their administrators as soldiers do their officers, can they at the same time be considered associates rather than subjects? Have they the feeling of being associated in a common task, or do they feel that they are subject to an anonymous power, exploited by the rich or by the state?

## The Production System

Men produce to live, they do not live to produce, although certain societies sometimes give the impression that production is a goal in itself. But a community is not considered modern, and does not look upon itself as such, unless it produces efficiently. Whatever the regime, industrial efficiency presupposes the organization of numerous workers into huge units. The factory itself, where actual

2. *Sommaire appréciation de l'ensemble du passé moderne*, included as an appendix to Vol. IV of the *Système de politique positive*, 1851.

production in the physical sense takes place, may not necessarily be gigantic – according to the area, the optimum size seems to vary – but its controlling financial and administrative apparatus usually embraces several factories and may include a distribution system. Called a *corporation* by Americans, an *entreprise* by the French, this has become the typical institution of the twentieth-century economy.

It is not important to know what percentage of the work force is directly employed by such corporations. In the United States the gigantic firms that organize production lines from which millions of automobiles pour each year also place orders with hundreds of subcontractors, and their product provides a livelihood for hundreds of thousands of gasoline retailers who, even though they may be financially connected with a huge oil company, still escape, at least physically, from the characteristic organization of modern society.

As Comte predicted, industrial operations, as well as those production and distribution complexes we call corporations, have indeed undergone an indefinite expansion in the course of the last century. To be sure, the whole of industry has not become *one* army, and the Marxist-Leninists have learned at great cost that it is not possible to run an economy by methods suitable for the management of *one* factory or *one* company. Even so, the law of expansion common to both the military and industrial orders has been confirmed.

Other resemblances are more easily seen today than a century ago; the more an army uses the complex 'hardware' manufactured by industry the more it must borrow from industry techniques of organization and action. In its wartime mobilization from 1940 to 1945 the United States demonstrated that innumerable 'civilian capacities' answered the needs of the military establishment. Twenty years later the most powerful and costly military establishment in the world was headed by a member of the President's Cabinet drawn from the upper ranks of industry, a telling symbol of the close kinship of problems common to the management of these two orders.

The hierarchic parallels between army and industry are increasing. From one rung to the next of the *same* ladder, the requisite knowledge and talents sometimes become different rather than unequal (but the remuneration for, and the prestige of, this different knowledge or ability are unequal). The superior may no longer be capable of certain tasks, material or intellectual, which his subordinates perform with ease. The specialization of duties is no less striking or rigorous in the hierarchical order than on the horizontal level.

Alexander was admired by the German historian Delbrück as perhaps the last of the great war chiefs who physically engaged in battle. Today's industrial leader, who long since has lost all personal contact with manual labour, is not always capable of following the studies of his research departments. According to the hierarchy and the level within each hierarchy, decisions change in nature. At the top they are *synthetic* and *venturesome*, they require taking into consideration multiple and heterogeneous arguments, and they tend to reduce, but rarely eliminate, a coefficient of uncertainty, whether they pertain to introducing a new automobile model, a weapons system, or a strategy for innovation or deterrence.

The character of decisions made at the highest level explains one of the apparent paradoxes of our civilization: the important role held by non-specialists in industry and in the government – the subordination of engineers and technicians to non-professional heads of businesses who often rise from the ranks of salesmen, of generals to civilian government officials, of the physicists who made possible the manufacture of atomic bombs to the elected politicians who ultimately decide upon their use.

At the head of an enterprise, military or industrial, there are leaders who possess, or are assumed to possess, certain specific personal qualities, although these qualities may not lend themselves to a precise definition. This is why the radical contrast established by Auguste Comte between *commanding* and *leading* is at the very least open to question; at all levels, this contrast, valid in the abstract, is apt to lose its clarity in actual practice.

To those who are part of it, an organization always appears more or less as a system of men commanding other men; technical or administrative necessities become embodied in individuals, and those who submit to them by performing humble or disagreeable tasks have difficulty distinguishing between rational requiremen ts and the orders of their leaders. Rationality takes on the aspect of those who interpret it: sometimes it is rigorous and abstract; sometimes, on the contrary, it is tempered by a desire for communication or equality. These remarks aim simply at suggesting the central theme of the sociology of organizations, civil or military. Analysis of the theoretical or legal structure, like the schematic representation given by tables of organization, leaves in the dark the essential: the true, unofficial, beneath-the-surface relations between performers of the various roles as distinguished from their purely formal or official relations. The contradiction between formal and informal relations in an enterprise is the equivalent of the contradiction between a constitution and its application in a political regime.

The dissimilarity of objectives – combat in the one case, production in the other – makes it impermissible to push too far any comparison of the two orders, military and industrial. The military order most resembles the industrial in its supporting activities (transportation, ordnance, logistics) and in the so-called 'learned' services in which the officer tends to become an engineer and the enlisted man a technician. Aside from push-button war, the danger of death, the degree of privation, and the margin of initiative which the commanding officer of a small unit and the private soldier himself still have, make the experiences of combat and labour basically different. In view of the emergencies that constitute the *raison d'être* of the military organization, it is impossible to think of substituting, even ideally, *direction* for *command*, that is democratic-style command for command in the authoritarian or unconditional style.

Military discipline tends to bring under its subjection not just the soldier as the performer of an assigned role but the whole person. This tendency derives perhaps more from a tradition than from objective necessities. The soldier, when not on duty, remained a soldier. To use the language of the sociologists, the military order did not carry through to the end its potential and logical universalism. Not that, in theory, it refuses to promote anyone to any rank; not that promotion conforms to any principle except that of merit. But the officers, especially in armies of aristocratic origin, found it difficult to give effective recognition to the specific nature of the military role. They exercised a total, person-to-person command rather than leadership of a specific kind. Certain regulations of the new German Army in the Federal Republic imply the concept of a citizens' army. The new German soldier spends part of his day at the barracks just as the labourer works eight hours at the factory; away from the barracks, it is set forth that the soldier owes no more to his chiefs than the labourer owes to his engineer or foreman. He is no more required to wear his uniform than the labourer to wear a white or blue collar. In this sense, as it becomes specific, the military order seems to resemble the industrial order, although the military has not eliminated command.

The attitudes and motives of workers and soldiers are different. The soldier who is indifferent to worldly goods, who obeys out of duty and consents to sacrifice with the joy of self-fulfilment, is a historical figure and not just a legendary character. But such could not be the psychology of the worker, subjected to the pitiless law of output: after all their strenuous attempts to approximate the ideals of socialism, the leaders of the Soviet Union admitted that 'in a peaceful period' the mass of labourers did not behave like soldiers – that even this proletarian elite, once victory had been won, gradually wearied of the austere virtues of asceticism, so that finally inequality of reward was, in a modern Soviet economy, accepted as indispensable and inevitable. The proletarians proved to be men, not angels; those revolutionaries who at first thought otherwise ended up treating them like animals. But the effort to introduce into industry a mode of discipline characteristic of the army also failed, even though Soviet leaders did not hesitate to use the severest means. One triumphs over the nature of society only by obeying its laws.

To preach scorn for riches in a civilization which preaches the gospel of production is against human nature. Of what avail is the unceasing effort to marshal the use of scarce resources as economically as possible, of what use are estimates of the precise time required for each industrial operation, if the workers do not obtain in return better living conditions? In time of war or revolution, the task of producers is transfigured by the grandeur of the objective – the salvation of the country, the building of a new society. In time of peace, the industrial order must be equitable, it must conform to the rules of universalism, it must be the living embodiment of *meritocracy*.

Actually, this ideal industrial order does not exist, and the one we do have never seems to everyone to be what it should be. Inequalities imposed by society at the very beginning are too great, no matter how powerful the trend towards speeding up social mobility. The correlation between each man's merits and the position he occupies in the hierarchy, or between the services rendered and the gratification received, is always subject to controversy. Whether in workshop or office, at all levels, and especially near the top, the qualifications of the engineer, the organizer, and the salesman are so heterogeneous that they cannot, in the last analysis, be exactly compared and weighed. In the West, the head of a business enterprise is sometimes the owner of the means of production; with decreasing frequency he may even have inherited the business. Such a manager can justify his power only through a claim of legitimacy which is clearly foreign to 'industrial meritocracy'.

Auguste Comte was not unaware of these inevitable tensions: he conceived of the submission of the entrepreneurs to moral law – thereby likening business enterprises to a public service – as the means of making the workers aware that they had become the associates of their boss. The founder of Positivism thought that each man would accept the position to which fate or his aptitudes had assigned him. The feeling of a duty fulfilled and services rendered would take the place of material reward. Wise men would teach others that the only hierarchy that really counts is the hierarchy of moral worth. The rich would be powerful, but power would impose obligations on them, not privileges. Unfortunately, Comte's utopia also demands an unselfishness which is inconsistent with the nature of the socio-industrial order.

Even more than in motives or attitudes, soldiers and workers differ in their acknowledged rights. Both are integral members of an organizational hierarchy, but workers do not belong wholeheartedly to the business enterprise. They are citizens and, as such, can join unions, which are now a common feature of the social order, whereas soldiers' unions, or soviets, have never lasted longer than the revolutionary circumstances from which they have sprung. The army of the Soviet Union has retained political commissars, but it has re-established the external insignia and internal authority of military rank.

We have identified three major principles of differentiation between military and industrial social structures; organizations typical of modern civilization have reached their logical end; they are universalistic, specific, and, in theory, emotionally neutral. The worker hires out his working ability for a fixed period, at a price arrived at by negotiation, but he does not involve his entire personality; he is not the servant of a master but the performer of a task, and, by law, all jobs are open to everyone according to each man's capacity. Moreover, however constraining the organization may be in its planned efficiency, it must also be as intelligible as possible; an effective remuneration for merit must, to the greatest possible extent, take the place of threats of punishment. Finally, the unions serve the function of making demands on or maintaining communication with the corporation and the economy as a whole. They negotiate with the heads of industry and eventually they oppose them; this is part of an ongoing effort to reconcile the needs and desires of the workers with the enterprise's available income. The worker has the right to remain morally isolated from the company that employs him; the unions serve as spokesmen who address the few responsible for the administration of the productive unit, thus guaranteeing some kind of collective representation of the employees in the councils where decisions are made.

Does this triple differentiation suffice to justify Auguste Comte's optimism? Has the protagonist become an associate? Does the individual have the feeling that he is achieving self-fulfilment through his work and through union participation? Or has an association embracing all men – from the unskilled labourer to the wealthiest manufacturer – remained as remote a dream as it was a century and a half ago?

*The Myth of Collectivism*

The development of industrial civilization has not eradicated certain myths which, in the last century, held a considerable fascination for European thought – notably the myth of collective ownership, with its corollary myth of self-rule by the workers.

Looking back, it is somewhat surprising to find that superior minds pinned their hopes on what were called structural reforms but actually were but juridical regulations controlling the means of production. Why should ownership laws determine the organization of work, the conditions of workers, the level of pay? During the initial stages of modernization, the myth had some relationship to necessary or desirable social changes. If a part of the land in vast agricultural holdings is not cultivated or is badly cultivated, if the owners of land or factories use their profits – which represent a substantial percentage of the national product – for conspicuous spending on luxuries and prestige, a revolt against rights acquires historic significance as well as economic effectiveness. Even in an industrialized country, laws regulating ownership still have ideological significance, because they influence the selection of heads of enterprises and the relationship between the order of production and that of commerce. But, clearly, no property laws can do away with submission to a rational discipline which entails the domination of one man by another, as well as the administration of things.

Along with the myth of a new era to be ushered in by collective ownership of the means of production the old illusion of worker self-rule has vanished. In retrospect, one can clearly perceive the three possible directions socialism could take: the assumption of power by the so-called proletarian party; reforms within the framework of a parliamentary democracy; and revolution by trade unionism itself on the work site. We know the provisional outcome of the first two.

Soviet practice has not abolished the subjection of the workers to the imperatives of technology and output, but it has instead done away with those trade-union and political liberties which, in a Western regime, guarantee the workers, besides their jobs, a certain kind and degree of freedom. A creation of the party, not of the proletariat, the Soviet regime perhaps succeeds in convincing the workers that they are working for themselves and for the future of their children, while under capitalism they would be making fortunes for the 'monopolists'. In certain circumstances, the humblest task can be transfigured in the eyes of the man performing it if he has the feeling that he is contributing to a grandiose scheme. However, there is nothing to indicate that the most effective totalitarian propaganda can make such a transfiguration long lasting.

The outcome of the second possibility is just as familiar to us, and in the case of Sweden, for example, it has proved more lasting than the present state of Sovietism. The four essential factors of reformist socialism – social security, trade union strength, redistribution of income to reduce inequalities, and accession to power of parties that received a huge majority of workers' votes – these are present simultaneously only in the Scandinavian countries. Elsewhere, each one of these factors is emphasized to a greater or lesser degree. Social security has been stressed more in France, and, until lately, less in the United States. Nowhere have the separate functions of labour and management been unified as was envisaged by revolutionary syndicalism. Nowhere have the large corporations become workers' communities, for the inevitable hierarchy is incompatible with the utopia of free association.

The end of myths is not the end of hope, on the condition that hope does not transcend the possible. For a long while yet the majority of workers, manual labourers or others, will do relatively simple, fragmentary tasks. Will they discover self-fulfilment in these tasks? Will they want to become integrated with the enterprise, or will they, on the contrary, want to withdraw from it? Will their occupation represent the very core of their existence or a disagreeable necessity whose duration they hope primarily to reduce? It is difficult to answer these questions, despite the wealth of empirical studies which may do no more than demonstrate that it is impossible to apprehend universal tendencies.

Experience does reveal certain facts, facts that are at once indisputable as well as superficial. The living standard of industrial workers has risen. (In the underdeveloped countries the proletariat is often a relatively privileged class, compared with the peasants.) Physical working conditions have improved almost everywhere. Types of industrial organization have succeeded one another without the new organization ever completely eliminating the preceding one. The professional worker, surrounded by helpers, was characteristic of a certain phase of industry and of trade unionism as well; then came production lines, where 'specialized workers', trained in a few weeks, epitomized a period of 'piecework'. This is being succeeded by complex machines maintained by specialists, which in turn are giving way to wholly automated operations requiring only a few professional personnel. Taking into consideration the various types of organization and the level of pay they provide, is it possible to forecast what future attitudes will be towards management and private enterprise, toward trade union activity, and to determine whether workers will desire participation or withdrawal?

The way in which work is organized and the level of rewards – wages and working conditions, in the trade union phrase – are certainly two of the principal factors conditioning workers' attitudes. Some of the excessive reactions against rationalization, such as the destruction of machines in the eighteenth century, are scarcely conceivable today in Europe and the United States, even though union resistance to worker displacement through automation is often very strong. One reason is that workers and their union leaders have a better understanding of the mechanics of economic progress. Although they are not necessarily willing to accept short-range loss for long-run gain (the theory that automation will create additional jobs after having done away with some), they now no longer think of themselves as prisoners of their individual situation; their horizon is gradually encompassing the entire economy.

These two principal determinants of worker attitudes always act in conjunction with particular circumstances – in the shop (the role of the foreman), in the factory (the manager's way of wielding authority), in the community or region (union traditions), in the nation (the position taken by the government, the influence of ideologies and political parties). The working of the causes suggests trends, not laws; information is not lacking, but uncertainty is inscribed in reality itself.

Manual labourers often remain in a world apart, as though a line of demarcation were drawn between dirty hands and white collars. Whatever the dissimilarities created among them by technical progress might be, they still preserve, for the most part, characteristics peculiar to them; they are part of an organization which seems the more oppressive the less they understand of its overall rationality.

Wages continue to be their essential concern; at times they are obsessed by the gap between their actual income and what they require to meet their needs and desires; at others, they attribute the malaise and discontent they feel to the meagreness of their personal resources; and at still other times, they are eager to find in their role as consumers all that their work does not give them – some meaning, some satisfaction.

In all countries there subsists, it seems, a barrier between manual labourers and other strata of society, and this distance entails a widespread malaise. In Germany, investigations have shown that labourers buy scarcely any paperback books, whereas white-collar employees, whose incomes are no higher, do buy them. In France, students from the petty bourgeois levels of society are more numerous than those coming from the working class, although their incomes may be the same. In each generation a number of working-class children move upward on the social scale, and with the speeding-up of general economic progress and increasing educational facilities, the number is increasing. However, working-class dissatisfaction and isolation still appear to be inseparable from the socio-industrial order.

The worker's dissatisfaction or his state of alienation does not normally express itself in rebellion or revolution any more. Many other reactions have been observed. The job is considered merely as a livelihood and it does not have to be 'interesting' provided it 'pays well'; the real gratification will come from the family or from leisure. Or the worker continues to consider his job his principal activity, something which occupies the greater part of his time and should give meaning to his life; if in fact his job is boring, monotonous, and insignificant, then nothing will right the balance. In such a case, the individual may feed on some hope of escaping, of rising in the hierarchy, or of participating in a collectivity. What remains uncertain is the long-range influence of technical progress: to what extent does it further acceptance of an occupation merely as a livelihood, or, on the other hand, rejection of work that holds no future promise or significance?

Two ways of looking at the facts, both schematic, haunt the literature. According to one, scientific and technical progress will gradually reduce the length of the working week; according to the other, it will divide workers between unskilled labourers and machine operators. In either case, the overall production system will become more and more external to those we call the producers. The individual will discover his own identity outside his productive activity, during his leisure time. But would not the refusal to be morally identified with a collective effort represent a renouncement of sorts? If the individual ceases to be productive, in the literal sense of the term, will he not become a mere consumer? Will he not lose his sense of civic responsibility as a member of his union, political party, voluntary associations? Will he still be a citizen?

It is impossible to determine the incidence of the various attitudes toward an occupation solely in terms of technical progress. The interest a worker takes in his job obviously depends upon the nature of his work; interest tends to increase with the level of skill required. The machine operator dreams less often of setting up on his own and becoming a small shopkeeper; he aspires, for himself or his children, to a better knowledge of the technical milieu in which his professional life is lived, to an increased participation in the collective effort. This participation is expressed in various ways, in the shop or in the union.

Union ideologies and practices vary from country to country, depending upon the political climate and the nature of the workers' parties. However, the demands voiced by these organizations provide a partial answer to our question: Do workers tend to become members of the enterprise? Do they wish to?

American unions have many millions of members, although their number has decreased during the last few years. Despite their wealth and power, or because of these, most of them are hostile to any concept of 'co-management'. Occasionally union leaders may take on the role of technical advisers to management and willingly suggest reforms for companies in economic difficulty; but except in these rare cases, they stick to the principle of the separation of function: one cannot engage in management and at the same time contest the decisions made by management. If spokesmen for the workers are to be free to make demands, they cannot and must not assume even partial responsibility for management. Responsibility towards the workers is incompatible with responsibility towards the stockholders. The large central unions have nevertheless a political role to play; they represent one pressure group among others within the plural society and they take an active part in public affairs at both the local and national level. It cannot be said that the American type of trade unionism assumes the task of transforming employees into associates.

The same is generally true of unions in the Federal Republic of Germany and in Great Britain. The limit of co-management, as it is conceived in Germany, provides for a director, chosen from the workers' representatives, who deals with workers' problems, thus perhaps giving some of the workers a sense of equality or participation. However, a director who comes from the working class cannot fail to become gradually identified with the interests of management; inevitably he moves further and further away from those who originally chose him. The distance between employers and employees springs not from ill-will on either side but from the very size of the operation, from the contrast between the prospects of workers occupied with compartmentalized, fragmentary tasks and those of the managers.

In Great Britain, the unions continue to finance the Labour Party, although approximately one-third of the workers cast their votes for the Conservative Party. The workers' organizations behave in the same way toward employers or the government regardless of the party in power. The unions have become so bureaucratized that workers often express their wishes by illegal strikes inspired from below, without, or despite, orders issued by responsible union officials.

In France, unions are at one and the same time weak and ambitious, divided, and, at least verbally, extremist. The intellectuals associated with them try to hit upon some middle course between the Marxist-Leninist belief in the millennium and the prosaic nature of union bureaucracies devoted solely to making demands on behalf of the workers. Initiative within the movement – which is both ideological and social – has come more from the intellectual *cadres*, from union leaders, and from the worker's aristocracy than from ordinary workers. On many occasions these *cadres* have joined strikes or at least have assumed an attitude of benevolent neutrality towards the strikers. Sometimes they have sought to protect an entire industry threatened by competition of other industries (coal), sometimes they have acted on behalf of the technicians of research bureaux or assistant managers who were directly affected by financial measures imposed by directors from the outside. More often, they have expressed a bitterness at being excluded from the places where important policies were being elaborated. Capable of understanding the needs of the company as a whole, they demanded a right to participate in the major decisions affecting it, and high officials, legislators, and advocates of traditional private enterprises once again took up a discussion that may be of interest to the entire Western world.

In all the developed capitalist countries, the production unit is the enterprise or corporation. Juridically, the company belongs to the stockholders or to the state, but whatever its legal status may be, the ownership of big business matters less than its management. Is it possible to give employees the feeling that they are cooperating in a common effort and that they are not controlled by others or, worse still, by an anonymous organization?

The debate involves one purely economic factor: the degree of concentration of ownership. In the United States, the number of holders of corporate stocks has increased rapidly since the last war. The number of stockholders in 1952 stood at 6.5 million. In 1969 the number increased to more than 20 million (22 million in 1967). Of these, 3.5 per cent are workers. In Europe the standard of living probably does not, as yet, permit this 'capitalism of the common man'. Even should economic progress make this possible, I doubt that it would be well received. European reformers have another plan in mind: the consequence of the self-financing of the big corporations is that a considerable share of the profits is reserved for the stockholders. Would it not be equitable to distribute among the employees a part of the increase in assets resulting from the reinvestment of profits? This idea is as attractive in theory as it would be difficult to put into practice.

In any case, the essence of the debate is not economic. If it were, foreseeable increases in pay would bring about a short- or long-term solution. To return to the terminology of Auguste Comte, the problem is to convert the *worker* into an *associate*, and no one is in a position to suggest a simple, categorical solution. At the lowest level of the hierarchy, the state of mind of the worker depends largely upon his immediate surroundings, his fellow workers, his foremen, his salary, the microscopic relations, formal or informal, which are part of his daily life. At a higher level in the hierarchy, other factors intervene: the disparity between his more or less conscious ambition and the limitations of the task imposed, his desire to create rather than merely to perform. This antithesis – to create or to perform – is obviously a simplification. Any worker is likely to hope for autonomy. And, on the other hand, we would be wrong to attribute to all those who perform relatively important functions a desire for responsibility. I merely wish to suggest that the contrast between democracy and oligarchy, already apparent in our analysis of society as a whole, stands out still more clearly in the analysis of business enterprise.

Equality before the law, the accessibility to all of every occupation, translate the democratic ideal into actuality, but without eliminating the apparent or real concentration of political power in the hands of minorities situated at strategic points. In business enterprises, the cards have already been dealt for most individuals and inequality of power is organized according to a bureaucratic hierarchy; depending upon the level, the problems are seen in a different light. Only those at the top can survey the whole. Society is run by ruling groups that quarrel among themselves even as they work together and that need the support of ordinary people. The industrial firm is run by directors who are less subject than the government to a written constitution, to the resistance of pressure groups, and to the censure of public opinion. Not that the big firms have no written constitution; they do have their legal articles of incorporation. However, in so far as the selection of directors is concerned, these bylaws are but a fiction as long as the majority of shareholder-owners show no interest in general meetings. In the big firms, power is transmitted by co-optation within a relatively closed circle. For those who reach or hope to reach this circle, the affective neutrality of the industrial occupation turns dialectically into its opposite.

In the upper reaches of the hierarchy, work becomes the reason for living, and in order to reach his goal the successful organization man is willing to subject himself and his whole personality to a discipline that eventually culminates in conformity. Actually, this dialectical process affects only a small number. Nevertheless, there is reason to fear that in the foreseeable future the feeling of autonomy and responsibility will be reserved for a minority alone. Unions do more to favour the social elevation of their own bosses than they do to associate the mass of workers with the collective activity. Oligarchy will always represent an imperfect conciliation between universalist principles and the necessity for an industrial, hence hierarchical and authoritarian order – a conciliation which will be less imperfect to the degree that selection conforms more closely to the ideals of a meritocracy. Neither revolt, nor even sustained dissatisfaction, will be the inevitable consequence of an organization that combines the administration of things with the government of persons. But the observer may wonder whether he hopes or fears that the workers will be content with their lot. Would such contentment represent a positive gain for society or mere subservience, liberation or the triumph of manipulation?

## The Personalized Task

Are productive and administrative work essentially alike? Do they belong to the same kind of social order? Must we not dispel the confusion, implicit in the preceding analyses, between workers who have to do with materials and those who deal with other men?

Let us return to the comparison with the military order. In a modern army, only a minority has direct combat experience.

Every aeroplane pilot or tank driver requires dozens of supporting military personnel. Similarly, those engaged in research, sales, advertising, and public relations provide services that have to do with production. But those so employed have lost contact with work in the physical sense known to those who work with materials in the production process. The utopia of push-button war has its counterpart in a wholly automated society which no longer uses manpower to produce material goods. Unfortunately, the first utopia would be easier to realize than the second: destruction is incomparably less costly than production.

State agencies, like those that administer the postal service, finance, and social security, permit a rationalization that does not differ in kind from industrial rationalization, and the increasing use of electronic machines will accentuate the similarity. Techniques of organization, inspired by psycho-sociological research, make such work less arduous, and reduce friction between individuals who must observe strict regulations and who occupy positions requiring them to remain essentially anonymous. If salaries are good and prospects for promotion favourable, such employees will not inevitably feel resentful or oppressed; but they will feel even less like associates or members of the enterprise than do the workers. And, of course, it may be that it is not in fact desirable for them to become totally involved in a task that is essentially impersonal.

The contradiction between rationalization and personality becomes altogether different in character in many areas of commerce or, more generally, in public relations. These are the occupations that lend themselves most fully to a sort of false personalization either condemned as a form of alienation or approved as a sign of good manners. The salesman in a big department store does not know the customer he serves, who is but one among countless others. But the technique of hidden persuasion demonstrates the effectiveness of an apparent personalization and this well-known device lends itself to innumerable variations. Should we prefer this comedy of personalization to the cold truth of impersonal contacts? Is it better to keep one's distance, when such a distance actually exists, or create an artificial climate of equality? Each person tends to answer such questions according to his own temperament, personal tastes, and experience. The 'style' of such individual interrelationships may vary from region to region and from country to country, although I have often been struck by the emergence of a style peculiar to journalism and television which cuts across national boundaries and spans oceans. Most often, however, it has seemed to me that the mode of such relations is mainly attributable to the imprint that social class and nationality leave on the individual. The stereotype of the German civil servant, imbued with the importance of his task, represents in the abstract one possible solution to the contradiction between depersonalized work and the person. Far from separating himself from his role, the individual finds satisfaction and dignity in identifying himself with it. The French have the reputation of oscillating between opposite solutions, going suddenly from strict impersonality to an informality which is theoretically incompatible with the obligations imposed by their occupation. The Americans freely say of themselves that they practise with great skill the art of apparent personalization.

In a certain measure, this apparent personalization is inevitable. These protagonists who express themselves in the realm of personal relations are obeying precise directives; they must adopt predetermined attitudes in order to exert upon others a predetermined influence. The salesman seems to improvise a speech which he knows by heart so that his customer answers these calculated remarks as though they were addressed to him alone. This sort of comedy would assume the degrading character its more severe critics attribute to it only if the protagonists infused their roles with the very meaning of their existence.

Moreover, it would be absurd to disregard the fact that many excellent people find pleasure and fulfilment in numerous non-manual occupations created by industrial civilization. Intellectuals tend to think that activities which seem mediocre to them must also seem mediocre to those who perform them. Empirical studies do not yet permit us to determine the percentage of contented and discontented people, of optimists and pessimists, in the industrial civilization now taking shape around us. In any event such figures would have only a limited significance; is not the worst form of alienation, the critic must object, alienation unconscious of itself?

With all these reservations, the fact remains that the new techniques of production and administration have lessened men's labours, but appear to have given only a minority a joyful awareness of performing a creative act. Many of the liberal professions, traditionally chosen out of a sense of vocation, are now being absorbed into vast, impersonal organizations; examples are to be found among teachers in large universities as well as among persons engaged in administrative or research bureaucracies. These professions are not stripped of their essential significance, but they do not readily give the individual the opportunity to feel that he is functioning as a person in contact with other persons. For many so situated, the will to be oneself freely is transferred from the occupation to activities of what is called leisure time.

In the preceding pages I have used the term 'work' or 'occupation' in a neutral, social sense; not as a divine punishment, nor as a moral obligation. Work is seen as an activity carried on most often away from home, with a wage or salary in view. It seems to me this definition mirrors the dominant conception of our time; it would be impossible to define leisure as simple inactivity when so many vacationers or tourists impose duties upon themselves (how many do what they think is proper when actually they have nothing to do!). It would be equally impossible to define leisure in contrast to specific occupations, since so many leisure activities constitute the sum and substance of work for other men. Whether one is repairing an electrical installation, indulging in gardening, or playing a Beethoven sonata, it is the intention, not the activity itself, which determines whether it is to be classified as work or leisure. And during the period of non-work one can still dream, like the young Marx, of escaping specialization; one can still be in turn a hunter, a fisherman, or a reader of Plato.

In the most highly developed countries civilization is no longer altogether a civilization of work; for work, as such, is no longer sanctified. Still less is it a civilization of leisure. Yet contemporary society thinks of itself in this duality of terms that are more complementary than antithetic. Production, the collective achievement of machines, is now too detached from individual physical effort for work to remain surrounded by the aura that characterized it even a generation ago. But nowhere has the problem of production been wholly resolved; nowhere has the gap between desires and purchasing power disappeared for all or even for a great number. Whatever the theoretical possibilities of redistribution of income, current reality demonstrates that a general increase in wealth provides the best chance of improving the condition of the least privileged. The manufacture and distribution of goods (in a Western economy distribution is considered just as productive as manufacture) continue to mobilize the bulk of manpower, and the scientific, technical, and productive exploits of the industrial order have lost none of their glamour. It matters little whether public opinion admires them in themselves, as an expression of human genius, or for the power and wealth they promise to the nation. Economists (and moralists) are right in attacking the resulting irrational reverence for rates of growth and in reminding us that distribution of the national effort, the allocation of resources among the various fields of employment, is now perhaps as important as the volume of the national product as estimated by statisticians. But they would be wrong in imagining that the growth of this volume is no longer important.

If we pass from the collectivity to the individual, the only general proposition warranted by the facts is so banal as to be scarcely worth formulating: the use each person makes of his free time at the end of the day, on weekends, during his paid vacation, can be understood only in relation to his work and his mode of existence in the city. The share devoted to sports, to amusement, to keeping himself informed or to cultural enrichment, to solitude or the group, varies according to occupation, fashion, and the individual. The choice is free in the sense that it is imposed by no regulation. But it is not necessarily the expression of a freedom: the person himself submits to prohibitions and obligations that he has internalized.

Every society has games that are just as revealing as its customs. Certain sociologists have outlined a typology of games as they relate to the diversity of social types. The socio-industrial order clearly favours games of competition and chance. On both sides of the Atlantic, the games played on television comprise a combination of the elements of *agon* (contest) and *alea* (chance): the $64 question is as much a matter of chance as an intellectual test. These combined elements are manifestly akin to the pattern of modern societies' economic and political regimes. In theory, the social hierarchy sanctions the results of fair competition, but in fact the competitors have not all started from the same point. Good or bad luck has determined their fate (in both senses of the word fate).

The field of sports, whose tremendous popularity is one of the enormous phenomena of our period, is primarily competitive (although the notion of luck is never altogether absent). In other respects, it is complementary to the socio-industrial order. It reinstates and glorifies qualities which now have scarcely any appreciable value in social competition. Physical strength, skill, endurance, eliminated from work (and from combat) first among the upper echelons of the hierarchy, then progressively among the middle and lower echelons, are, thanks to sports, again in vogue, esteemed in their own right. Tools and machines have substituted for hands in the factories; but the body once again comes into its own and is worshipped in the stadiums where the crowds throng. Some sports have not passed beyond the borders of a nation (cricket), others are scarcely indulged in outside narrow social circles (golf), but many sports, whatever their national origin, have gone around the world and have been adopted as an integral part of an expanding civilization.

Country farms, old houses transformed into second residences in French villages, the *dachas* around Moscow – all are evidence of the same spontaneous attempt at compensation for the deficiencies of industrial civilization. Prisoner of the artificial milieu created by technical advances, the city dweller seeks elsewhere for solitude, contact with nature, and less impersonal, less falsely personalized social relations than those of the factories or offices. Hunting, fishing, and camping spring from the same need, a need sincerely felt, whatever part imitation may play in their popularity. Tourism in all its forms, whether it merely entails a move to a vacation residence or the search for new scenes, signifies escape, a chance to experience different ways of life.

Now the quality, the very freedom, of leisure is being challenged no less than the quality and freedom of occupational existence. In each milieu individuals believe they are obliged to fill in their free time in a certain manner. Those who want a change of scene fall once again victim to organization: visits to cities and museums, conducted by professional guides, become an exhausting bore; there is often less pleasure in actually seeing than in enjoying in advance the satisfaction of having seen. In short, the banal criticism of radio and television develops into a criticism of the 'leisure industry' – a criticism that is neither entirely false nor entirely convincing.

In the present state of our civilization men often have time off from work. But it is not enough to give almost everyone a stretch of empty time to be filled in such a way as to enrich the individual. In the eyes of the moralist, the quality of the 'filling in' does not compensate for the mediocrity of the occupational life and may only reflect it. It cannot be otherwise until the time comes when the majority will have received the kind of intellectual training that raises them above their occupation and inspires them with the desire and courage to be what they are. And even then they will have to escape on their own from the clutches of the growing 'culture industry' that has arisen to exploit the increase in leisure time.

It is not easy to strike the right note on this topic. Whatever the commentator says or writes, he feels guilty. He is suspected of complicity with the businessmen of these industries if he notes that they do not create their audience even though they may attract it by low means; or he is suspected of scorning his fellow men if he affirms that so-called mass culture is not always contemptible, that it brings to many the only means of information and amusement they are capable of employing. It is useful to recall that all societies, including the wealthiest, continue to train *the men they need*, but that none, despite its proclaimed objectives, *needs* to have all men realize their individual potentialities. No society *needs* to have many men become personalities fully capable of freedom in relation to their environment.

Many of the occupations in industrial civilization require only a so-called elementary education for the average individual; such occupations not only do not require but do not tolerate initiative or originality. To the extent that 'qualifications' are no greater than what is required, one may well say that the majority of workers are usually capable of doing better. The disparity between what people are and what they might be depends sometimes upon the inadequacy of their education, sometimes upon the very nature of their occupational activity – more often the first than the second, at least in our day.

The disparity between what each man has become, given the circumstances in which he has found himself, and what he could have become in the most favourable circumstances is, by definition, irreducible. It is not possible for *all* individuals to be placed in the *most favourable* circumstances. All patients cannot be treated by the best doctors, all students taught by the best teachers. Surgeons are not all capable of successfully performing certain operations, nor do all parents have the means of giving their children the help which would allow them to complete their studies successfully. To assure the fulfilment of everyone's potentialities is, and will remain, an unattainable goal.

The distance between reality and this ideal will not remain constant. The prolongation of schooling accompanies progress. Technical methods will enable the same number of instructors to teach more students, even if this means the depersonalization of perhaps the most precious of interpersonal relationships, that of teacher and student. Industrial civilization, especially in the phase through which it is passing today in developed countries, requires better manpower training at almost every social level. Old civilizations, such as France and Germany, are as short of skilled workers as they are of teachers or researchers. Industrialized agriculture, automated factories, efficiently organized administrations, have little use for illiterates or unskilled workers. In this sense, then, evolution is advancing toward the ideal: from generation to generation, the percentage of those who continue their education and go on to higher learning is increasing. A facile kind of extrapolation might nurse the illusion that, in the long run, industrial civilization inevitably leads, not to republics of scholars, but to a society of *honnêtes hommes* or 'gentlemen', to use the eighteenth-century term, or 'cultivated men', as we say today. Such an extrapolation would be hazardous for many reasons.

The richest societies are still very far from any utopia. No one knows the percentage of individuals genetically or psychologically capable of pursuing higher studies. In the foreseeable future, there will still be a large number of tasks which are detailed and fragmented rather than arduous, and which constitute part of the complex system that inhibits any real expression of originality. There will remain a considerable number of men engaged in such occupations who consider themselves unjustly relegated to inferior status. No one can foresee precisely what percentage of the various levels of intellectual training in the total population would be required to maintain a balance with the needs of the community.

Let us return to the present. Think of the millions of workers or employees who work eight hours a day and whose elementary education was mediocre. Why should we be surprised that they mainly desire relaxation, diversion, or similar compensation when the work day is over, and are satisfied with what intellectuals view with contempt? Not that I wish to deny the obvious – that the search for as large an audience as possible sometimes leads to a disheartening competition in low practices, in the use of 'techniques' of entertainment inspired, if not by contempt for mankind, at least by a pessimistic assessment of human nature. It is pleasant to imagine a 'didactic state' which would shun both 'commercialization' and 'politicization'. For the time being, certain countries sometimes avoid the one, sometimes the other. In countries where individual freedoms still subsist, the sensational press and the trivial electronic media still dominate mass communication.

A few simple observations will serve to delimit the scope of the foregoing. The number of people who appreciate good painting or good music is increasing both absolutely and relatively, along with the growing number of persons receiving higher education. If more people purchase recordings by popular musicians than by classical artists, it is still true that classical music has never had so large a clientele. Millions are amused by the exploits of comic-strip characters and television heroes; even Jean-Paul Sartre admits that he gets more pleasure from reading Paul d'Ivoi than the philosopher Wittgenstein. Readers, radio listeners, and television viewers do not all attribute the same significance to the messages the identical means of communication offer them. Thus the fact that the same culture is offered to everyone does not necessarily mean that everyone participates in the same culture. This proposition will annoy pessimists who denounce the elite's descent to the level of the masses, and it will disappoint optimists who would like to perceive the possibility of unification of the entire population through the enjoyment of identical intellectual and aesthetic values.

The fact is that the new electronic media do not inform listeners or viewers 'exactly', nor do they offer them 'authentic' culture. Was the general public better informed or more cultivated before the advent of radio and television? Criticism is more convincing when it compares what is with what could be than when it measures what is against what was.

## The Industrial Society

The concept of the industrial society dates from the beginning of the nineteenth century. After having been overlooked for several decades, the term now is a part of everyday parlance. Definition of society in terms of a socio-economic regime was rejected by capitalists as well as socialists. Capitalists, with their future assured, preferred to attribute the collective increase in wealth to liberalism; the socialists did not accept this masking of the fundamental conflict between classes. However, the partial similarities between Soviet and Western regimes and, still more, the contrast between developed and underdeveloped countries have imposed the use of a concept which, despite equivocal definitions, designates an unprecedented social type: societies that strive to produce as much and as efficiently as possible by renewing the instruments and organization of work in accordance with the progress of science.

The effort to produce, the progress of science, the wedding of science and technology to the means of production – all these phenomena have progressed at increasing speed during the last thirty years. Preceding bourgeois society, with its mutually hostile classes and its small units of production, hardly deserved to be called industrial prior to the advent of the internal combustion engine, which made possible development of the techniques of transportation, communication, production, and destruction that are the primary characteristics of our age.

A controversy over the precise birth date of industrial society would have little significance. A historian, in quest of origins, will place this date far in the past. A sociologist, more mindful of the originality of the contemporary society, will place it closer to us. One fact admits of no doubt: the first half of the nineteenth century saw the great spread of the very concept of industrial society, accompanied by recognition of the two major developments of modern times – democracy and industrialism. The drive for social equality paralleled the application of science to production. In these terms one can clearly trace the growth of the gross national product in the United States and in the major countries of Western Europe. However, the way for these developments obviously had been prepared during the two preceding centuries and the historian is thus justified in going back to the Age of Enlightenment, indeed even to the Renaissance, in order to identify their intellectual origins.

Most nations did not enter the modern or industrial age simultaneously, and so each of them employed somewhat different techniques at homologous stages of their development. European societies did not possess internal combustion engines, planes, or electronics when the value of their product per capita was more or less the same as that of many underdeveloped countries of today. What makes a coherent theory of subsequent stages of development almost impossible, however, is that it would have to take into consideration at one and the same time *the volume of the national product*, *the socio-economic regime*, and *technical progress*.

The question often asked today has to do with the next phase in the most advanced countries. Is it possible to discern the precursory symptoms of a continuing scientific and technical revolution so profound that it would upset the socio-industrial order? The sociologist is hesitant to answer and is tempted to leave the responsibility for such prophecies to physicists, biologists, and technologists. Most of the progress announced by scientists, spectacular though it may be, represents the continuation or acceleration of movements launched some time ago. Whether the discoveries or inventions result in new raw materials, improved means of transportation, the exploitation of new sources of energy, or the manufacture of foods from the wealth of the sea, these forward steps will not by themselves change the nature of the socio-industrial order. They only emphasize one of its already visible features: the organization of research and development (one is tempted to say the science of scientific research).

Some observers now conclude that in the realm of scientific technological innovation the universities may play an increased role at the expense of the industrial and business sectors. The science of scientific research, it seems to me, demands and will demand the cooperation of the state, the entrepreneurs, and the universities (or research institutes). The institutional form this collaboration will assume will not necessarily be the same in all countries. What seems hardly arguable is the increased importance that will be given in the course of the next decades to what is now called 'research and development'. This attitude will persist until the moment, maybe closer than we think, when a point of saturation is reached, when the sums devoted to the exploration of the unknown can no longer be increased for lack of human resources rather than of money.

Society will be scientific to the second power not only by the application of science to production but also by the scientific organization of scientific progress, and so we must assume that society in the future will be still more heterogeneous than it is today; intellectual inequalities will be even more accentuated. The amount of manpower employed in the physical process of production will continue to decrease, even though industrial productivity will be more than ever the prerequisite of expansion in other sectors, and agriculture, like administration, will be industrialized. However, none of the banal expectations such as automated factories and bureaucracies regulated by computers, portend a change in direction for society. At most, what is in question is the point at which the change in quantity might begin to entail qualitative modification.

A qualitative modification, many times prophesied but still only a possibility, would affect the meaning of work, the relationship between work and leisure. Even in advanced countries, fragmented work activities, which in our eyes are denuded of human significance, are still the most numerous. If we except the two thirds of mankind who have not gone beyond the initial stages of industrialization, if we assume that humanity will not use the means of destruction which the scientists keep offering, and if we extrapolate the strides made by automation and do not extrapolate the current growth of the world's population, we can conceive that men will find non-work their reason for living: with long training periods, short working days and weeks, and long periods of retirement, leisure would come to occupy the greatest part of the existence of most men. The share of themselves which some (or all) will subject to the 'reign of necessity' (as Marx called work) will not prevent anyone's fulfilling himself in freedom. In this way industrialization would, so to speak, rise above itself. The classical dictum that an industrial society no longer needs slaves because servile tasks devolve upon machines would at long last be strictly true.

Everyone imagines in his own way, according to moment and mood, the paradise or the hell of a society that would train individuals only in order to turn them over to themselves, that would finally reconcile the two Marxist ideas: the *administration of things* and the *anarchy of persons*. But this utopia lies beyond the foreseeable future, and most thinking men judge the socio-industrial order harshly. When they envision the future they are less apprehensive of the possible boredom that would lie in wait for a civilization of leisure than of the superhuman power which biology, in the wake of physics, may give to humanity tomorrow.

Already mankind is capable of annihilating itself, of adulterating the genetic patrimony of millions of men yet to be born. Will it be capable of modifying this patrimony, of controlling genetic chance? Perfected by physicists, nuclear weapons have been put at the disposal of statesmen. On whom will fall the burden of manipulating the hereditary patrimony if biologists should ever acquire the power to do so?

# 6 On Social Criticism: Anomy and Alienation

Members of contemporary society believe in 'their know-how and their power', but they do not always believe in themselves. Scientists do not doubt the continued progress of science, be it physical, chemical, or biological; technologists are quite sure that they can send astronauts to the moon by 1975, if not before;[1] we are provided with quite specific forecasts of impending weather control, substitution of synthetic proteins for food, exploitation of biochemical agents against bacteria and viruses, use of chemical agents to eliminate hereditary defects, and so on. To sociologists of philosophical bent or advanced opinions is left the thankless task of social criticism, and their usual pessimism is often judged severely by the physicists and biologists.

The economists occupy a position midway between the technologists and the sociologists, perhaps closer to the first than to the second. They, too, practise the art of forecasting and, starting with growth rates observed over a certain period, they calculate what will be the gross national product, or the product per capita in twenty, fifty, or a hundred years. Thanks to a great growth and standardization of economic statistics, they have practically done away with the myths that used to plague them and have almost overcome conflicts between various schools of thought.

All of this has thrown important new light on the principal contentions of the traditional enemies of capitalism as to the inherent contradictions of private ownership of the means of production and market mechanisms. They denounced, on the one hand, the divergence between potential and actual production, the loss of wealth as a consequence of capitalist anarchy, and on the other, the unequal distribution of income, the concentration of wealth in the hands of the few, and the poverty of the many.

1. This book was first published in 1968.

The significance of both these accusations has been reduced by experience.

While many defenders of capitalism underestimated the possible increase in production and productivity under the impact of the new technology, many socialists tended to overestimate it. The latter saw abundance as within close reach; the problem of production, they said, is finally solved, and it is only the imperfections and basic injustice of the established capitalist regime that prevent humanity from enjoying the material well-being that could be available to all. This myth was never taken seriously by professional economists, although it had a long vogue in revolutionary circles. The difficulties and inevitable losses of the centralized planning made possible by government ownership of the means of production have been demonstrated by the experience of Soviet Russia. In the West, meantime, there has not been any real depression in the course of more than twenty postwar years, and the previous falling off of production as productive capacity increased has not recurred.

To be sure, no country, capitalist or socialist, can be entirely confident of complete mastery over its economic processes. The gap between actual production and the theoretical potential of production has not disappeared, although it is no longer wide enough to justify the illusions of the early theorists of abundance. No regime can do away with this gap because in essence even the most stringently regulated regime is imperfect; no economic machine can produce at 100 per cent.

Inequalities of income continue to be considerable, and here socialist criticism still has a point. In most countries, as we have seen, even in the wealthiest, the predicament of the forgotten man – of the neglected victims of the general prosperity – stands out more or less sharply. The racial heterogeneity of the American people, the vastness of the country, and the very nature of its regime have aggravated the problem in the most affluent of capitalist societies. But, however tragic this may be in some of its aspects, it has little pertinence for the Marxist theme of absolute or relative pauperization. Even though not everyone shares in the general enrichment, the majority profits more or less.

Of all the arguments that impressed economists of the pessimistic school during the last century, Malthusian theory still carries the most weight. Enlightened people, taking a world view, still ask themselves whether the surplus of production is not being wiped out by the greater number of consumers. In the last century the Malthusian thesis was refuted in parts of Europe by economic progress that moved faster than demographic growth, and in others by the emigration of several tens of millions to a rapidly expanding America. But today the cost of large-scale health services is relatively slight and the results are considerable; while it is impossible to give everyone expert individualized medical care, it is possible to reduce infant mortality drastically and to increase average longevity by wholesale public health methods. Thus, many underdeveloped countries undergoing the initial phase of modernization have maintained the very high birthrate (35–40 per 1,000), which is in keeping with the experience of tradition-bound societies, while acquiring the low mortality rate (10–15 per 1,000) characteristic of industrial societies. Some countries show demographic growth rates of two to three per cent per year, which are wholly unrelated to economic progress but stem entirely from hygienic techniques introduced from abroad.

Aside from this race between size of population and quantity of resources, the problem of numbers remains none the less critical to those who look objectively at the actual facts; it remains *the* major problem. It is not inconceivable that one can feed six, ten, or twenty billion people on this planet; the scientists promise us artificial proteins and the exploitation of marine riches before the end of the century. But even if these miracles are achieved *in time*, grave social issues will remain.

First of all, during the course of the next twenty or thirty years the so-called underdeveloped countries will have to be satisfied in the main with economies based primarily on ordinarily agricultural products improved by the advances in biology and chemistry; that is, they will have to continue to rely on cultivation of the soil and husbandry. Such countries will not remain *completely* poor; in many, economic rate of growth will often exceed the demographic rate. But they may grow poorer in comparison to developed countries, as the gap between rich and poor nations grows wider.

Moreover, especially if one takes the long view, *quantity* even in the developed countries runs the risk of impairing *quality* – that is, of reducing those qualities which cultured men throughout the centuries have held to be the highest. Great questions arise. Are states composed of hundred of millions of men compatible with the known forms of political democracy? Would the actual participation of the citizen in public life, which is already so filled with malaise, be tolerable? Can men avoid an increasing and almost abstract rationalization of bureaucracy and the extension of impersonal relations to new domains – to universities, for instance? Some distinction again is inevitable between the *small number* of highly gifted individuals who warrant and may obtain special treatment and the *large number* who will receive only the training necessary to perform their jobs effectively. Is it feasible to think of educating everyone so that each man can realize his full potential, if not in work, at least in leisure? Or is it not more likely to foresee a society in which these millions and millions of human beings will be able to enjoy certain comforts, but will be condemned to the creative existence of termites?

Most economists have not been converted to the pessimistic neo-Malthusian outlook by the facts and speculation we have just cited. In the Third World, the value of the product per capita rises slowly, but it does rise nearly everywhere. A high birthrate can be said to constitute an obstacle to progress, but one that is usually overcome. More and more, economists refer the problem of numbers and quality to biologists and sociologists. The professional university economists look askance at those of their colleagues who do not differentiate between social science and social criticism.

As for the sociologists, some of them seem to take the pessimistic view less because of the setbacks than because of the successes of industrial civilization. It is a source of bitterness, to those intellectuals who share the Marxist faith, that the working class is no longer revolutionary. They judge mass culture more harshly the more the standard of living rises. Sometimes the severity of the criticism is due to the excessiveness of the demands they make on society, and certainly it is true that even the least imperfect societies are still far from realizing their ambitions.

Nevertheless, social criticism has two authentic motives, one of a sociological, the other of a metaphysical order. What is the price of economic progress? Is it not true that the instability of living conditions, and the intensity of demands fed by impatient desires and invidious comparisons create a climate of dissatisfaction? The neurotic, the anxious, the maladjusted, the criminal – is not their number on the rise, and especially in the United States, where industrial civilization is most advanced? Are not the people living in this immense and mysterious universe being driven out of their minds, repeating as they do the advertising and political slogans that assault their consciousness, unable to escape the pressures of their social surroundings which are all the more irresistible for being insidious and seductive? If this is so, *anomy* or *conformism* may provide the two alternative responses from which only a minority will escape. A radically secularized society that is not founded on any transcendent truth, that accepts itself as only one among many, and does not know the purpose of its own becoming is in essence unsure of itself. In questioning its present and its future it also questions human destiny. The apparently illogical alliance between Marxists and existentialists in Germany, later in France, and here and there in the United States, can thus be explained.

The existentialists are primarily concerned about the eternal condition of man; the Marxists want to upset the economic and social order. In one sense they are at opposite poles. They both descend from Hegel, but the existentialists reject the *system* and give primacy to the human being and his living experience, while the Marxists claim they are about to translate into reality the final plan foretold in the intellectual system. The fact is that the existential element was already present in the Marxist system. Marx did not denounce capitalist anarchy or private ownership of the means of production in the manner of an efficiency expert or a moralist. He was not satisfied merely to pronounce judgements on the inefficiency and injustice of capitalist institutions; he spoke also as a philosopher who criticized the condition imposed upon man by a regime: work degraded to the status of a commodity, the worker separated from his tools and from the product of his work, the entire economy delivered over to the blind forces of accumulated capital and competition. Socialism, in the eyes of the young Marx, and even of the mature Marx, was not only a system without precedent but also a solution of the metaphysical problem. In Heidegger's way of speaking, man is that creature who questions himself about the meaning of his being; in the existentialist-Marxist language, man, a historic being, wonders about the meaning of history, not as to the direction in which it is evolving, but rather the significance it presents to the very people who make it or live it. After 'the death of God', philosophically-minded critics demand much more from the social order than did philosophers of the past.

This calling into question the very concept of industrial civilization seems to be an integral part of the social order itself. It is governed by two themes: that of *anomy* and that of *alienation*. Neither of these two concepts is devoid of ambiguity. The instability of industrial civilization might give rise to the dissolution of those common beliefs and internalized obligations without which the individual may slip from isolation to deviation and delinquency. But at what point does this kind of anomy, implied by an individualist and changing order, become pathological?

The term *alienation* is even more ambiguous. In the strongest sense, an alienated man is, so to speak, a stranger to himself. He has lost his essence, he is in search of his being. But if alienation can be reduced to a malaise of sorts which an individual feels because he is not wholly committed to the existence he leads or to the institutions to which he submits, who does not, to some extent, feel alienated? A collectivity in control of its own destiny, which would organize its own development according to a plan, might perhaps not feel alienated – but is there any guarantee that as individuals the majority of its members might not feel so all the more?

In spite of these ambiguities, or perhaps because of them, these two concepts reveal the perplexities of industrial civilization.

*Breakdown of the Norms*

The modern concept of anomy[2] was formulated by Émile Durkheim between 1890 and 1900 at a time when he was devoting himself to the study of contemporary society with a concentration on the division of labour. This led him to the phenomenon of suicide, and in his book on the subject he makes a distinction between three types: selfish suicide, altruistic suicide, and anomic suicide. Analysis of the last type will illustrate the general meaning of anomy.

Statistics show that suicide varies in inverse ratio to the degree of religious, domestic, and political integration of a society. Durkheim wrote:

The weaker the groups to which an individual belongs, the less he depends on them, and, in consequence, the more he is answerable to himself alone and will recognize only those rules of conduct that are based upon personal self-interest. If, therefore, one agrees to designate egoism as that state in which the individual 'I' asserts itself excessively against and at the cost of the social 'I', we might call this type of suicide, which stems from exaggerated individuation, an egoistic one.[3]

The term 'altruistic' is suggested by numerous examples of suicides which may be described as voluntary sacrifices, as in India and Japan. The individual wants to strip off his personal being in order to steep himself in something which he regards as his true essence. In modern societies the suicides of the military belong to this type; instead of the individual killing himself because he is left to his own resources, because he has detached himself from his group and has sought in himself alone the guiding principle of his life, he kills himself because he has not yet acceded to individuation, because he has become totally fused with his group and has failed it in these terms. 'It is the suicide of inferior societies that survives among us, because the military

2. According to an essay by Herbert McClosky and John H. Schaar (*American Sociological Review*, February 1965) the word was currently used in the seventeenth century and spelled *anomy*. American sociologists, in particular R. K. Merton, picked it up again from Durkheim and for a long time used the French *anomie*. English authors use either spelling.

3. *Le Suicide*, Presses Universitaires de France, Paris, 1960, p. 223.

code of morals is itself, in certain respects, a survival of primitive morality.'[4]

Statistics on the third type turn on variations of the frequency of suicide due to economic circumstances. The rise in the number of suicides during an economic crisis is easy to explain, but that it should also rise in a period of rapid expansion, as it did in Prussia after the war of 1870, from 1875 to 1886, seems very surprising at first. The interpretation that has since become general refers to the fundamental structure of modern society, especially to the economic order. Here is Durkheim's analysis:

> Industrial and commercial life escapes all regulation. One no longer knows what is possible and what is not, what is just and what is unjust; which claims and hopes are legitimate and which are beyond the limits. Because of a rising prosperity desires are pitched higher. The more substantial the prey offered them, the more it stimulates them, makes them more demanding, more impatient with any regulations, just when traditional rules have lost their authority. The state of lawlessness or of anomy is therefore reinforced by the fact that passions are less disciplined at the very moment when they need to be more firmly held in check.[5]

Without denying a kind of kinship between egoism and anomy, Durkheim differentiated between them, for he was anxious not only to take into account statistical correlations but also to stress two aspects of the social malaise that are related but different. The egoistic suicide occurs chiefly in intellectual milieus, the anomic suicide in industrial and commercial professions. The egoist thinks only of himself because he is not deeply enough integrated into such societies as would impose a discipline on him and would give a meaning to his life. The anomic is perpetually in quest of new sensations and inaccessible possessions. He is agitated and ambitious, always dissatisfied and vulnerable to the vicissitudes of fate.

Émile Durkheim fully approved the principles of modern society, the inevitable specialization of functions and the autonomy of individuals. He pleaded the cause of the professional man against the anachronistic ideal of the gentleman. The individual obeys moral as well as social dictates when he dedicates himself

4. ibid., p. 260.
5. ibid., p. 281.

entirely to a definite occupation. To be sure, professional specialization requires training, which again is specialized; it forces
everyone to sacrifice some aspirations, to restrict his intellectual
horizon. This is the price which contemporary man has to pay.
But, while subscribing to these modern values, Durkheim also
feared the weakening of a discipline originating in and guaranteed
by society, without always clearly distinguishing between the
external pressure exercised by the group and the imperatives
internalized in the course of years of training. He attributed the
social malaise to two principal causes: the decline of religions on
which traditional morality was founded; and the anarchy of
economic life, uncontrolled, organized, and conscious of the
collectivity. True to the tradition of Saint-Simon and Auguste
Comte, he dreamed of founding an ethic, almost a religion, on
sociology and of giving a moral authority to professional associations which he called *corporations*.

The therapy suggested by the French sociologist to cure the ills
of modern society is now only a historical curiosity. Associations
comprising both employers and employees and which may properly be called *corporations* in Durkheim's usage do not exist in any
democratic society. Even authoritarian regimes, with the excep-
tion of Fascist Italy, have preferred to bring the trade unions to
heel rather than to embody them in such corporations. Trade
unions are nowhere centres of moral authority. If ever workers
and management should some day unite to form genuine communities, these would probably have as their framework business
concerns[6] rather than an economic sector. As for economic
organization by the state, it has indeed progressed. This organization seems to have attenuated the fluctuations of the economy,
but it has not subjected the individual to any form or degree of
moral discipline.

The concept of *anomy* became familiar to American sociologists
half a century after it was first formulated. R. K. Merton is
perhaps principally responsible for importing the idea from
Europe, and he has, in a sense, broadened its meaning. According
to Merton, anomy means

6. Such is the case, up to a point, in Japan.

a breakdown in the cultural structure, occurring particularly when there is an acute disjunction between the cultural norms and goals and the socially structured capacities of members of the group to act in accord with them. ... When the cultural and the social structures are mal-integrated, the first calling for behaviour and attitudes which the second precludes, there is a strain toward the breakdown of the norms, toward normlessness.[7]

Merton retains one of Durkheim's ideas: the obsessive desire for success, the incessant quest for unattainable possessions, unrestrained competition – all characteristic of our time – shatter the authority of social norms. But the distinction between *egoism* (through the disintegration of family, professional, or religious groups) and *anomy* (absence of internalized norms), between individuals who avoid collective discipline because they think only of themselves and those who avoid it because their boundless ambitions are never satisfied, tends to become obliter-ated. At the same time divorce, suicide, crime, and juvenile delinquency, psychic disturbance, and phenomena whose only common denominator is to point up to some kind of failure in socialization, all are ascribed to anomy.

This extension of the term results from the immediate reaction of the sociologist to apparently pathological phenomena, which is like that of the doctor who makes his diagnosis, analyses the causes of the illness, and seeks remedies. Whether they are ideal-ists or Machiavellians, all sociologists hope to reduce the frequency of crimes or suicides, even though they do not all agree on the best way to go about it. In the implicit ideology of Amer-ican society *consensus* provides a central theme: a society pre-supposes the commitment (unconscious before being conscious) of all its members to common values, transmitted by the family and the school. A nation which has been formed by the accultura-tion of millions of immigrants of varying language backgrounds spontaneously comes to regard society as the product of social-ization. It pays greater attention to socialization because it operates, so to speak, in broad daylight and remains imperfect only in so far as it allows the diversity of its origins to subsist.

7. *Social Theory and Social Structure*, Free Press, New York, 1957, pp. 136–9, quoted by Herbert McClosky and John H. Schaar (see footnote 2).

The consensus which the Saint-Simonians and the Positivists wanted to establish over and above the collapse of gospels of salvation becomes again, a century and a half later, the implicit ideal of a nation which must overcome the heterogeneity of its population, the immensity of its land, the youthfulness of its statehood, and the disorders of an industrialization advancing more rapidly than anywhere else.

A person is assumed to be socially integrated when, in obeying his own wishes, he also behaves in a manner that conforms to social morality and thus satisfies the needs of the collectivity. Total integration would obliterate any trace of his own personality and, in fact, is impossible in a complex society where, because of the multiplicity of social strata and occupational groups, the individual, when he reaches maturity, must recognize the extreme diversity of opinions, ways of living, and values. However powerful the initial process of socialization might be, contemporary man is forced to make a choice between different life styles and, within certain limits, to decide for himself.

In general, the older societies have not fared any differently from American society. The present culture of European nations is the result of a kind of historical sedimentation. The layers of culture, each belonging to a more or less recent century, are fused rather than superimposed in the unconscious of a limited group or an entire nation. The different groups have not all rejected, assimilated, or transformed the heritage of every bygone age in the same way. Here, too, fortunately, integration is incomplete. Creative dissatisfaction springs from the contradictions in values.

No society in history has lent itself to a complete assimilation of all its members. But modern societies increase the causes of anomy, if one may define anomy in the most general sense as *the absence of a system of values or of behaviour patterns which would at once impose itself with self-evident authority*.

In the vague sense we have now given this concept one can find a certain degree of anomy in all contemporary societies: in some, because they are overwhelmed by the example set or the impact made by the developed countries, Western or Soviet; in others, because they are in the process of growing and hence changing rapidly. But when one tries to substitute statistics for impressions, quantitative analyses for descriptions, difficulties multiply. None of the indications of anomy is incontestable, none permits categorical affirmations.

Take, for instance, divorce statistics. Divorce in itself is not necessarily a symptom of social disintegration or even of family disintegration, although it can, of course, in certain circumstances, hamper the process of socialization and, therefore, the normal integration of children. But the statistics that highlight well-known facts hardly reveal either the immanent tendencies of industrial civilization or tendencies pertaining to a phase of this civilization. Between the prewar and postwar periods the annual divorce rate per thousand inhabitants – aside from the exceptional period of 1945–9 – has risen a little in France, but risen slowly; it was 1.10 in 1935–9 and it was 1.26 in 1963. Since the rise in the divorce rate can be attributed either to very young couples or to couples over forty, it cannot even be proved that the propensity of couples married since 1950, that is, since the return to normal conditions, has risen. The U.S. rate (4.44 in 1957) and the Swedish (2.40) are higher than the prewar rates but in the first case lower than divorce rates immediately after the war. It is in Soviet countries that rates have risen most: in Czechoslovakia 2.14 in 1957 compared with 1.09 in 1935–9 and in Hungary 3.62 compared with 1.14.

We know that the frequency of divorce, all other things being equal, tends to rise with the introduction of modern ways of life, and that it varies considerably from country to country for different reasons (religion, system of values, customs). It is permissible to assume that some major causes will increase the frequency: the slackening of moral reprobation, the increase of life expectancy and therefore of the duration of marriage, and the decrease in the percentage of non-urban population. But the statistics do not allow us to admit that this tendency is universal, irresistible, or dangerous to society itself.

To balance this, the statistics reflecting the family patterns for Negroes in North American cities, as they stand at present, leave little doubt as to the pathological character of the situation. The percentage of illegitimate births in 1963 was 3.7 for the white population and 23.59 for the Negro. Such figures are evidence of a social disintegration which the divorce rates do not show, even the high rates of the United States.

Nor do the suicide rates in the developed countries allow us to infer a growing anomy (including under this head the two Durkheimian types, egoism and anomy). In France this rate (per million inhabitants) was lower in the 1950s than in the 1930s (195 in 1936, 159 in 1960). The rates in Switzerland are higher than those in France or the United States. To interpret these differences it would be desirable to have precise and accurate statistics concerning mental illness, psychoses, neuroses, and criminality. But some of these statistics are missing and others are not easy to compare. The statistics for criminality are compiled variously from country to country. The number of sentences pronounced or of cases closed is not a precise indication of the number of crimes.

In the United States the authorities and the press have been alarmed for years about the growth of crime. According to Federal Bureau of Investigation statistics, for instance, the number of premeditated homicides increased by 8 per cent between 1963 and 1964, rape by 21 per cent, thefts by force or violence increased 12 per cent, assault 17 per cent, and automobile thefts 16 per cent. According to the kind of statistics Americans prefer, premeditated homicide was committed every forty-two minutes in 1951, every forty-one minutes in 1954, but only every fifty-seven minutes in 1964. In contrast, in 1964 rape was committed every twenty-six minutes (forcible rape only) compared to every thirty-one minutes in 1951 and every twenty-nine minutes in 1954 (all rapes). If we assume that there is indeed an increase of crime in the United States, it is due to a large extent to the disentegration of certain social milieus, and not to the anomy of the entire population. Neither can it be proved that the rates for all crimes (assuming that they are meaningful) are higher in the United States than in Europe.

In the area of crime the only change of the last fifteen years that is incontestable is the rise of juvenile delinquency. This phenomenon is plainly evident in Sweden, Great Britain, and France. In these countries it accompanies a prolongation of schooling and a drop in the rate of unemployment and can therefore be variously interpreted: by the relationship between the generations, the attitude of young people towards the family and society, the autonomous organizations of adolescents, plus the disintegration of the family in certain milieus.

Statistics do not allow us to conclude either that industrial societies disintegrate progressively or that social integration gathers strength along with economic progress. These remarks are not meant to refute the social criticism of anomy. They are intended to correct the pessimism of certain observers and to reintroduce, in another form, an idea of Durkheim's.

He stated that crime, that is the act that violates a general prohibition, is sociologically normal; no society exists without crimes or criminals. Just as statistics show that every year a percentage of 'abnormal' children is born (a *percentage* which we call 'normal'), in the same way statistics show that every year a certain number of murders and armed robberies occur. This number may be considered normal if it is observed to occur regularly in the majority of societies which have reached the same stage of development. Sociologists have given up making broad distinctions between the normal and the pathological, since they are not able to discern clearly the various types of society or their phases of evolution. The rate of divorce or suicide is higher in urban civilizations than in predominantly agricultural regions where the people live in villages or small towns. But no one can say what is the normal rate, or even whether there is a normal rate.

Some American sociologists, rejecting the vague definition of anomy used above, have attempted to give the term an exact meaning. Anomy has nothing to do with some vague form of social disintegration, but with a psychic state like that which Durkheim attributed to suicides caused by anomy, namely 'normlessness', as the Americans say, although I would prefer 'absence of internalized norms'. This means, to use a current expression, that certain individuals do not know what to hold on to, they have the feeling of being carried away by an irresistible movement towards an unknown future; they no longer believe in the values of their fathers, and have found no others to replace them.

A study by H. McClosky and John H. Schaar in the *American Sociological Review* of February 1965 marks a return to the Durkheim method, that is, a moral interrogation. Instead of seeking social indices of 'anomy', the authors, using the modern technique of the questionnaire, attempt to discern by means of answers to questions,[8] the psychic state of 'anomy', 'normlessness', the absence of imperatives and prohibitions internalized by the conscience. Answers to some of the questions revealed a lack of firm convictions, the feeling that it is difficult to distinguish between true and false, good and evil, in a complex world, to determine what is chaotic and what is merely changing. Defined in this way, anomy has no direct relation to the rate of divorce, crime, delinquency, alcoholism, or suicide. It is not proved either that anomy (in the sense of state of mind) produces these results or that a large proportion of these acts can be attributed even in part to anomy. The conclusion of the study, the technical details of which we cannot elaborate, is that anomy, in so far as it is a state of internal anarchy (not knowing how to regard oneself, feeling lost), is produced in certain cases by the social context, in others by the structure of individual personality, and again in others by a combination of both. People of the upper classes, with a high level of education, who have a better understanding of the society in which they live, have a better chance of avoiding anomy. But even among the advantaged groups there are some anomic individuals who are anxious, dogmatic, or pitiless. Quick to condemn their fellows, reluctant to forgive human weaknesses, they will often appear anomic, even if they have a university degree and hold a high position in society.

This study is valuable in that it parts company with the sociologist's professional equation. Whether concerned with children's academic achievements or the frequency of anomy, the sociologist usually explores the social determinants and consequently runs the risk of neglecting the genetic or psychological factors.

8 For example: 'With everything so uncertain these days, it almost seems as though anything could happen.' 'Everything changes so quickly these days that I often have trouble deciding which are the right rules to follow.' 'People were better off in the old days, when everyone knew just how he was expected to act.'

Depending upon inherited disposition or aptitude, people sharing the same environment will succeed or, on the contrary will fail – will find their place in society or, on the contrary, will experience a kind of inner emptiness.

It is obvious that there is no reason to choose between an explanation based on environment and one based on personal predisposition. What must be decided is how much to attribute to the one and how much to the other. Similarly, the conclusion of the study by McClosky and Schaar does not call for a radical repudiation of R. K. Merton's classic thesis. The anomy manifested by a fraction of the people questioned, judging by their answers (more numerous in the lower classes, but present in all classes), is the symptom of a failure in the process of socialization and in the means by which such socialization is achieved (communication, interaction, education). Perhaps the process of socialization is more difficult, and failure more frequent, when individual aspiration is not limited by custom and when mobility and the worship of success seem to open unbounded prospects to so many individuals.

By way of this digression we return from 'objective indices' and 'inner emptiness' to the vague definition of anomy, the malaise of our civilization – to use an expression current during the last century. There is no doubt that this malaise is identifiable to the majority of social critics, writers, philosophers, physicians, and psychologists.

Integration implies a *system of values and an ensemble of models of behaviour which are at once imposed with all the authority of evidence on the conscious or unconscious of all the members of a community, and which ensure peaceful coexistence between individuals*. The rapidity of material changes, and hence of adaptive behaviour, the contrast between family and local traditions, and the demands of industrial and urban life apparently constitute major obstacles to such integration.

In non-Western societies in the throes of modernization the clash between two cultural worlds is always evident, although the results are variable and uncertain. The Kabyle peasant, accustomed to a subsistence economy under the strict rules of the family and village community, will never again be entirely 'at home' after he has come in contact with a monetary economy and the technical equipment of modern civilization. He will live in two worlds, one which he carries within himself, shaped by the living experience of his first years, the other, the external world to which at all costs he must adapt himself if he wants to survive. Of those who belong to two worlds, some will in their hearts remain faithful to their tradition, even if they work in a streamlined factory; others will end up converted to the modern socio-industrial order. By definition, archaic societies on the road to industrialization are all more or less anomic (in the vague sense). The perpetual transformation of the technological environment repeatedly challenges this double culture even for a generation already moulded by cities, a challenge sometimes all the more difficult because the norms of socialization in certain working-class neighbourhoods have neither the clarity nor the power of traditional norms. The least favoured classes (and they exist in all industrialized countries, even those that are racially homogeneous) are, as it were, excluded from the community. In addition, the socio-industrial order inevitably gives rise to a certain percentage of failures. All modern societies are competitive, even those which do not make success the supreme value. There is no failure without bitterness and resentment on one side, and on the other accusations of a kind all the more odious to the victims because it seems to them at once anonymous, unjust, and falsely rational.

The ethics of an acquisitive civilization, in which worth can only be measured by success, promotion, or wealth, inevitably abandon to themselves and to their daemons those whom fate has betrayed. In this respect, the difference between systems is not as great as it would seem. In an entirely state-controlled economic regime which, at the same time, would like to conform to the principle of equal opportunity for all, the competition between scholars, universities, and bureaucrats is as great as in the West. The stiffness of the examinations which open the doors to the university is greater in the Soviet Union than in liberal democratic countries, even supposing that the children of the upper classes are less advantaged. Apart from periods of revolutionary exaltation, individuals in bureaucratically planned societies are themselves engaged in a permanent struggle whose stake is the place they will finally occupy in the hierarchy.

Joseph Schumpeter illuminated the basic paradox of capitalist industrial society. In theory to the extent that each man acts in his own interest, the good of all is attained. But the 'invisible hand' does not transmute common lead into pure gold save on two conditions: selfish people must respect the law; they must be surrounded by people – officials, policemen, judges, politicians – whose motives and codes have nothing in common with those of the *Homo oeconomiens*.

It is impossible, in the present state of our knowledge, to place an appropriate value on the various factors: the victims of economic progress, the lower strata excluded from society as a whole either because they belong to a handicapped ethnic minority or because they include individuals whom heredity and family environment have reduced to poverty; the heterogeneity of the cultural worlds enclosed within each conscience and within society as a whole; the relative weakness of those norms deprived of religious or traditional foundation; the contradiction between the ethics of success and respect for ethics; finally, the isolation and bitterness of those who have not climbed the steps of the social pyramid, or who have come down a few. It is also impossible to affirm that the combination of factors creates insoluble problems for a growing number of people. The Western societies of Europe *seem* more integrated after twenty years of growth than they have been for at least a half century.

It is fashionable to imagine that it is possible to discern on the horizons of history the peaceful mediocrity of a middle class which has grown to envelop all the social classes, or a bureaucratic crystallization which reproduces in the industrial age the rigidity of earlier theocratic hierarchies. Criticism of anomy reminds us that these visions are beyond our foreseeable future, a future in which societies will be agitated by the multiplicity of cultural norms, by competition between individuals, and the mobility which the egalitarian ideal makes mandatory from the outset.

*Alienation*

For several decades, in Germany, in France, in Western Europe, now even in the United States, the word alienation has been used and defined in so many ways that it would perhaps be better to discard it. We take it up again here only because it enables us to pose some special problems; even in its ambiguity it is a part of our own society's critical consciousness of itself.

In French or in English, the word alienation is used to translate three German words: *Veräusserung*, *Entäusserung*, and *Entfremdung*. The first of these usually has a juridical meaning, as does the equivalent French word; it merely describes the sale of property, especially real estate, or an inheritance. One does not 'alienate' a refrigerator, one sells it; but one alienates a family estate. The other two words, which Marx uses almost indiscriminately, do not have the same root; one refers to externalization (*aussen* – outside), the other to strangeness (*fremd* – alien).

*Entäusserung* means externalization, the creation of a work which exists outside its creator. Externalization equals alienation when the work becomes or seems alien to its creator.

Without going back to the religious origins of this concept, let us recall that the young historian Marx kept his distance in regard to Hegelian philosophy, especially in considering the mystery of historical alienation. According to Hegel, as interpreted by Marx, human history is the last stage of the Becoming of the Spirit; it was projected into Nature, and then was alienated from it in order to return to itself in a unity in which subject and object are fused. All externalization is alienation, and alienation will be overcome only with the end of history and the return of the Spirit to itself in absolute knowledge.

Marx refuses to admit that all externalization is alienation, in other words, that alienation is a metaphysical process. Man, as physical anthropology looks upon him, belongs to the animal kingdom; he created himself in the course of the centuries as he discovered more and more effective means of production. But, in creating himself he also lost himself; alienation is the historical adventure of humanity divided into antagonistic classes. With the advent of the capitalist regime the adventure reaches its final phase: gradually the evolution of the means of production and the accumulation of capital will eliminate the destitution which forced the many to make sacrifices for the comfort and well-being of the few responsible for the progress of culture. Never has humanity been so estranged from itself as in the capitalist regime, never has it been so close to putting an end, once and for all, to alienation, to the divorce of men from the social order in which they live.

This reminder of well-known ideas suggests the richness of an elusive theme. All institutions, all events are the work of men, but neither an economico-social regime nor a great war is the work of *one* human will. According to the common saying, men make their own history but they do not know the history they make. They create their societies but do not know the society they create. The more complex and changing the society, the more will men feel themselves strangers to it. If one calls alienation the experience which millions of individuals have of the distance between conscience and social life, is not alienation irreducible, the price to be paid for the conquests of civilization itself?

How did Marx, in his youth or in his mature years, conceive of a non-alienated existence? No one can say with certainty. After 1844 even the term *Entfremdung* rarely appears in his writings. In the *Economic and Philosophic Manuscripts* (1844) and in previous texts, all human creations – religion, philosophy, politics – seem to be seen as so many alienations. According to this hypothesis, non-alienated man would, in the last analysis, be nearest to nature, the worker indistinguishable from his activity. In *Capital* the principal expression of alienation is the substitution of a merchant economy for direct relations between producers: planned organization of production and trade would put an end to the power of the creation over the creator, the mechanisms of the market over men.

Marx's conclusions are of little moment; they will always be controversial. In contemporary social criticism, the idea of alienation has, for the most part, lost philosophical acceptance. For lack of a definition of human essence, sociologists, and particularly those with Marxist leanings, do not denounce the non-humanity of the life men lead in an industrial society as evidence of man's loss of his *essence;* they denounce the divorce, conscious or unconscious, of individuals from their social being. We have written *conscious or unconscious* deliberately, for the critics of alienation refuse to see the acceptance of the established order as proof of man's reconciliation with his environment. At times they stress objective reality, at others, inner experience. Sometimes alienation is defined by the sociologist himself, at other times it is experienced by the social protagonists. The meaning which the word alienation has in psychopathology (*madness*) is, in principle, entirely different from the meaning the critics of modern society give it; but a kind of kinship is more or less discernible between the psychiatric alienation – separation by madness, from others and from himself – and the alienation of men sound in body and mind who are not reconciled to their own existence.

All the problems of the socio-industrial order lend themselves to interpretation in terms of alienation. Allegiance to a capitalist class is social alienation; the subjection of a worker to one set of tools which are not his own and which he does not understand is technical alienation; the separation of the producer from the product is economic alienation. One must also add political alienation to the extent that the regime itself, whether democratic or authoritarian, is felt by its subjects or citizens to be a power that is at once foreign, unintelligible, and anonymous.

This interpretation has the advantage of illustrating a basic problem of modern civilization; it has the disadvantage of furthering its confusion. Every society that is technically complex is *depersonalized*, the individuals performing anonymous duties are, in certain respects, treated like things and have no communication with each other save through the intermediary of objects manufactured by all and external to all. An industrial concern might appear to the individual worker either as a power system in the service of one class (capitalists, directors, the Communist Party) or as an organizational system that obeys only its own rationality. The separation of workers from their tools, producers from their product, constitutes a structural characteristic of industrial civilization.

The private property system, however, is not without influence on the way individuals endure this separation. A worker who sees the world in terms of Marxist ideology experiences alienation more intensely than a worker placed in objectively identical circumstances but with a different attitude towards his environment. Every society seeks to convince its members of the virtues of its own regime, although democracies accept what totalitarian regimes outlaw – self-criticism.

What then, are the means of seeking not the total elimination of man's divorce from his social life but an attenuation of this state of affairs? The answer seems to me as simple as it is banal: raising the intellectual level. *Men will become less alien to their destiny to the extent that they come to understand it.* This does not mean that they will not necessarily be less dissatisfied; dissatisfaction, clearly felt, and expressing itself by a desire for definite reform, cannot be called alienation. It is the human response to an order which is, in essence, imperfect.

Alienation, as we have previously defined it, is less an isolated aspect of the social order or of collective psychology than it is the product of the ever present threat of rationalized techniques in complex organizations and in heavily populated societies. Tens of thousands of young men and women, assembled in universities, read the young Marx and see alienation as the loneliness of the man in the crowd, the loss of personal contacts with the organization itself – symbolized for them by lack of personal interchange with their busy or disinterested professors. Sometimes they feel themselves estranged from their lot as students, not because it is too harsh but because it is predetermined. A destiny, even a comfortable one, remains external to a man who has not made it by himself; modern civilization gives no one certainty that he will find his bearings in his changing environment. No country I have visited has given me the feeling of political alienation I experienced in Poland – by which I mean the divorce between the established system of government and the institutions and processes that would correspond to the wishes of the governed. The indifference which so many citizens show towards their state and their rulers in countries where there is representative government may be in sharp contrast, but it also may indicate a similar gap between men and their institutions, and it probably attests to a latent uneasiness which might suddenly explode in a crisis of wild passions.

Man, said Bergson, was *naturally* made to live in small closed societies. In modern civilization, however, we must say that man has definitely lost the naïve certitudes which led him to make no distinction between his private and his social being. The Marxist utopia of man's reconciliation with himself and his environment symbolized the yearning for a return to the ideal of primitive communities, which would be possible with the coming of plenty, and the unhampered fulfilment of each individual, at last delivered from the curse of faceless industrial labour. Perhaps the utopian ideal is not dead, but merely clothed in a new form: it is not the taking over of power by the proletariat or the advent of central economic planning that should mark the end of prehistory, but automation carried to its extreme, which would reduce to a minimum the time men must devote to work. During their leisure, men would find liberty again.

## Non-Alienation

In the preceding pages we have avoided any metaphysical discussion of alienation and confined ourselves to dealing with the sociological meaning of the term. But, implicitly, the critics of alienation entertain a certain notion of non-alienation, or of the non-alienated man. What is this notion? Or rather, what are the various notions? It seems to me that one can, by simplifying, distinguish three tendencies: one which is based on classical Marxism, a second of existentialist inspiration, and a third that stems from Freudianism, either orthodox or as revised by the culturalist American school.

The first tendency attributes psychological and social malaise to specific features of the capitalist regime: private ownership of the means of production; accentuation of the commercial, competitive, and advertising aspect of industrial civilization; manipulation of the masses by means of the communication media; and the existence of a capitalist power elite. This Marxist criticism of alienation does not avoid the arguments raised by non-Marxist criticism, but it puts all the blame on the regime.

It relegates to the shadows the possibilities of similar alienation under other regimes. Radio and television provide a leading example; these mass media inevitably are either public or private. In the first instance they are subject to political exploitation; in the second they are open to the risk of degradation to the level of advertising propaganda. One cannot utterly shield them from the one or the other danger at the same time; actually, neither is ever completely eliminated because while the media that put all men in touch with one another are and probably always will be under the control of the few, they cannot be effective unless they are responsive to the tastes of their mass audience.

In the same way, it is easy to emphasize the ambition of individuals in a capitalist regime: the organization man, ready to devote body and soul to his enterprise so as to scale the last rungs to success; young university graduates solely concerned with quick promotion; the upstart rich, striving to acquire the glittering status they think glamorous, and know to be precarious; and the old families attempting to erect a barrier of status quo against these new competitors. Some of these phenomena, which are the subject of much popularized sociology, seem to be peculiar to the United States, related to the special traits of this heterogeneous nation, composed of immigrants who arrived at different times. But in every society the ambition to succeed inevitably results from a decrease in the permanence of social status. The art of rising to the higher rungs of a bureaucracy is not exactly the same in the Soviet Union as in a great American corporation, but in both it demands respect for the established order and acceptance of its values. Organizations require conformity from the moment they cease to be limited to a specific goal; they may be set these requirements anonymously as part of an obvious rationale, or they may become caricatures of communities, oppressive to all those who do not subscribe to the religion of socialism or of General Motors.

The Marxist criticism of alienation none the less preserves a double meaning, even for those who side with the opposite camp. It separates the specifically *capitalist* causes of the feeling millions have of living in a world that has become alien to them; we know that under another regime the same or other causes evoke a similar feeling. It is important, nevertheless, to be reminded of the actual causes of alienation in the existing regime. And there is value in the Marxist teaching that points to at least one way in which men might be reconciled to their work: to reduce the distance between the worker and the social framework in which he works, and to offer those who prefer participation to isolation a better opportunity for commitment to the common task.

The writings of Jean-Paul Sartre, in particular *Critique de la Raison dialectique*, are the most revealing exercises in existentialist philosophy. If we set aside the repetition of purely Marxist themes, such as the analysis of capitalism, of private property and trade, we find that Sartre limits himself to proclaiming the definitive truth of *Capital* without adding anything of his own. However, contrary to the preceding school which was satisfied with a sociological interpretation of alienation without defining what a non-alienated existence would be, Sartre clearly delineates the principle of his criticism, the origin of alienation, immanent in the history of mankind. Consciousness, the active subjectivity (called *praxis*), is in essence freedom, the determination of its aim as well as its means in a context that it defines itself. This liberty, which is part of our humanity, has been constantly wrested from itself, ever since the beginning of history. Each person remains free because he *is* freedom in the strict, metaphysical sense, but because of the scarcity of goods, man becomes the enemy of man. The living have ensured their survival by causing or allowing their fellow creatures to die in great numbers; the master has transformed his slave into an instrument; the creation escapes its creator because *another* takes hold of it or determines its significance; the product no longer belongs to the producer but to another who uses it as he sees fit. The *other* is never himself, there is always *another* beyond the *other* in a society where the world of objects and institutions, which is called practical-inert, encloses all and sundry in a network of reciprocal restrictions, anonymous interdictions, and technical and administrative obligations.

Social existence is *alienated*. Freedom moves under conditions of enslavement. Revolutionary action, that of the crowd storming the Bastille, marks the return of liberty to itself, the origin of non-alienation. All individuals act together, they have a single common objective. Although each consciousness remains locked in itself, it is no longer an object to others, the meaning of its design has not been adulterated by others. The consciousness of all converges in a single design; everyone has made the same choice, victory or death. Mass movements have been severely criticized by banal theories of crowd psychology – that of Gustave le Bon, for instance, who held that individuals, even superior ones, would lose their self-control, give in to their emotions or to the general violence of the populace. Sartre, on the contrary, perceives in revolt the beginning of humanity. Revolt overcomes at once the separation between the consciousness of individuals and the subordination of consciousness to things, a separation and a subordination characteristic of all social orders and especially of the capitalist order.

We see here another meaning to modern criticism of alienation, another nostalgia that man harbours in our civilization: in the complexity the individual loses himself, he belongs to no one and to all, a slave to objects theoretically at his service.

In a society that no longer has a religious foundation, imperatives become degraded into customs which nobody quite understands but which each obeys because others do. Conformity becomes sacred because conformity to the beliefs and the behaviour of the group is the only guarantee of values. Contests in which auditors and viewers of television are asked to choose not the song they prefer but one which will be preferred by the majority are symbolic of a society in which each individual subscribes in advance to judgements of public opinion. This opinion itself is created by a kind of forward light in which each person submits in advance to the mediocrity which he attributes to others. Ortega y Gasset condemns this servility to the masses, in the name of aristocratic values. Jean-Paul Sartre, steeped in democratic values, seeks salvation in the revolutionary masses which he transfigures. United by the same desire for action, the militants avoid alienation by the existence of others and by the actuality of things (techniques and institutions).

Humanity, which begins with revolt, Sartre writes, inevitably ends, at least during its transitional phase, in a totalitarian party and a cult of personality. Here, too, let us disregard the dialectic acrobatics by means of which the philosopher strains to show the inevitable character of events which he could not foresee, and the existence of which he was willing to acknowledge only after the fact. What interests us is that he points up the mechanism by which radical revolt against alienation paves the way for totalitarianism – that is, the total power of one party, embodied in one man, over all men, in their total being.

Industrial civilization, in effect, implies a kind of widespread servitude, if seen in the light of the existentialist conception of pure liberty. All individual consciousness, all the subjectivities in action, are like ants, caught inextricably in a network of social distinctions, authoritarian organizations, technical apparatus, and institutional inequalities. Like Jean-Jacques Rousseau, and in a sense nearer to him than one might think, Sartre might exclaim: man is born free, and everywhere he is in chains. He has forged these chains himself; why should he not throw them off once and for all? Eternal illusion! This network of the practical-inert is society itself in which man, to quote Tocqueville in his melancholy wisdom, 'is neither entirely independent, nor entirely slave. Providence, it is true, draws a circle of fate round each man from which he cannot escape, but within these outer limits, man has power and freedom.' The dream of absolute freedom quickens totalitarian revolutions.

The third school owes as much to Freud as to Marx, and perhaps more. The liberty in whose name it condemns the alienation of modern civilization is not that of consciousness or of individual *praxis*, translucid to itself, but that of the instincts which the family, dominated by the father, and a competitive society continue to repress. Non-alienation is defined by this school in psychological terms: that person is alienated who has not the strength or the courage to be himself, to give free rein to his desires, to solve his problems, to denounce the contradictions which confine his very soul. Neurotics, although not alienated in the clinical sense of the word, are not masters of themselves, torn as they are between their deep ego and their social being, occasionally unaware of having sacrificed what they truly were for conventions or ambitions.

Social psychology, sociometry, psychoanalysis, psychodrama and sociodrama – all the studies of the behaviour of individuals and small groups – are determined by the distinction between the formal and the informal, between visible relationships and feelings experienced. Thus this school of psychology is all the more interested in what happens behind the social façade because individual relationships seem condemned to a kind of anonymity. The distinction between the person and the role constitutes the most favourable historic climate for psychological studies that have as their aim, or their therapeutic means, the freeing of repressions; such studies are concerned with the dynamics of those interpersonal relations hidden from view by the rigidity of administrative or technical organizations.

This psychological interpretation of alienation leads to quite different judgements on industrial civilization. One can sort out, it seems to me, the *neutrals,* the *reformers,* and the *radical critics.*

The first abstain from all positive or negative assessment of the social order. This order is a fact. The psychologists help individuals to adapt themselves to it; the sociologists advise those responsible about reforms that will attenuate friction, give individuals a better chance of expressing themselves, and reduce to a minimum the inevitable suppression of desires that are incompatible with the discipline of the organization. Sometimes the neutrals incline towards optimism. Compared with the authoritarian bureaucracies of the last century, with the military hierarchy, with the first technicians in the scientific organization of work who misunderstood the human factor, has not the socio-industrial order, in factories as well as in offices, been cured of the infantile disease of rationalization?

Reformists (I am thinking of the cultural school of psychoanalysis, epitomized by Erich Fromm), are at once more severe about the present socio-industrial order and less resigned to the social order, such as it is. They attribute to social conflict more responsibility for the genesis of psychic disorders than do the orthodox Freudians; they denounce tensions, repressions, and frustrations, the causes of psychic troubles which are increased by a society in search of possessions, power, and prestige. Their object is to encourage the full flowering of personalities in the existing order or to reform society in order to encourage such a flowering. But they do not try to destroy or evade the realm of U.S. society or industrial civilization, where self-criticism is typical.

A man like Herbert Marcuse, whose ideas derive both from German Marxism (prior to 1933) and Freudianism is one of the last representatives of radical criticism. True to Marxist ideas, he upholds the *great refusal* in his book *One Dimensional Man*. Too clear-thinking to imagine that his hopes have been realized in contemporary Soviet societies, too honest to credit the proletariat with a revolutionary will, he has to admit that the radical negation of reality is no longer embodied in any political movement. Only a few people are determined to say *no* and are proud of not yielding. As long as the machine of production continues to turn and to bring more goods to almost everyone from year to year, the masses will accept their fate passively. But this acceptance represents alienation none the less and for two interrelated reasons. Civilization still treats men like objects; it permits the commercial or political manipulation of consumers or pseudo-citizens; it maintains a climate of competition between individuals and nations even though the productive capacity would be sufficient to secure a simpler and less frantic life for everyone.

Apart from this criticism, whose themes are well known, Marcuse returns to Freud's writings which assail not only industrial civilization but all civilization. Has not civilization at all times been conditioned by the repression of instincts, the primacy of the principle of reality in the form of parental authority, and the relentless discipline of work? Marcuse is against the culturalist school of psychoanalysis and the turn it has taken in the United States. The social dimension of psychic disturbances is present from the beginning in the training provided by the family. This initial process of socialization consists in a repression of fundamental instincts, the sacrifice of pleasure to work, of Eros to reality, of freedom to discipline. The malaise of our civilization can be healed only by a radically different civilization, which he is not even sure can be achieved. So writes Marcuse, after Freud.

Thus Marcuse borrows from the two great destroyers of myths and illusions, Freud and Marx, the weapons he needs to destroy the myths and illusions of a civilization both liberal and appeased. Individuals continue to be enslaved by the process of family socialization. Wealth seems to accelerate the mad course of overproduction and destructive power.

It remains to be seen whether radical criticism, far more than reformist criticism, is not fed by a myth of its own – that of a socialization without repression – and by the ancient illusion of a humanity capable, were it united, of acquiring for the first time mastery over its own ventures.

*Part Three*

# The Dialectic of Universality

One forgets that each of the tens or hundreds of thousands of societies that have coexisted or succeeded one another on this earth since man first appeared has made use of a moral certitude – like that which we ourselves can invoke – to proclaim that even if it were nothing more than a small nomadic band or a hamlet lost in the midst of a forest, it nonetheless embodied all the meaning and dignity of which human life is capable.

CLAUDE LÉVI-STRAUSS
*Le Pensée sauvage*

Humanity is now, for the first time, experiencing a common history. This fact has become a commonplace and in its external manifestations it is obvious. Both the United Nations and the Olympic games symbolize a certain unity within the human species; all the nations send their athletes to the Olympics as did the Greek cities more than two thousand years ago, and most countries are – or should be – represented in the United Nations. So athletes of every nation compete in sporting events on a basis of equality, just as the emissaries of every country mingle socially at official receptions. This 'transnational' society tends towards universality, and the system of interstate relations is developing around the entire planet. If two countries in the modern world do not maintain diplomatic relations it is not because they are unaware of one another's existence but rather because they pretend to be; the refusal of the United States to recognize Communist China constitutes a diplomatic combat weapon and therefore is itself a form of dialogue.

It is also a commonplace to stress the technological and economic causes of what we might call 'globalization' or 'planetarization'. When civilian airlines introduce supersonic equipment it will take only three hours to fly from Paris to New York; it took Tocqueville as many weeks to cross the Atlantic; the speed of the trip will have been multiplied by a factor of 168. The means at men's disposal for travel and the transport of goods have altered our entire concept of space, while instantaneous communication has obliterated time. Statesmen from the northern and southern hemispheres, in Washington, Tokyo, Peking, Moscow, London, Paris, Cape Town, and Buenos Aires, are closer to each other than were European monarchs to their own subjects a century ago. English has become the lingua franca of this planetary civilization as French was the language of European civilization, but with a considerable difference: only a small elite mastered French, whereas today the number of people who understand and speak basic English is – absolutely and relatively – incomparably larger.

The classic notion of the unification of mankind through this new technology of production, transportation, and communication is part of our common awareness. How could it be otherwise when anyone sitting in front of a little screen in his own living-room can see what is happening thousands of miles away? The ubiquity of the visual image and the quick transmission of news give, or ought to give, people today a sense of their capacity to become part of a single world. Certainly the masses take pride in the new power of communication which seems to them all the more limitless since they do not understand its origin and look upon it as miraculous.

But this unification, which we might call material, has less real impact than superficial observers are wont to believe. Even if all families had television sets – and this is far from the case on a world-wide basis – their interests would still be limited to a narrowly restricted social sphere. The poverty and misery of distant peoples, the daily catastrophes that occur all over the world, the strange customs the mass media purvey in such lively fashion – none of this, whether written or visual, affects the average viewer or reader as much as a quarrel with a neighbour or a colleague at the office, or the fluctuations of his own personal fortune.

It is entirely legitimate to speculate on the universality of modern society, but the phenomena we allude to here do not represent the sole or even the primary justification for raising such questions. In any event, the true universality of technology is linked to that ideal of modern society which we have dealt with in Part One and which can be summed up by the twin terms: *scientific truth* and *individual equality* (or, if you will, scientific rationality and democracy). But the internal contradictions of our study take on quite a different focus when we move from a national to a human frame of reference.

In 1965 two East African states brought an action before the International Court of Justice at The Hague against the Republic of South Africa, challenging that nation's administration of the League of Nations mandate in former German South West Africa. The terms of the mandate recognized implicitly the right and duty of the mandatory power to work for the progress of the 'natives' and to further their welfare. In following a policy of discrimination between the dominant white minority and the

Negro majority, South Africa was accused of violating a principle which since has been accepted by the conscience of mankind. To this accusation the representatives of South Africa replied that the principle of non-discrimination – citizenship for all and equality before the law – was applicable only within a politically organized community, or at least within a community sufficiently homogeneous to be aware of itself as such. When ethnic groups, thrown together under the same sovereignty by accidents of history, differ too drastically in their ways of life and their degree of material progress (hypothetically, modern industrial society provides the goal), the absolute power of one ethnic group is inevitable (unless a radical separation between ethnic groups exists), and this could eventually become the most beneficial resolution for the backward majority ethnic groups. However repugnant this argument may be to egalitarian theory, it raises questions not yet satisfactorily answered by any nation.

As we have said, historically, the principle of equality has produced two kinds of consequences: either non-discrimination within a single political body under a centralized regime, or a federated form of government. During the last fifty years the nations of Europe, except for Portugal, have renounced the 'white man's burden' – the task, which they assumed by right of conquest, of 'civilizing' (in their own meaning of the word) the peoples of Africa and some of those of Asia. There were many reasons for the renunciation of this colonial mission, most of which have no relation to the stated ideal. The end of colonialism, however, has an inescapable relationship to a dialectic that is internal to the principle of equality: the same obligations are imposed on each and everyone, the same rights are recognized. But how could laws be the same for the Muslims of Algeria and the French minority, for the Bantu and the whites? When ethnic groups are so very different from one another, the principle of non-discrimination logically calls for separation, not integration.

The principle of equality thus has been transferred from individuals to collectivities which, because of a variety of circumstances, are regarded as national, that is, worthy of becoming a politically organized nation. At no time prior to the first decades of world history have so many states emerged in so few years.

How then can we refrain from asking the following question: Is humanity, now divided into more than a hundred states, each of which, according to the charter of the United Nations, possesses sovereign equality, actually moving in the direction of a *single* society? Is technological unification merely a thin coating which conceals a fundamental diversity? Or, to use another figure of speech, is technological unification more than just another of the many currents of history – and not necessarily the strongest?

The tendency of industrial society to encompass all of mankind has its origin in reason and its handmaidens, science and technology. Does not technology, as the creator of the means of destruction, divide humanity, even though wisdom would call for unification? As the creator of the means of production, is not technology responsible for an inequality among peoples which is at once less open to question and less acceptable than at any time in the past? Sovereign states have not been created by these techniques of destruction and production, but represent the accomplishment of human beings who for thousands of years have lived in politically sovereign units; have the new techniques which threaten the old patterns fostered or hindered the unity, or at least the peace to which men of goodwill have always aspired?

This is another way of pointing up the themes of the first two chapters. One thermonuclear bomb dropped on a large city would kill several million people; yet increasing numbers of states demand a sovereignty which theoretically is defined by their right to choose between peace and war. The same means of production are available to all peoples, but all are not able to make good use of them. There is nothing to prevent all men from becoming enriched together, since riches can be wrested from nature rather than from other men; but for the time being (for how many decades or centuries will this continue to be true?) inequality of progress characterizes the dawn of universal history.

The interstate system is torn apart by conflicts between sovereign states, just as the world economy suffers from disparities in development. Must we not go a step further and ask – and this is the theme of the final chapter – if humanity can be said to be united in pursuit of the same goal? The rulers of every state would like to participate in some way in modern industrial civilization, but do production, welfare, and such modern scientific miracles as space exploration lend a meaning to human existence? No one would want mankind to accept a dismal uniformity in order to put an end to its quarrels; but while it is easy in theory it is extremely difficult in practice to distinguish between *cultures* which should acknowledge each other's values and politico-economic *ideologies* locked in a death struggle. Religions of salvation that addressed themselves to all men as individuals were once involved in the great conflicts between state collectivities. Today, secular religions, even those inspired by the ideal of universality, temporarily divide those they claim to unite. No one knows how long this phase will last.

# 7 The Anarchical Order of Power

Men continue to belong to political units pretending to independence. Hence, there is no 'planetary society' or 'human society' comparable to Pueblo or French society, or to the society of the United States or the Soviet Union.

The examples just given intentionally illustrate the diversity of the 'political units' or 'societies' of which the state claims to be the sovereign expression. A historian of the school of Spengler or Toynbee would contrast 'national societies', naïvely proud of their originality, with the 'intelligible field' that makes up a whole civilization', such as ancient civilization or Western Christian civilization.[1] An ethnologist would reply that the truly intelligible field lies below and not above politically organized society. A state such as the Soviet Union encompasses many ethnic groups or cultural communities whose past, customs, and even creeds remain different in many respects.

We shall, none the less, take the multiplicity of legally sovereign states (according to the Charter of the United Nations) as the characteristic trait of the 'asocial society' or the 'anarchical order' of mankind. The former expression goes back to Kant; the latter borrows the notion of anarchy from the banal critique of the system of rival sovereignties. Both seek to emphasize the *essential imperfection* of 'human society', to assume the existence of a 'society' of all mankind in the sense that the city-states and empires of the ancient world and the nation-states of Europe constituted one.

This essential imperfection is not corrected by the growth of commercial transactions between countries and continents. It is in vain that telecommunication satellites transmit words and images instantaneously; it is in vain that scholars and intellectuals

1. Toynbee prefers to use the term society in designating these 'intelligible fields'.

meet at conventions. However useful relations transcending national borders among private individuals may be – whether in the domain of sports, science, tourism, religion, or business – and whatever influence these individual relations may exert over a long term on the 'reserved domain' of relations between states, international relations still remain today what they have been throughout history: they have not entirely left the state of the law of the jungle. A sovereign collectivity is one which makes its own laws and whose leaders acknowledge obedience to no one else in certain matters – those affecting so-called vital interests, which in certain circumstances involve the choice between war and peace. The state is not solely, but it is at the very least and in any case, that agency which possesses the monopoly of legitimate violence. Now this monopoly must be effective and not merely legal. What army would be capable of fulfilling for the whole of mankind the function entrusted to the police force in nation-states? All civilizations (or societies, in Toynbee's use of the word) have known a violent history whose mainspring has been the relations between states. Modern civilization, while planetary in its technico-economic dynamism, has not eliminated or even morally modified interstate relations, which, despite our individual condemnations of their cruelty and our desire to shake off their yoke, continue mercilessly in their unreasonable rationality to forge our common destiny.

'Asocial society', 'anarchical order', 'unreasonable rationality' – these apparently contradictory expressions are not dictated by a taste for paradox or literary affectation. The society of sovereign states is in essence asocial, since it does not outlaw the recourse to force among the 'collective persons' that are its members. Order, if there be one, in this society of states is anarchical in that it rejects the authority of law, of morality, or of collective force. In an anarchical society, why would any individual entrust to someone other than himself the concern for his security? On the other hand, when one thermonuclear bomb alone has more power of destruction than all the bombs or shells used during the Second World War, is it not unreasonable to risk a war whose sole possible benefits would be insignificant compared to the certain costs?

It is easy to elicit enthusiasm by contrasting the spirit of science with the unenlightened parochial spirit. Jets fly at over 500 miles an hour; tomorrow supersonic planes will fly at Mach 2 or 3; ballistic missiles cover nearly 10,000 miles in an hour; and customs officials continue to guard borders; armies, incapable of protecting populations, consume resources that would be better used to combat hunger or underdevelopment. How long will the contradiction between the universal diffusion of technology and the survival of traditional diplomacy persist?

The entire planet alone is scaled to the technology of the twentieth century: the conquest of outer space testifies to this even more eloquently than thermonuclear bombs. It does not necessarily follow that the continuation of traditional diplomacy is merely a 'survival'. Or at least – before hastening to condemn – we must attempt to understand the anarchical order of the international system, as it has been for millennia and remains today (though not without substantial modifications due to changes in thought and events).

## The Social Animal

Man is *naturally* a social animal (the word nature here being understood in the meaning given to it by biologists). Human young depend on their mothers for a long period; the family by itself is weak and threatened. The species can evolve towards the full realization of its potentialities only in and through societies capable of preserving what preceding generations have acquired, and, thus, of promoting the further accumulation of knowledge and power. The so-called archaic societies that came into being with the Neolithic revolution were limited. Each placed itself spontaneously at the centre of a universe it interpreted both arbitrarily and intelligibly. Defined by a system of values, a way of life, indeed a world view, each tended to regard the others as foreign and, therefore, strange, though this strangeness did not necessarily provoke hostility. In this sense, Bergson is wrong in affirming that collectivities are like wolves to one another (*Homo homini lupus*), while members of the collectivities are like gods to one another (*Homo homini deus*). The most closed societies were not devoid of internal conflicts and were not perforce dedicated to a struggle unto death with near-by or distant societies. So long as the strictly political organization – borders, laws, central power – is imperfect, the limits of the societies themselves do not stand out clearly, and often one hesitates over the meanings of the words used to designate its groupings (family, clan, village, tribe, and so forth). But these semantic uncertainties, reflecting ambiguities inscribed in reality itself, do not eliminate the major fact: mankind began by division and not by unity. Every human society grew conscious of its originality in developing a culture – it established itself by distinction from the others, proud, rather than anxious, to discover itself different from others.

The interstate relations one observes throughout the several thousand years of major history (of so-called higher civilization) are a work of culture, and as such they may be called artificial if one equates the nature of man or of societies with their initial state. Even biologists would condemn such an equation: man is an animal species which, being organized in stable groups, has a history. This history does not mark the end of the biological evolution of the species, but it is no less evident than that evolution. The history of civilizations and the evolution of the species react upon one another, whatever interpretation one makes of this duality, according to one's metaphysical or religious beliefs.

Conflicts between states, more or less regulated by tradition, custom, or law, form an integral part of civilizations; they belong not to the biological but to the human order. This proposition is not in contradiction with the theory common among the classic philosophers, according to which the relations between states derive from the *state of nature*. The latter stood in contrast to the civil society (*l'état civil*), and both sprang from culture, not from animal nature. The concept of nature, in this sense, is ambiguous because it contrasts at times with convention, at other times with civil society, and most times with both together. In contrast to conventions, the state of nature is characteristic of man qua man, leaving aside the infinite and arbitrary diversity of mores. Hence, natural laws are universal laws – those applying to all men, irrespective of the norms to which an individual is subject by virtue of his membership in a particular society. In contrast to civil society, the state of nature excludes a supreme authority, a tribunal entitled to render verdicts, a police authorized to enforce them: therefore each man is responsible for his own security, free in his decisions, including the decision to take up arms.

The concept of the state of nature represented an interpretation of the behaviour appropriate to historical man, a pessimistic or optimistic metaphysics. Some philosophers described the state of nature as the war of all against all; others, on the contrary, depict man as peaceful and benign outside society. Some proclaim that the state of nature knows no other law than that of might; others, claiming that man by himself tends toward the fulfilment of his reasonable nature, placed the laws of nature above civil law. But all made a distinction between the state of nature where each man, separate or sovereign, can count only on himself, and civil society where law reigns, where justice is rendered by tribunals, where the police suppress violence.

This distinction does not at all suggest that the present style of interstate relations represents the survival of a primordial situation of individuals or societies – the war of all against all: archaic societies were not all bellicose, and the struggles in which they engaged were often ritualized to the point of being closer to our competitive games than to death struggles of the industrial age. Nor does this distinction imply that interstate hostilities derive through the mysteries of the collective unconsciousness, from the enmity that primitive man spontaneously felt for the foreigner: it is simply the product of historic experience, confirmed by the study of all civilizations. City-states and empires alike were established through violence; the maintenance of peace was the first task of those in power within politically organized units, but peace among these units was never imposed by the same method. All international systems have been anarchical, in the strict sense of the term: they have not been subjected to an *archē*. Once an *archē* is recognized, the political units are deprived of their constructive principle – auto-nomy, in-dependence, the ability of making their own decisions involving their destiny.

This distinction in essence does not exclude a similarity in the realm of practice. Within states, too, individuals and groups rival one another, and there is a permanent danger of recourse to violence. And it is true that there is not a single state which has not been established by violence, from narrower collectivities of differing cultures. The homogeneity of a people has been the work of centuries, meaning, most often, the work of force. Only the United States of America has a slightly different history. Leaving aside the wars against the Indians, then against Mexico and Spain, U.S. nationality was forged by a constitutional law established for nearly two centuries. Millions of immigrants freely decided to join this *commonwealth*, this community.

In short, the philosophical distinction between the state of nature and civil society expresses a permanent fact of history: men live in society, but there have always been many societies and not one society. Every historic society has been distinctive and in more or less regular relation with other societies. Within each of them, the rival ambitions of individuals or groups, ethnic heterogeneity, and opposition of interests created a permanent danger of illegitimate violence. Between societies, recourse to armed force was legitimate since, in the absence of civil authority, each could count only on itself to ward off perils and to survive.

It is scarcely necessary, in order to explain the endemic character of wars, to endow man with greater aggressiveness than that of other primates: the conditions, constant throughout history, of the political organization of mankind suffice to explain the precariousness of peace and the frequency of wars. Peace could be safeguarded only, and always temporarily, by the balance of rival powers or the victory of the strongest and the establishment of an empire.

The 'natural' character of the specificity of interstate relations (legitimacy of recourse to force), as confirmed by historical experience, imposes no conclusion regarding the future of human society; it merely prohibits an illusory extrapolation. The transition from *many* sovereignties to *one* sovereignty is neither logically nor materially impossible, but it would be *essentially* different from the transition from city-state to empire. Empires eliminated or integrated sovereign states; they did not eliminate all external sovereignty. United under one sovereignty, mankind would no longer have any enemy – unless it be on another planet.

This would be a mutation *of* history itself and not a mutation *within* history.

A world state is not in contradiction with the biological or social nature of man, as it has been revealed throughout the centuries. If Rome was able to spread its domain to the British Isles and to Byzantium at a time when legions travelled by foot, modern techniques for movement on land, on sea, and in air make a planetary empire materially possible. What excludes such an empire today and for the foreseeable future are the historic protagonists. By historic protagonists I mean the politically organized collectivities, the minorities governing them, and perhaps the peoples themselves. Heads of state hold fast to sovereignty – that is, to their freedom of action internally and externally, of which the term sovereignty represents the juridical or ideological expression. Peoples respond to the call for 'national independence', some because they have barely emerged from a colonial regime, and others because they are nostalgic for their lost grandeur, or because the official ideology depicts classes and states engaged in a death struggle.

If we use the word *nationalism* here to indicate the will of politically organized collectivities, established in a territory and subject to a state, to maintain vis-à-vis other similar collectivities a liberty theoretically total and at least equal to that of others, then we would have to say that the planetary expansion of technology and of modern economy does not result in a universal state. Peoples or states act on the stage of history like individuals who *refuse* to submit to a master and *do not know how* to submit to a common law. In seeking to establish or maintain a universal state one encounters the same obstacle. To establish a universal state, in the absence of consent, it would be necessary to break the resistance of states, as the resistance of the feudal barons was broken by the armed force of the kings, or that of the Greek city-states or of Macedonia was broken by the Roman legions. But the monarchic precedent has no value as an example so long as a universal sovereignty must encompass heterogeneous peoples; the Roman precedent might serve as a model, but it inspires terror. At what price and with what consequences would unity be arrived at through the defeat of all the pretenders to empire save one?

But let us suppose that the universal state has been established: it could survive only by the effective monopoly of legitimate violence. It would have to possess enough weapons to prevent provincial groups from resorting to force or, at least, to prevent the spread of conflicts, if these groups preserved an army. But could the army of the universal state succeed in *restraining* local armies by the threat of nuclear weapons alone (supposing that these were a monopoly of the universal state)? Or are we to imagine the estates reduced to the level of administrations, virtually disarmed? Under this hypothesis, one requires of these administrations (ex-states) a confidence in the loyalty of its people (ex-citizens) of which our period provides few examples. In both cases, one assumes that the main problem has been solved, namely, the consent of the peoples and the states to surrender to a universal state a portion of the autonomy that has been held essential over the centuries. But all indications are that they do not fear the nuclear apocalypse enough to abdicate their sovereignty.

Lord Russell gave mankind a deadline of a few decades, until the end of the century, to choose between a world-state and annihilation. But at the end of the second decade of the atomic age, a third path has appeared.

## Forms of Warfare

History has thus far refused to pose the ultimate choice between collective suicide and the abdication of states. It has gradually brought a certain order out of the anarchy common to all international systems, an order favouring the limitation of armed conflicts, subject to an oligarchy camouflaged by democratic symbols.

This order results in the first place from a quasi-control of interstate violence – a control as novel as the historic conjuncture itself. There are three sorts of weapons available today, corresponding to three combat methods: let us say, symbolically, the submachine gun, the tank, and the atomic bomb – the first being adapted to guerrilla warfare, the second to regular army fighting, the third to thermonuclear exchanges (or push-button warfare, to adopt the terminology of science fiction). In terms of power of destruction, there is nothing in common between the guerrilla fighter, the tank driver, and the crew of the Minuteman missile, any more than between a wrench used by a garage mechanic, a conveyor belt in an automobile factory, and the equipment of an atomic plant. But more recent techniques, while they may be most characteristic of the present age, do not eliminate former techniques, and this is for two reasons. Automation (where it is possible and profitable) is so expensive that it can only be partial and gradual. Large sectors of the economy continue to remain refractory to the new technology, and the mechanic's wrench, even the shovel and the pick, continue to remain symbolic. Similarly, the thermonuclear bomb and the ballistic missile have eliminated neither the machine gun of the guerrilla fighter nor the coolie who transports on his back the rice and munitions of the combatants.

The individual weapon – light, effective in short-term operations, in ambushes, and in man-to-man fighting – was the response of the colonized peoples to the colonial domination of the European states. The white man imposed his domination on the peoples of Asia and Africa thanks to the superiority of his technology and science, thanks also to his prestige. Once that prestige has been eroded by familiarity, domination tended to have no basis other than force. The Vietnamese, Indonesians, or Congolese could not defeat the regular armies of France, the Netherlands, or Belgium, but they could deny the colonial regime's security. If they have the sympathy and complicity of the masses, a few thousand guerrillas can strip the rich few of the desire and ability to rule. In the twenty years since the explosions of Hiroshima and Nagasaki, the machine guns of guerrillas have changed the map of the world much more than have tanks or atomic bombs. At Dien Bien Phu, these guerrillas had become soldiers, organized in divisions, who dealt a death blow to the French expeditionary force, worn out by seven years of struggle against elusive combatants. Thus ended an empire.

Wars, all limited and local, between regular or quasi-regular armies, have all ended since 1945 in armistices that have not been followed by peace treaties. The demarcation lines give sanction to the accidental results of combat operations at the time of the cease-fire: such is the case of the border between India and Pakistan in Kashmir, between Israel and the Arab states in the Near East, and between North and South Korea after three years of fighting. The contrast is striking between the victory of the rebels over the Dutch or the French in Indonesia or Vietnam, and the stalemates or armistices without peace treaties at the conclusion of hostilities between regular forces.

Need we add that the reason for this contrast is more political than military. The guerrillas won nearly everywhere because the 'imperialists', morally and materially weakened by the Second World War, no longer believed in their mission, and because the empire becomes too costly when it entails economic obligations towards conquered peoples. Israeli tanks could have gone on to Cairo in 1956; if there had been enough of them, American tanks could have reached the Yalu. The Great Powers of the international system wanted, above all, to arrive at a compromise when they confronted one another directly or through satellites interposed prudently between them; generally they stopped military operations between secondary states as quickly as possible; they prevented weapons from fulfilling their secular function of deciding otherwise insoluble questions. By their intervention, they have perpetuated situations that, in other times, would have been deemed absurd: the division of Jerusalem (before the Israeli military action in 1967) or of Kashmir. The limitation of hostilities has seemed to be the prime object of the Great Powers during this period, if not of the interested parties.

Is the guerrilla fighter a vestige of the past who will disappear with the disappearance of underdevelopment itself? To be sure, when one observes the relations between Israel and the Arab states, the punitive expeditions undertaken by units of the regular Israeli Army – between 1949 and 1967 – in response to operations by the fedayeen, one is tempted to draw a sort of correlation between the level of development and the nature of weapons, between the type of society and the mode of combat. This correlation is indeed linked to particular circumstances, without being entirely accidental. As soon as guerrillas have won the war, driven out the colonialists, and founded a state, the state seeks to create a regular army equipped with heavy weapons, tanks, pursuit planes, and bombers. Each new state does so because other states that have preceded it in the career of independence have done so before it. Concern for prestige? Not entirely. A regular army protects the new state against other guerrillas who might be recruited among the veterans or among those who expected that the end of domination would usher in a new era, a sort of golden age. It is also useful in the border disputes that threaten to break out after the end of colonialism and hence of anti-colonialist solidarity. Finally, it must not be forgotten that even in industrialized countries, during times of oppression, there have been snipers and guerrillas.

In truth, the guerrilla belongs to our age as he belongs to most ages of human history; but he assumes a novel form in the industrial age. He incarnates the antitechnical to the extent to which he defies the instruments of massive destruction developed by science, but he utilizes weapons and means of communication that have also been forged by the modern age, and he has likewise developed rational methods of action. If technology refers not only to the material objects made by machines but also to a form of thought – a sort of pragmatism pushed to its extreme – guerrilla warfare, as taught by the Chinese after long experience, is henceforth conducted according to technological principles. These entail a technique of organization, a technique for the psychological manipulation of the masses, appealing to terror and to hope. To be sure, the guerrilla, more often than the soldier in uniform, is left to his own devices; he must therefore be capable of initiative, and he must retain in solitude the sense of his own responsibility, as well as the consciousness of a solidarity with his dispersed comrades. But, the more guerrilla warfare becomes organized, the more the guerrilla resembles the soldier. The discipline he is subject to will never have the same physical immediacy as in regular armies, but its distant and diffused character is compensated for by its merciless sanctions. Leaders are nowhere and everywhere. There is, so to speak, no longer any question of the *degree* of crime or punishment. The difference between guerrillas and soldiers remains; the tendency toward their rapprochement grows out of a like desire for effective techniques.

As an isolated volunteer, the guerrilla seems superior to the soldier in human qualities. Although heroic, he is not necessarily holy: all depends on the cause for which he sacrifices his peaceful existence or his life. Since 1940, the guerrilla has symbolized the struggle against the Nazis, then against the 'colonialists'. He has profited from the sympathy of progressivist opinion despite the often inevitable cruelty of his means. He has been David against Goliath, the Pekinese or Kabyle peasant, barehanded against planes or tanks, the soldier in the shadows destined more for martyrdom than for glory. Should this same guerrilla serve a doubtful cause, or the population for the most part be against his cause, or should his victory bring to power a detested regime, he would become again, in the eyes of all defenders of the established order, whether Occidentals or Afro-Asians, what he has been in other times – the outlaw, closer to the bandit than to the soldier, the man who kills unexpectedly and often randomly, the man who introduces a reign of suspicion and terror, who confuses the essential distinction between peace and war, between law and violence. When faced with mechanical monsters, he incarnates the grandeur of the resistant, rebel, or heretic. When faced with the norms of civilized existence, he incarnates the aggression – animal or human, primitive or permanent – that society must control in order to survive.

The triad of the submachine gun, the tank, and the ballistic missile with a thermonuclear warhead, of the guerrilla, the soldier, and the crew of the ballistic missiles buried in silos, will have tomorrow, as today, a historic significance. The complex dialectic linking each of these three types of weapons to the other two will continue symbolically, at least until mankind substitutes the rule of law for that of violence. Each of these three weapons, each of the three methods of combat will preserve its meaning. Nuclear weapons exclude a repetition of the total wars that have occupied the first half of the twentieth century. Regular armies remain the guarantee of internal peace in all states that cannot do without an eventual recourse to force. At the same time, they provide strategists with a means of avoiding the alternative of all-or-nothing, of passivity or the apocalypse. States aspiring to play leading roles on the world scene can no more do without nuclear weapons than without conventional weapons. Guerrilla rebellion, the supreme and often the desperate response to injustice, poses an ironic challenge to the omnipotence of machines.

Does the dialectic of the three weapons serve to constitute an international order? During the postwar period it has been the principle of what has come to be called variously the Cold War or bellicose peace, precarious order or endemic disorder. Contemporaries have denounced this constant ambiguity; there is no outbreak of major war, but true peace is neither imposed by a victor nor arrived at together by rivals. In retrospect, the historian tends to place a more balanced judgement on the first two decades of the atomic age, and indeed he may even indulge in the secret hope that this ambiguous conjecture, this limitation of violence, should continue.

## Nuclear Diplomacy

For twenty years, from 1945 to 1965, only two states were worthy of the title of nuclear powers. Great Britain, while possessing nuclear weapons, has not conducted an independent diplomacy. France and Communist China have exploded atomic bombs, but do not possess the combination of bombs, missiles to carry them, and a network of alert and communication without which the weapons cannot really be effective military or diplomatic arms. At the time of the Korean War, the United States had only a limited stock of nuclear weapons, including neither thermonuclear bombs nor tactical nuclear weapons. From 1953 on, as Stalin's successors perfected and completed their new armaments, they spoke more and more willingly of peaceful coexistence. They were tempted, between 1958 and 1962, to obtain a modification of the status quo in Berlin through threat of force, under the protection of intercontinental missiles. They never risked carrying out their threat. When they were forced by a U.S. ultimatum to withdraw their ballistic missiles from Cuba, they immediately gave up their Berlin operation. The two major powers – thermonuclear duopolists – became aware of their common interest not to become involved in a war of annihilation; in other words, they understood that none of the stakes of their conflict was worth the cost of a war in which nuclear weapons would be used. Let us consider the terminology borrowed by rational strategists from economics: they compare cost and profit – that is, the losses in lives and goods that a war would entail on the one hand, and the possible fruits of victory on the other (the latter being appraised on the basis of a coefficient calculated in terms of the uncertainty of the outcome). The higher the losses, the fewer the advantages of victory, even if the risk of defeat is slight, and the more the rational strategist is inclined to prefer the drawbacks of peace to the risks of war.

On the whole, the optimistic argument based on 'peace through fear' remains valid, no matter how many nuclear powers there are. States producing these weapons will discover at the same time both their power and their impotence, the capacity they have acquired to destroy and the vulnerability of their own population and cities. There is nothing to prevent us from conjecturing about the spread of wisdom that might accompany the proliferation of nuclear weapons.

It would none the less be imprudent to overlook the circumstances that have favoured the logical use that the two major powers have made of their nuclear weapons. In the first place and above all, both the United States and the Soviet Union were victors in the war, satisfied with the result, having neither a defeat to avenge nor territory to conquer. The Soviet Union, seizing the opportunity to exploit its victory, had subjected 100 million Europeans to its Marxist-Leninist regime. The United States, despite the call for a rollback, resigned itself to this *fait accompli* and confined itself to preventing any further advance of the Soviet forces in Europe. The success of containment was acceptable to both of the major powers, since each could interpret it as a success: the Americans because they had achieved their stated goal, and the Russians because they had never wanted to do more than consolidate their hegemony over Eastern Europe, including East Germany.

To be sure, despite the fact that the stakes of their rivalry were not *national* in the narrow sense of the term (neither begrudged the existence and the territory of the other), the two major powers still remained enemies in that each claimed their ideologies to be universally valid. In certain cases, the most inexpiable struggles are those involving the confrontation not of national interests (a province, a border line) but rather this non-material good – the glory of pre-eminence, the power, at last uncontested, of no longer having a rival at one's side. No one can say whether, in the absence of nuclear weapons, the victors of the Second World War would have resolved their conflict by force. There is little doubt that possession of these weapons contributed to a preference for peaceful solutions.

In many respects, duopoly is a less unpredictable situation than one involving numerous participants. The situation was all the more stable as long as each of the duopolists exercised virtually uncontested power within its own camp. The United States and the Soviet Union avoided direct confrontation as much as possible. West Germany, the state least satisfied by the status quo, has not had an autonomous diplomacy *vis-à-vis* Pankow or Moscow. In Asia, until the schism between the Soviet Union and Communist China, the leaders of the Kremlin, sole possessors of a nuclear force capable of counterbalancing America's, retained, in case of crisis, the means of influencing the decisions of the North Koreans and the Chinese. Thus the two major powers imperceptibly acquired the habit of pursuing their politico-ideological rivalry while keeping the risks of an 'unthinkable war' at a minimum.

Technico-strategic precautions reinforced political prudence. Analysts in institutes and universities envisioned the possibility of a war involving the use of nuclear weapons which neither side desired. U.S. statesmen, especially, did their utmost to take precautions in order to attenuate such a danger. Security mechanisms were developed to prevent the accidental explosion of a bomb and to prevent an officer, no matter what his grade, from making the decision to utilize nuclear weapons without having received an order from the President of the United States (the latter alone has the legal authority to make such a decision and, thanks to electronics, these weapons are for the most part physically impossible to use without that decision), and finally to prevent extreme escalation if, by some misfortune, in spite of every effort, an atomic bomb should be set off.

These sophisticated technico-political precautions are the expression of a strategic concept that is not so much new as renovated. The two major wars of the twentieth century had been, from a certain point of view, total wars: the First World War, having broken out over an obscure conflict in the Balkans and spread through the alliance system, had, to the surprise of most of the generals and statesmen, lasted over four years, thanks to the improvised mobilization of all able-bodied men in combat units and factories. The close relationship between the military and industrial spheres foreseen by certain sociologists at the beginning of the nineteenth century was readily apparent. The diplomatic system of Old Europe, the centre of the world system, crumbled under the weight of the war and the revolutions it brought with it. The Second World War was still more total since the Japanese attempt at empire building had accompanied that of the Third Reich, and the very existence of the sovereignty of the defeated states had been suspended for a period that the victors themselves reserved the right to determine.

Public opinion and the private views of statesmen were haunted by the spectre of these total wars, and tended to be limited to an absolute alternative of peace or war. Since 1945, because of thermonuclear bombs, the efforts of strategic thinking, the cunning of reason, those responsible for world politics have finally understood the lesson of Clausewitz: absolute war – one resulting from unlimited escalation – is not a model, but a menace, a menace that can be warded off as long as the means of force remain in the service of policy, the 'intelligence of the state'. It falls to this intelligence to weigh the risks that must be run, and the sacrifices that it is legitimate to accept to attain a goal.

On the one hand, the blurring of the distinction between war and peace has brought about the bellicose peace: the permanent mobilization of the nuclear apparatus, the limited use of military force here and there throughout the world, the qualitative race for armaments, with each of the major powers devoting billions and billions of dollars to the development of bombs, missiles, planes, and ever more sophisticated conventional weapons. It has also made total war less probable – that monstrous and absurd war in which thermonuclear powers heap upon one another, as in an orgy, all the means of destruction at their disposal. The strategy of the flexible response has become a fact at times of crisis – the strategy of all nuclear powers, despite the fact that in periods of calm certain states will proclaim the doctrine of massive retaliation – futile talk so long as the hour of reckoning does not sound.

For twenty years, nuclear weapons have constantly been placed at the service of a defensive strategy; in their military concept they are not a primary but a final recourse. The very term *deterrent* suggests this defensive use. To deter someone is to prevent him from taking certain action under threat of sanctions. Why would the sanction be necessarily or immediately unlimited? For ten to fifteen years, the obsession over the preceding wars, the confusion over nuclear weapons, and the strategy of deterrence was such that the weapons themselves were called a deterrent, as if any weapon were not, in certain cases, a deterrent in the hands of a determined man. Neither of the two nuclear powers has ever tried, until now, to obtain a modification of the status quo at the expense of the other or the surrender of a non-nuclear power by the threat of using these weapons. In Cuba, the United States restored the *status quo ante;* in Berlin, the Soviets finally accommodated themselves to the military presence of the West in West Berlin.

Circumstances have likewise favoured limitations on the use of conventional weapons. The nuclear powers alone possessed large stocks of these, and after the Korean campaign they feared to use them wherever there was a possibility of escalation. Elsewhere, the states involved in conflicts possessed relatively few weapons. The United Nations served as an intermediary between the two major powers and the states directly involved, standing behind the peace efforts made by one or another of the major powers, or even by the member-states as a whole.

Finally, the submachine gun has been widely used to prosecute wars of liberation, and these have, for the most part, ended in the victory of the guerrillas. There have been exceptions, however – in the Philippines and in Malaysia. But these wars have tended to result in the independence of countries formerly subject to colonial domination. Now U.S. and Soviet opinion were in agreement with Afro-Asian countries in condemning *en bloc*, on principle, the governing of coloured peoples by white men (even though the same condemnation did not extend to the governing of Asian peoples by the Russians). The Europeans never went the whole way in using their military force in these colonial struggles. The French, who fought from 1946 to 1954 in Indo-China, from 1954 to 1962 in Algeria, never attacked the logistical bases of the guerrillas in China, in Tunisia, or in Morocco. In one case, they did not have the indispensable military resources; in the other, they were paralysed by a guilty conscience, by the opposition of their allies and that of a segment of French opinion. Nonetheless, in 1962, thanks to the fortified lines along the borders, the isolation of Algeria had succeeded in choking out the guerrillas. The French government consented to Algerian independence not because the guerrillas had won on the battlefield but because, politically, no other solution was feasible in the long run.

From the moment that wars of liberation take on as their objective not the winning of independence from a colonial state but the installing of a regime identified by U.S. public opinion with Communism, the guerrilla ceases, in the estimation of that opinion, to be a freedom fighter and becomes instead the perhaps sincere but blind militant of a despotic party, and the rules by which wars are fought are, and will be, changed. North Vietnam experienced the horrors of large-scale bombing because it supported the action of the Vietcong in the South.

The dialectic of the three weapons has, for twenty years, maintained peace among nuclear powers, favoured decolonization with minimum diplomatic upheaval, and restrained the use of conventional weapons. Will this dialectic play the same role in the decades ahead?

### Dialectic of Weapons

As far as thermonuclear weapons are concerned, there are three sets of conditions necessary to the prolongation of 'peace through fear': *technical* – the maintenance of the balance of terror; *strategic* – the acceptance by all heads of state of the doctrine of so-called graduated response, progressive retaliation; and *political* – the nature of the conflict and the stakes.

The concept of flexible response by a cool head during a period of crisis requires that nuclear weapons be sufficiently dispersed or protected so that a first strike cannot eliminate the capacity for retaliation by any one of the states involved. This kind of stability depends therefore on the qualitative armaments race so far as the major powers are concerned, and on the acquisition of a nuclear apparatus (weapons and delivery vehicles) by new members of the atomic club.

The two major powers of the two decades after 1945 are both opposed to the proliferation of atomic weapons – the United States, with an ostentatious passion, the Soviet Union more discreetly. According to the law of probabilities, does not the danger of an explosion increase along with the number of bombs – or even more, with the number of states possessing them? This is irrefutable reasoning on an abstract plane, but far from reality: it assumes that the problem is resolved – in other words, that other states have decided to leave to two, three, or four among them the exclusive possession of weapons that are considered decisive in any modern conflict.

In theory, according to strict Machiavellian logic, the United States and the Soviet Union could have or even should have opposed at all costs the development of Chinese nuclear capability. However, the informal Russo-American alliance against atomic proliferation does not suffice to eliminate politico-ideological enmity. Furthermore, just as the nuclear powers have never used their supreme weapons offensively to compel the surrender of a state without such arms by imposing a choice between submission and annihilation, so too they have never attempted by such a threat to prevent the development of a new atomic force. All indications are that they will continue to respect the sovereignty of states – whether out of weakness or because of their mutual political antagonism – and resign themselves to an evolution contrary to their common interest.

Proliferation probably will not stop with the fifth nuclear power (China), but this does not mean that it will be unlimited, at least in the foreseeable future. Switzerland and Sweden would use such weapons to protect their neutrality – in other words, they will not be playing for the highest stakes. India will one day follow the lead of China, Israel that of France or Switzerland. This proliferation will not be without risks: one would have to be blind or to believe in the rationality of all statesmen to deny this. But the error of too many specialists is to confuse these numerous and diverse threats with the probability of the unthinkable war. The danger is probably smaller for the superpowers of today than for less important countries, who will have joined the atomic club without sufficient resources.

Under what conditions is peace through fear most stable? Where the forces of reprisal are least vulnerable, the states have both the will and the means to apply the doctrine of graduated response, and the disproportion between the cost and the stakes, between the risk of war and the violence of enmity, is enormous. All the conditions that further peace through fear are met in the case of the relations between the United States and the Soviet Union. Short of an improbable technical breakthrough, they will persist during the decades ahead. They will not be met to the same extent elsewhere, in Asia or the Near East. But the United States and the Soviet Union will not allow themselves to be dragged unwillingly into a war of annihilation. The dissemination of nuclear weapons increases, to a degree that cannot be precisely assessed, the danger that, one day or another, nuclear weapons will be used militarily on some battlefield or other. At least for the next twenty or thirty years proliferation should not threaten the military foundation of the present order – the existence of arms so terrifying that even those who possess them keep them on reserve to be used only as an ultimate course. The greatest threat to mankind, then, is not that a few more states should come to possess nuclear weapons but that statesmen should begin to make a different use of their weapons in the diplomatic game.

The foundation of the present order of power, this anarchical order that tends towards the limitation of violence, is in the final analysis *psychological*. One reads in a report made to UNESCO that war begins in the minds of men. Such a simplistic theory is more false than true; in our times, one is tempted to state that the citizens of one state detest those of another because they have fought or are fighting them, rather than vice versa. In any event, if diplomatic conditions require a reversal of alliances, a well-designed propaganda campaign is sufficient to overcome collective passions or to direct them toward another goal. On the other hand, when some states possess means of destruction against which all the others cannot protect themselves, and to which they cannot respond, the essential focus lies predominantly in the minds of men, especially in those few who are responsible for the diplomacy or strategy of the nuclear powers.

The strictly defensive or deterrent use of atomic weapons is dictated by a certain logic. It has been rightly said that the very limitless nature of these weapons renders their effective utilization difficult. It has been rightly said that there is no common ground between the capacity to destroy and the ability to convince, between *strength* as it is measured according to strictly military potential and the *power* of a state to obtain the submission or consent of other states. It has been rightly said that never before have states so superior in strength as the United States and the Soviet Union been defied with impunity by dwarf states like Albania and Cuba. It has been rightly said that from now until the end of this century no state will even come close to attaining the economic and military potential of either of the superpowers. China and India, both larger in population, have not even gone beyond the first phase of industrialization. All the other states either have a much smaller population (and among industrialized countries, the Soviet Union and the United States have a relatively high demographic rate of growth) or a much lower per capita income. An American writer caused a scandal in 1964 by declaring that by the end of the century the two superpowers of today would outstrip their potential rivals even more decisively. The statement none the less was incontestable, provided two conditions prevail: that the Soviet Union and the United States maintain the same internal coherence and political will within their borders, and that potential resources be identified with military strength and diplomatic power.

In reality, what ought to have caused an outcry was not the very plausible prediction of a continued or enlarged gap between the resources at the disposal of the two major powers and those of other states, but rather the transition from resources to power and strength. At the beginning of the 1960s, observers were struck by the disintegration of the blocs, by the impunity of the smaller states, by the apparent uselessness of nuclear weapons in daily relations or even in struggles for national liberation. It is to be hoped that this disproportion between the power of destruction and the power of persuasion might be prolonged and increased, but it is not determined solely by the nature of weapons or by the dialectic of the three weapons. For the time being, happily, statesmen are paralysed by the 'atomic taboo'. The atomic weapon, like the gold reserves used to back currency, is buried in the ground and accumulated in stockpiles, although always ready to be used. To paraphrase Clausewitz, one might say that nuclear weapons allow firm commitments to be honoured and credit operations to be paid in cash. But nuclear weapons are not employed physically, any more than gold is removed from the storage vaults. The crisis – with its exchanges of threats and messages, its dialogue of affirmations of will – is the equivalent of what Clausewitz called commitment.

The true question concerning the future thus involves the continuation of this fragile order, founded at once on a strategic doctrine gradually and spontaneously elaborated by the protagonists of history, and on prohibitions arising out of the depths of the human conscience – or perhaps, one might say, out of the collective unconsciousness. Will the superpowers respect the imperative of the solely deterrent use of nuclear weapons? Will not the inclusion of new members in the atomic club push them to re-establish, through defence against ballistic missiles or civil defence, the margin of superiority that the progress of the Chinese and the Europeans threatens to reduce? Will the smaller nuclear powers be capable of the same moderation if their so-called retaliatory force is vulnerable? Will not the states that have reduced their conventional weapons to a minimum in order to acquire a nuclear force be driven some day to the choice between passivity (that is, defeat) or a violation of the atomic taboo?

Finally, and above all, a question that one hesitates even to pose can hardly fail to haunt the minds of those who are concerned about the future. As long as war is and remains an act of violence in which one collective person attempts to compel another collective person, the offensive use of the nuclear threat is morally and even materially difficult: if the person one is bent on bringing to surrender remains indifferent to the warning shots, if 'Ruritania' allows first one, and then two of its cities to be destroyed rather than surrender, what choice do the superpowers have in ending destruction that becomes more futile than monstrous? It may be recognized once again that man is capable of preferring his reasons for living over his very life! The order of power in the atomic age is thus founded on the *atomic taboo*, the rational strategy of the major powers, and the courage of historic man. But what might happen the day when the states involved are no longer comparable to 'collective persons', each seeking to obtain the submission of the other, but to a Hitler bent on exterminating an entire race deemed to be a noxious animal species?

Heaven forbid that there should ever be a statesman who would view nuclear weapons not only as deterrent weapons – that is, instruments to be used in human dialogue – but also as arms of extermination.

## The Order of Power

An anarchical order is normally inegalitarian to the extent to which, in the absence of a common law or an impartial police, the powerful prevail over the weak. Thus, Plato's Callicles deemed natural (in conformity with nature) the domination of the most powerful. According to Spinoza and Hobbes, in the absence of civil society power determines rights. Philosophers did not ignore the fact that at least a principle of equality exists between individuals. The weak man is still able, in certain circumstances, to kill the strong man. Man does not act as man when he kills his fellow as the hunter kills his prey: the essential quality of victory is lost when the defeated is no longer present to recognize his defeat.

The anarchical order of the international system has always been inegalitarian. In the most complex system, that of the Greek city-states or of the European states prior to 1914, the great powers constituted a closed club with membership reserved to sovereigns possessing a minimum of military strength. The question attributed to Stalin during the last war – 'How many divisions does the Pope have?' – roughly interprets a traditional doctrine. A great power would feel it had been offended if it were not consulted when an important affair was discussed. Eventually, the great powers settled affairs involving lesser powers among themselves; sometimes they imposed a status (neutrality) or borders upon smaller states solely to avoid or to settle their own conflicts.

Nuclear weapons have not decisively modified this customary order of power. The present order is both more and less inegalitarian than international orders of the past. It is less so for two reasons. The first is the egalitarian ideal of modern civilization. The likening of 'political units' to 'collective persons' is suggested by the language we use, by the reigning ideology, by our anticolonialist passion. No distinction is made between the liberation of peoples and the liberation of individuals (or rather, the former is placed before the latter). The separation of ethnic groups, as we have seen, is a means of eliminating inequalities among individuals belonging to one or another of them. The old principle of European *ius gentium* (international law), implying a certain equality between states – an equality arising out of the recognized sovereignty of all states – is reinforced and enlarged by the egalitarian design of our period. The international law of the last century did not exclude the protectorate, foreign concessions (so-called unequal treaties), or the managing of certain public services in an independent state by bureaucrats from other countries representing the so-called community of civilized nations. Again, following the First World War, the mandate principle implied a hierarchy among states, in that the mandatory states were by this very fact recognized as worthy of administering 'dependent peoples', of working for their welfare and development. The liquidation in two decades of almost all colonial administrations consecrated the triumph of the egalitarian idea on the world level, but at the same time it increased the real inequalities between states that were juridically equal, at least in their sovereignty, and it enlarged the divergence between the legal theory espoused by the United Nations and the realities of international politics.

The elimination of protectorates, mandates, or colonies, the equal voting right of 'Ruritania' and the the United States in the United Nations General Assembly, consecrates the triumph of the egalitarian ideal in our century. But this has not been the sole agent of our historic revolution. The unarmed member of the Resistance, or the man armed with a submachine gun, Gandhi or Giap, forced the Europeans to recall the ideal they had proclaimed in Europe; and nuclear weapons at first promoted the revolt of the coloured peoples because the two states that possessed them had no colonies in the ordinary meaning of the term (although the Soviet Union maintains a multinational empire carved out by great sweeps of the sword, while Latin Americans denounce U.S. hegemony, if not Yankee imperialism).

This double equalization – in refusing a hierarchy between ethnic groups or states and in the dialectic of the submachine gun and advanced weapons – is likewise a function of the heterogeneity of the international system, whose members are held to be equal, while from all points of view (extent of territory volume of population, per capita income, degree of development) they have never been so unequal in any of the systems of the past. We observe the denouement of this paradox every day: a combination of formal democracy and real oligarchy, to borrow our nouns from the Greeks and our adjectives from Marx. The two major powers, and especially the United States, possess all means of force – both conventional and nuclear weapons – and they can mobilize immense resources to back their foreign policy.

Anarchy continues to exist because there are two of them, and they cannot even agree to prevent the proliferation of nuclear weapons which is clearly in their common interest. The authority exercised by each of the major powers on its bloc is directly related to the fear aroused by the other. Peaceful coexistence therefore actually produces a loosening of the blocs. Elsewhere, in the Third World, the will of the major powers encounters the revolt of the masses and the submachine gun of the guerrilla.

The power of the two oligarchs is neither assured nor unlimited. Between now and the end of the century, two evolutions – the one probable, the other as certain as a historic evolution can be – will tend to curtail that power. Nuclear weapons have not been used militarily, but without them the Chinese Nationalists would not retain Quemoy and Matsu, and American bombers would not attack North Vietnam. The United States owes its freedom of action in Asia and even in Africa to its nuclear supremacy. It is probable that the military gap between first-rate and second-rate nuclear powers will decrease within the next decade and, by virtue of this, the planetary system will be less unified than it is today. Even though they may not be capable of striking American territory, the Chinese nuclear force will exercise a certain deterrence on American diplomacy. The superpowers will have to resign themselves to giving up their presence in the four corners of the globe.

One aspect of the deterrence which is not in doubt is the rise of China; this will almost certainly bring about the dissociation of the Soviet camp and the 'nationalization' of the Marxist-Leninist party religions. It is permissible to speculate on the consequences of this prime factor, on the realignments that it will give rise to, on the relative weight of East and West, of Asia, America, and Europe in the world of the year 2000. But such is not within the scope of this chapter.

Our objective was more modest. The order of power – that is, the interstate order – has always been anarchical and oligarchical: anarchical because of the absence of a monopoly of legitimate violence, oligarchical (or hierarchic) in that, without a civil society, rights depend largely on might. We asked ourselves how this traditional order has been adapted to technological civilization. Our conclusion is that this order has been transformed, but not overturned. Pessimists prophesy the collective suicide of mankind failing a kind of historic mutation such as would be denoted by the renunciation of military sovereignty by states. Optimists believe in peace through fear, in the end of the domination of peoples by peoples, since domination does not pay.

We have no grounds to decide in favour of one or the other. Mankind has always lived dangerously. The dangers are no longer the same, but they have not disappeared. One mankind, united under a single rational administration in order to exploit natural resources, would constitute one possible end of the human adventure. The adventure is still far from this final state, conforming not to *the* logic of history but to *a* partial logic that fascinates because it at once attracts and repels. Would man achieve fulfilment or perdition were he to arrive at the promised land of the world-state of technology?

# 8 The Inegalitarian Order of Progress

The conclusion of the preceding chapter may be summed up in this way: the means of transportation and communication bring the various segments of mankind closer together, whereas the means of destruction pull them apart. Since a thermonuclear bomb of a few megatons can pulverize a city, security – assuming that the word still has any meaning – depends primarily on having these frightful weapons, not in order to use them but to avoid becoming their victims. This irrefutable argument first put forward in the United States and the Soviet Union will convince the heads of other states, apparently, just as it did the leaders of Great Britain, France, and Communist China.

In reality, as we have shown, such reasoning is not irrefutable. As long as nations can acquire only a vulnerable nuclear force by reducing their conventional arms to a minimum they will run the risk of increasing rather than decreasing the dangers to which they are exposed, unless they have the indirect protection of their allies' conventional or nuclear weapons. The atomic taboo, the common concern of the two superpowers to confine themselves to a politically defensible use of their nuclear arms, provides the other states with temporary protection against the risk of blackmail ('capitulate or your cities will be destroyed'). Under present conditions, the other nations want to join the atomic club primarily to avoid dependence on the great powers. This statement is certainly true of France and Great Britain, although it is probably less so of Communist China. China might possibly have been satisfied with the protection afforded by her alliance with the Soviet Union, but this alliance, although it protected her from a nuclear attack by the United States, also robbed her of all freedom of action. The men of the Kremlin fearful that they might be drawn by Chinese imprudence into a serious clash with 'the atomic-toothed paper tiger', fully intended to maintain strategic control over the entire Soviet bloc. They let Mao Tse-tung know this in 1958 when he was threatening military action against Quemoy and Matsu.

It would be incorrect to conclude that the spread of atomic weapons is due exclusively to irrational and anachronistic desires for independence, or that it can and must be stopped. These desires are *perhaps* irrational and anachronistic (although rationality in such matters is not easy to define), but they *certainly* represent an obstacle to the establishment of world unity. Nuclear weapons in themselves do not further such unity. How is it possible not to be apprehensive and therefore distrustful of any nation that can without warning reduce any large urban centre anywhere on earth to radioactive rubble and ashes? To what international organization can one entrust these accursed arms? The possibility cannot be ruled out that the least objectionable solution is a balance of terror between two or, if need be, several powers that deal cautiously with one another and try to prevent the extension of local conflicts. It matters little in this connection whether these weapons – the natural consequences of a technological civilization – in themselves further or hinder the establishment of an order different in kind from the immemorial balance of power. In the twentieth century it is not the fact of nuclear weapons but the existence of many sovereign states that blocks the establishment of a world state. These atomic missiles came into being in a world already divided into states that have insisted and continue to insist on their sovereignty. They were immediately put to political uses which were neither more nor less self-seeking than those of the past. Atomic arms have neither created the anarchic order of power nor replaced this secular order by a new one.

## The Order of Growth

What influence do the means of production – which are simply another expression of our technological civilization – exert on the planetary unification of human society? For the short run, at the beginning of the last third of the twentieth century, the answer is obvious. Inequalities in progress have never been as great as they are in our time. To put it more precisely, the very concept of inequality of progress is quite recent and has no meaning outside the context of industrial civilization. It would be absurd to claim that there was no technological progress during the five or six thousand years that elapsed between the era of the great empires of the Near East and the beginning of this century. Whether we are concerned with tools or weapons, with the organization of workers or soldiers, all the evidence indicates that the roots of our modern society can be traced across the centuries; despite regressions, there has been some general historical forward motion that may be called progress. But never before has this technico-organizational progress been important enough to give primacy to the drive towards productivity, and thereby to strip conquest of its value.

To be sure, wars have often been disastrous to nations, even to the victors. But it is not true that *any of the evils that war sought to prevent were as great an evil as war itself.*[1] The costs of war were not always greater than the gains; political domination made possible by conquest was frequently profitable. The exploitation of slaves enriched their masters, whether Roman, Spanish, or English. Sometimes an empire contributed to the welfare of defeated peoples by the mere fact that it put an end to ceaseless strife and guaranteed security of trade in an enlarged market.

Today's banal theory of progress is a far cry from *The Spirit of Laws* or even from *The Wealth of Nations*. This theory, which has become an integral part of the awareness men have of themselves and of their collective destiny, calls for a fresh interpretation of societies and their history. It leaves no room for a permanent order, imposed by morality or sanctified by tradition. Nowadays, the order of change is the only acknowledged order and it is defined from the very outset by the term *growth*. In industrial societies, the individual, unlike his ancestors, no longer accepts the ups and downs of personal fortune or the continuance of an acquired status, but rather expects and demands a continuous

1. This view by the French writer Alain dates from the end of the first twentieth-century war. It is still untrue, even in our atomic age.

improvement of his lot. It is now presumed that production and income will increase from year to year, and each generation will have at its disposal a greater amount of goods than did the preceding one. The practice of forecasting economic conditions contributes to the spread of this obsessive vision of the future; men living in developed societies cling to this image of promised abundance and, because they are imbued with the technico-economic originality of our age, tend to break with the past or, at any rate, to believe they are breaking with it.

The spread of this philosophy of history is recent. It dates from the last twenty years and has become, since the Second World War, a way of thinking common to intellectuals, semi-intellectuals, and statesmen of the Western world. It combines into a more or less coherent whole a multiplicity of elements. The primary objective, over and above all else, is to produce more and to produce it better. Rates of growth are virtually 'sanctified', they are cited as if they were an exact measure of the merit of a government or regime; the causes of growth and consequently the factors involved in productivity are sought out. This leads inevitably to science: to physics, which makes machines possible; to chemistry, which creates materials not found in nature; to medicine and hygiene which make it possible to prolong the average life span; and to the electronic technology which replaces the brain as well as the hands of the worker. Primacy of the future over the past, of growth over stability, the worship of science which is responsible for the welfare of mankind and the strength of our collectivities – all these to a greater or lesser degree permeate the awareness that modern societies have of themselves; in this sense, they all possess a single and identical purpose.

The first sociologists, Auguste Comte and Karl Marx, had correctly foreseen that modern society (dubbed 'industrial' by one, 'capitalist' by the other) tended toward universality. Comte spoke of mankind's *avant-garde*, whose temporary superiority, he urged, should not be used to establish empires that would be anachronistic even before they were created. Marx extolled the historic role of the bourgeoisie which, within a century, did more to revolutionize production and living conditions than all the ruling classes of the past had been able to do in the space of several thousand years. Both men were right, but neither had foreseen that progress, that is the transformation of society in accordance with the requirements of planned, efficient, and income-producing work was *bound to reduce the inequalities within economic units and increase these same inequalities between economic units.* (Save for a few exceptions, economic units are also political units, that is, populations established in an area of sovereignty.) The major problem during the first half of the nineteenth century was that of the proletariat who witnessed the existence of scandalous poverty in the very shadow of factories from which wealth flowed. The major problem during the second half of the twentieth century seems to be that of the inequality of progress – the scandalous poverty of entire peoples, while in the industrial nations all classes of society profit from the collective progress, although not all to the same degree.

In retrospect it seems it should have been very easy to predict this development. All one had to do was to accept the most elementary proposition of economic theory: there must be a certain proportionality between the output of labour and the purchasing power of wages[2] so that in a rationalized society all increase in the standard of living of almost everyone becomes in the long run virtually inevitable.[3] Inequality of progress becomes self-explanatory when one notes that different societies – if one assumes that all are pursuing the same course – have nowhere reached an identical level. How could these various societies have progressed at the same pace when some were creating the institutions of industrial civilization while others endured the same institutions in humiliation, subject to the will of their conquerors; when some traditional cultures were alien and others more or less favourable to the spirit of experimental science and a rational economy?

Traditional cultures were *different*, they were not *unequal*. Each could believe in its superiority and each was right in believing in its unique character. Nations were free to treat each other with

2. I am omitting the subtleties – which are really not so very subtle – of average or marginal output.
3. Only a very rapid increase in the supply of labour would make this statement untrue.

contempt or to disregard one another entirely. Weapons alone established a hierarchy between collectivities, and gospels of salvation alone sanctioned or upset the hierarchies within these collectivities. It requires the conjunction, at once logical and contradictory, of pride in technology and the egalitarian ideal for the universalist design of industrial civilization to divide the very humanity it tends to unite.

Industrial civilization has the capacity to unite humanity since all societies, whether voluntary or not, now proclaim through the voices of their governments that progress is their objective. But this civilization cannot fail to be divisive since the distance of various societies from the common goal is *measurable*. Inequality among nations, expressed in quantitative terms (even if it cannot reflect reality accurately), is not open to question; rather, it assumes the rigidity of a scientific fact. Contrary to the ideal proclaimed by modern civilization, these disparities appear for the first time to be demonstrated in numerical terms. When all segments of humanity have, or claim to have, the same goal – that of producing more and better for the sake of well-being and power – they become rivals in a contest, subject to the impartial arbitration of statistics or statisticians.

Arbitration is not as incontestable as statesmen or statisticians would have us believe. Estimates of the rate of growth entail approximations and uncertainties of which the public is unaware. Unwarranted extrapolation of rates of growth observed over a period of several years enables the more backward nations to announce that ten, twenty, or thirty years from now they will be counted among the front-runners in the international sweepstakes. Some are more developed to begin with, others are developing more rapidly. Even if we limit ourselves to the figures (which can be manipulated), there are ways of making inequality appear acceptable by picturing a future that could redress the balance.

For the time being, inequality of progress, which, as we have shown in Chapter 3, threatens to paralyse the integration or even the federation of divergent ethnic groups, definitely precludes the unification of mankind on a planetary scale. The economic growth of underdeveloped peoples is not incompatible with the interests of developed peoples. Just as growth within each state, that is to say, an increase in the quantity of goods, brings with it the simultaneous improvement of everyone's lot, so, as long as land and raw materials are not in short supply (and we have not yet reached that point), the welfare of white Europeans and Americans does not depend on the poverty of the coloured peoples of Africa and Asia. The wealth which humanity possesses is not – as it was when productivity remained virtually stagnant – a fixed quantity of which the few can receive a greater proportion only if the amount received by others is decreased. The wealth of humanity as a whole can increase from year to year, and thus the inherent conflicts of scarcity can be reduced.

It does not follow, however, that inequality of development does not create genuine conflicts of interest. It is this inequality that still constitutes a barrier to the political unity which is the traditional dream of pacifists. The integration of ethnic groups with sharply varying birth-rates and degrees of development encounters the contradiction between the impossibility of subjecting these groups to the same laws (social laws, for example) and the virtual impossibility (moral rather than material) of violating the individualist principle of non-discrimination. *A fortiori*, the wealthy nation would refuse to accept majority rule, and the poor majority would refuse to submit to any other principle of government.

To be sure, a world state could allow considerable autonomy to regional or continental administrations; but even negotiations for the regulation of international trade illustrate, by the way they usually merely mark time, the clash between the demands of countries still in the first phase of industrialization and the interests of the more advanced countries. Whether it is a question of aid, the price of raw materials, or the lowering of tariffs by the developed countries to encourage industrial production in the underdeveloped areas, the resistance of national self-interest is difficult to overcome. And such self-interest is due less to the blindness of statesmen than to the peoples themselves and to the regime. Statesmen would be more willing to grant certain concessions if they were not leery of public opinion. Analysis of the influence exerted on world order by the means of destruction brought us to nationalism as it is manifested in the *desire for independence.* Analysis of the means of production brings us back, by way of inequality in progress, to nationalism as it is displayed in *the awareness of each historical community of its uniqueness and its will to live.*

We know that industrial progress breaks down the isolation of local communities and brings men into the cities. It imposes on each individual the obligation to learn to read and write and brings him into contact with the administration of the state. The official language, which may not correspond to his native dialect, becomes all the more important since private individuals expect and demand more from public services. Perhaps in a modern society there are not many *citizens* in Rousseau's sense of the word, that is, men who are concerned about the public good as such and willing to sacrifice their own interests for it. But the number of the governed is enormous; subjects or objects in turn, taxpayers or officials, students or employees – almost every member of the social body is related in some way to public administration. (Even organizations which are non-governmental none the less have some connection with the organization of the state.) The governed discover that citizenship has a positive value since their success depends upon the language of officialdom and the nationality of those who hold economic or political power. European writers of the last century were not wrong in claiming that nationalist movements were democratic; their mistake was to see in them a promise of peace.

## The Sovereign States

Does *nationalism,* the traditional desire for non-dependence or autonomy as expressed by rulers, and the *nationalism* associated with underdevelopment have anything in common save the name? The desire for non-dependence has been characteristic of 'political units' (or states, if one prefers the modern term) for centuries. These units, whether ruled by kings or elected officials, have insisted on being *sovereign.* Now, sovereignty has always meant the absence of a superior, the right to make decisions in times of crisis – in other words, the right to choose between peace and war. What has disconcerted and continues to disconcert many observers is that the bourgeois, who succeeded the princes in the places of power, have not conducted the affairs of state any differently than did the monarchs. Economists like Schumpeter, although imbued with a sociological turn of mind, believed for a long time that this was merely a vestigial survival. Why should the bourgeois conduct a diplomacy of prestige, of conspicuous consumption, perhaps more in conformity with outmoded aristocratic mores than with the spirit of a rational economy? Plainly, Schumpeter's analysis was false, or else it omitted something important: the desire for independence is characteristic of nations and not merely of monarchies. Perhaps states have never really been governed by the bourgeois (as Max Weber and W. Sombart thought of them), by men accustomed to negotiation, thrift, and calculation; even so, on the international scene, the nations that are ruled by a bourgeois minority behave no differently from those of the old regime. Surviving intact into the atomic age, we find this same desire for independence thwarting American and Russian opposition to the spread of atomic arms. And these weapons represent much more than a presumed guarantee of security; they also symbolize the greatness and dignity of the 'collective person', of the people organized as a state.

In the nineteenth century one could readily believe that when all nations became free they would reconcile their differences. In the twentieth century we have discovered that the principle of nationhood, like any other principle involved in the constitution of political units, gives rise to many occasions for conflict because of its intrinsic ambiguity and because of problems raised by marginal cases. (Should Alsace, which was Germanic in culture, be French because in 1871 its representatives solemnly proclaimed that they wished it, or should it be returned to the German Empire from which it had been wrested two centuries earlier by the armies of Louis XIV?) The titles of nations are often no less dubious than those of royal families. Moreover, so-called national states, that is, states with more or less ethnically homogeneous populations, could not survive in Central and Eastern Europe. The great war of 1914–18, which was the original source of the disorders of this century, was caused by quarrels over nationality, and while it resulted in the dissolution of multinational empires (Turkey, Austria-Hungary), it did not put an end to such quarrels in the succession states. The First World War was followed by still more terrible conflict, for which a totalitarian regime, appealing to race rather than nationhood, bore the major responsibility.

After the Second World War the revolt of colonial peoples against the European empires was also put down to the account of nationalism, which this time was a creditor, not a debtor. This great historical movement – whose interpretation should be as complex as that of the earlier and contrary movement of colonization – has produced more states than were counted among the total membership of the U.N. in 1946. Among them are but a few that merit the strict description 'national', in the sense that they include a homogeneous community and encompass the totality of that 'nationality' or 'community'.

In Africa the drive for statehood came from an elitist minority, usually dominated by people who had been trained in European schools and universities and who came to power by exploiting the widespread hostility of the masses to foreign domination. In Africa south of the Sahara, boundaries of new states were formed by slicing up old colonial administrations in a fashion that usually paid no attention to the lines separating tribal and *linguistic* communities. (These terms are inevitably vague because the social realities themselves are vague.) All the states of Southeast Asia have national minorities within their area of sovereignty. India is a subcontinent whose unity, realized by the British Raj, still requires the official use of the English language on the national level because none of the various Indian languages is acceptable to all the culturally identifiable groups within the population.

*Nationalist* states (states that are proud of their distinctive character and jealous of their independence) can, at the same time, not be 'national' (they are not based on an ethnic homogeneity aware of itself). Sometimes such states must be all the more 'nationalist' precisely because internally they are less than 'national', stressing all the more energetically their mission as an original, unique, collective person precisely because the description lacks reality. It is commonplace to say that nationalism is the childhood disease of underdeveloped countries. The contrast between the nationalism of Ghana, for example, and the European work of unification under the Common Market begun in 1950 illustrates and confirms this seductive theory.

Sometimes this theory is supported by another, equally attractive, which establishes a correlation between phases of development and economico-social ideologies. Nationalism – exaltation of a particular community, uncompromising affirmation of internal and external sovereignty, obsessive desire to be master within one's own borders and to obey no one outside them, even if he is stronger – provides a spur to economic development. The perhaps excessive pride fostered by nationalism creates within the political unit a sense of solidarity that either does not yet exist or might be stifled by the tensions of ethnico-cultural heterogeneity. In its early phases development requires the intervention of the state, which alone is capable of establishing the administrative infrastructure: the financing, the means of transportation and communication, and the supporting educational system indispensable to economic modernization. If the nation did not exist, to put it another way, if individuals felt they belonged either to a multiplicity of narrow communities or to an expanded but heterogeneous mass, the state would have to create a nation by invoking some variation of the spirit of nationalism.

Ideologies of the Marxist-Leninist type seem to meet the special psychological as well as the politico-economic needs of under-developed countries. In the popular form these ideologies take throughout the world they place total responsibility on the late colonizers for the poverty of countries previously colonized. 'Capitalistic exploitation' is held to be the major cause of under-development; the camouflaged imperialism of the Yankees is said to have prevented the development of Latin America just as the overt imperialism of the British or French stifled the development of India and Algeria.

Contrary facts do not blunt the appeal of this thesis. The leaders of former colonies are not interested in speculating on what the history of India would have been without British domination, or that of Algeria had it not been colonized by the French. The record shows that, apart from the exceptional case of Japan, the states of Africa, Asia, and Latin America which preserved their sovereignty have not all progressed more rapidly than did the states that lost their independence during the era of colonial domination. But the compelling factor seems to be that inferiority becomes less unbearable if someone else is to blame for it. But this is not all. Despite the existence of an objective measure of development, Marxism-Leninism makes possible a reversal of values.

The philosophy of history formulated in Marx's preface to 'The Critique of Political Economy' is evolutionist. Humanity, at least Western humanity, must journey through various economic regimes, from slavery to serfdom and the wage system, before reaching the promised land of socialism (or of a classless society). This evolutionist philosophy implies a sort of parallelism between the development of productive forces and the succession of regimes. The historical function of capitalism is to develop the productive forces; socialism will be its heir and will distribute to all the wealth which has been produced by the accumulation of capital. As for capitalism, it will finally wither, since it is incapable of providing any but the few with the fruits of the work of all. History has followed a different course. No developed country has become converted of its own will to Marxism-Leninism; no government in a developed country has been taken over by a party owing allegiance to this ideology. But there are two contrary interpretations of this contemporary history.

Marxist-Leninist orthodoxy, holding fast to the rule of the succession of regimes, puts the socialist countries at the head of the procession. These countries are perhaps inferior in terms of production or productivity, but they are superior politically and morally since they have liquidated capitalist exploitation and laid the foundations for the regime of the future. The inferiority of progress is cancelled out by the superiority of the regime.

The other interpretation has been popularized by W. W. Rostow's little book[4] which expresses in a summary and striking way ideas which have become quite widespread. Marxism was created in Europe at a time when social realities justified Marx's revolt and gave some plausibility to the predictions he made. It took quite a different direction when it became the ideology of a

4. *The Stages of Economic Growth*, Cambridge University Press, 1960.

revolutionary party that was master of a huge empire and necessarily dedicated itself to achievement of a task which should have been, and usually has been, the task of capitalism. Thus Sovietism in action, calling itself socialism, functioned as a substitute for, rather than the heir to, capitalism, and in Western eyes can be seen as a method of economic development and at the same time as a characteristic feature of underdevelopment. The party plays the role that entrepreneurs have played in the West: it provides for capital formation and at the same time gives the state the necessary authority for the radical changes industrial civilization requires – an authority the state founded on the principles of the *ancien régime* did not possess despite its absolutism. The party ensures the transmission of public decrees throughout the social body; it obtains obedience where it cannot command consent, employing the enthusiasm of a minority if not the assent of the majority.

This interpretation is Marxist in one sense: it limits itself to taking as its point of reference the development of productive forces (measured by per capita production) instead of the succession of regimes. The Soviets, in accordance with their orthodoxy, set their standards by relegating to the background the most advanced countries on the pretext that they have remained capitalist. Westerners in turn attribute the new nations' adherence to Marxist-Leninist ideologies to lag in progress as well as to childish manifestations of nationalism.

Westerners and Soviets cannot both be right but both could well be wrong.


*The Continuing Gap*

Just as nuclear means of destruction create a *common* danger for mankind but do not thereby create a human community, so the means of production perfected by science and technology, although they possess universalist potentials and do in fact tend to spread over the continents, divide humanity as much as they unite it. They are bringing men to live in the same material and even ideological universe, but it is a universe torn by conflicts inscribed in the very dialectic of industrial civilization.

Inequalities in the development of nations may be ephemeral from the point of view of Sirius or of an observer who reckons in centuries, but for the statesman or sociologist who confines his view to the twentieth century they are the reality of the age. Moreover, if one agrees to use the term *developed* only for societies that attain a certain value of per capita production ($600 to $700 was used as a bench mark in the mid 1960s) or possess the organization of facilities and division of labour characteristic of wealthy nations, many of the countries represented in the United Nations will not yet qualify as developed by the end of the century. In many respects it is far more difficult to reduce the gap between the *avant-garde* and the main body, to speed up the progress of the latecomers, than it was to first 'get things moving' in Europe, America, and even in the Soviet Union.

This statement seems paradoxical and it calls for a great many reservations. There are, certainly, some contemporary circumstances that facilitate development. The best evidence of this is that almost all countries, including the underdeveloped ones, have experienced over the last fifteen years an increase in population and production, and almost everywhere the increase in production has been greater than that in population. Present-day scientific knowledge and technology are incomparably superior to that of the last century. Thanks to the social sciences, the conditions necessary to progress are better understood than they were even at the beginning of this century. In what sense, then, and for what reasons does the gap between developed countries and the others seem likely to continue over the short term (several decades), and indeed even to widen?

The first cause is the acceleration of growth in both Western and Eastern Europe. Whatever reservations one may have about rates of growth they do provide an order of magnitude. For the last fifteen years they have been higher than the rates of the last century in both the West and the Soviet zone. This has come about as if the best handling of economic contingencies (lessening of crises), the most rapid technological progress (especially in agriculture), and new awareness of organization as a rational art had combined to double the rates of growth of the real per capita product (three to four per cent or more, instead of one to two per cent). In these terms the most advanced nations tend to advance even more rapidly; and if the laggards are not able to keep up the pace the gap widens. And such is often, if not always, the case.

The idea of underdevelopment, as we have said, has only a negative connotation. It applies to any country that has not reached a certain stage of modernization, but this negation is not enough to describe a social type. A small African nation south of the Sahara is underdeveloped; but so is China, the oldest empire with the most lasting civilization in history. It would therefore be unreasonable to seek the causes of underdevelopment or the obstacles to development as if causes and obstacles were everywhere the same.

I shall limit myself to a few simplified typical examples. Communist China has a regime, a ruling group, administrative and technological cadres, that have the determination and ability to modernize the economy and society. But, even supposing that the mistakes of 'the great leap forward' are not repeated and that planning is no more irrational than it was or is in the Soviet Union, a rise in the standard of living must be gradual for two reasons: the increase in population and the high percentage of resources earmarked for armaments. At the end of the century, barring unforeseen events, Communist China will be a great military power. The social organization will be modern and collectivist, but living conditions for most of the people will seem primitive to consumers in wealthy societies. The combination of military might and poverty, common enough in the past, is not typical of industrial civilization. But, for an ancient empire that has experienced a century of humiliation and is now belatedly becoming modernized, whose productivity has not kept pace with its population growth, this seems an inevitable course. China, and China alone, will provide an example, at least for the next few decades, of a state that in a military sense must be reckoned a great power, but still belongs to the underdeveloped Third World. If the principle of classification is per capita production it is this contradiction that makes China a military danger to all her neighbours, even to Japan, and a threat to the position of the United States in Asia.

India's situation is altogether different, despite one factor in common with China (a rapid increase in population, probably at the rate of two per cent per year). India also has the administrative and technological organization necessary for development, but it is confronted by systems of religious beliefs and practices radically contrary to rationalization. The power of the central authority does not extend effectively to the hundreds of thousands of villages that form the basis of Indian civilization. There are already significant modernized areas and these will spread, but an important part of the population will continue to live according to ancestral customs. So far statistics of the kind used by the U.N. show a rate of increase in per capita income that is scarcely higher than that of the birthrate, although there is reason to hope that in time the income growth figure will be substantially higher. But these figures will not reveal the internal reality that is of paramount importance; the juxtaposition of two widely varying sectors, the size of the modernized sector, and the way of life characteristic of those areas which have not been modernized.

Such a duality is likely to be even more pronounced in Africa south of the Sahara, if the bush is 'Africanized' while the coastal cities, plus certain agricultural and industrial enclaves, are modernized. In that part of the world numbers of people are not the stumbling block; space, climate, and the deficiencies of the ruling minorities are. In terms of the requirements of industrial civilization, the Europeans did not stay long enough; they began the task of education too late and they left too soon. They created too many states – some of them giants, in comparison to the administrative capacity of their rulers (the Congo, Nigeria), others dwarfs – so that small islands of modernity are all that one can look forward to in the remainder of this century. There is already reason to wonder how these small states will be able to absorb without endemic difficulties their young men who are being graduated from European universities, since politics and administration seem the only avenue open to well-paid and prestigious positions.

In Latin America the political contradictions are clearly visible. A country like Argentina, which had achieved a high level of per capita income thirty years ago, offers one of the rare examples in our century of arrested development. The cause is essentially, if not exclusively, political. The population of Argentina is European in origin; the country has not experienced the difficulties of integration which have beset most of the Latin-American states. It lacks neither space, resources, nor educated leadership. The follies of Perón, which were provoked by the blindness of the minorities in power before him, plus the semi-revolutionary situation created by the consequences of Perónism, resulted in the squandering of many opportunities and the prolongation of economic stagnation.

In the rest of Latin America, no matter how diverse the specific local conditions, development will require, first and foremost, a regime which is neither uniquely concerned with preserving the privileges of the propertied class (landed proprietors or industrial magnates) nor impelled by resentment to break with the United States and the loose grouping of American states, as Castro of Cuba did. At the beginning of the last third of the twentieth century, some countries – Mexico, Chile, Uruguay – are apparently developing (or are about to develop) a regime capable of stimulating and shaping development – or, at least, of not hindering it. It is possible, of course, that regimes stemming from Marxism-Leninism or the Castroist variant will spring up and perform the task of modernization despite the hostile reactions of the United States or of neighbouring nations whose rulers cannot remain in power without Washington's support. In either case the great issue is whether the principal countries of Latin America, although far from possessing Yankee wealth, will in this century reach the point where development has acquired an adequate pattern of self-sustained growth. In any case it seems likely that on this continent also shanty-towns will continue to stand close to skyscrapers, that oxcarts as well as large American automobiles will be on the road, just as the taxis on the streets of Calcutta must make their way in the midst of sacred cows.

Will Westerners, Soviets, and Japanese – in other words, the developed countries – have the power or the desire to alter these predictions? (The view will doubtless seem pessimistic to many readers, and would look quite different if expressed in the usual statistics.) Will accelerated enrichment of the 'have-nots' depend entirely upon the 'haves'? I would be tempted to say, paraphrasing Marx, that *the development of the underdeveloped countries must be the task of the underdeveloped countries themselves.* ('The liberation of the proletariat must be the task of the workers themselves.')

Apart from the unusual case of Cuba, the nations of the Soviet bloc provide only modest sums for aid to underdeveloped countries. They do this in the form of long-term credits. (The yearly total is of the order of several hundreds of millions of dollars, save for Cuba.) For some years private investment capital in the West has been primarily attracted to the developed countries where there is less danger of confiscation by nationalization and better opportunities for steady profit. American and European capital invested privately in the Third World is devoted largely to the exploitation of raw materials (oil and nonferrous metals). Directly or indirectly, these investments provide a primary source of funds for those states whose subsoil contains this natural wealth. But the sums paid in royalty by the operators and the taxes levied on foreign companies merely constitute a down payment. Depending on the way in which the dollars, francs, or pounds are spent, the consequences vary greatly. There is a great danger that the flow of capital will be used to create a glittering, artificial enclave of wealth instead of providing a nucleus for development from which the effects of modernization would radiate to the country as a whole.

The generosity of the Western nations in providing official governmental aid has frequently been a concomitant of the Cold War. This source of development capital is and will continue to be limited, subject as it is – under regimes based on universal suffrage – to the vagaries of public opinion. In a world-wide context, inequality among nations is more shocking in our day than the inequality of individuals or classes within a nation; but inequality among nations is so huge and vague a phenomenon that it remains virtually an abstraction. Inequality between classes or individuals represents the real experience of men, all of whom belong to their nation, and its correction is a national concern. This sentiment may be reversed in the case of aid at the government-to-government level, which may result in flooding the home market with cheap foreign products – threatening factories with bankruptcy, forcing workers into other jobs and placing an added burden on the taxpayer while imposing upon the government an additional payment to balance accounts. The rulers of the wealthy democracies are inevitably more sensitive to the demands and complaints of *their* pressure groups than to the pleading of economists or moralists who can preach the advantages of the long-term view, or urge a dominating concern with what ought to be.

Even if the wealthy nations were to do much more than they are now doing – even if they did everything possible – it would still be true that development finally must be the task of the underdeveloped countries themselves. Progress means a change of all of society. From the moment a state has been granted its independence the most it can expect is encouragement from the outside; it could be otherwise only if the colonial regime had been retained and brought around to functioning exclusively in the interest of the natives themselves. Historically, it is quite plain that this double requirement could never have been met; the colonizers would have balked at the material cost, and the natives at the moral cost of trading independence for progress.

Once the peoples of Asia and Africa had been organized as states, both large and small, wealthy or precarious, as nations historically constituted or in the process of becoming so, responsibility fell essentially to the minorities who were in charge of these new nations. They would have access to modern machines and methods, but development that is imported or imitative, as contrasted to the kind of spontaneous, evolutionary development that took place in Western Europe and America, presupposes initiatory and regulative action by states. And the fervent nationalism of the new states, however legitimate and inescapable it may be, serves to reduce and limit the possibilities of help from the outside.

Finally, the underdeveloped nations are affected by the ideological tides in the world at large. The United States is more concerned with halting the spread of Marxist-Leninist theory and practice than in fostering industrial development, just as the Soviet Union enters the arena in the hope of uncovering fresh evidence that non-socialist regimes are bound to fail. Development of underdeveloped countries is not the primary objective which activates the rulers of developed countries, nor is it the exclusive or always even the primary goal of the underdeveloped countries themselves.

Some of the rulers of the new states themselves proclaim their indifference to attaining the highest possible rate of growth; they insist that they put non-material values above all others. Development, whether defined by an increase in the total output or assessed on a per capita basis, by the division of labour or by rationalization, is an idea elaborated by economists and sociologists who have isolated the characteristics that industrial societies have in common. The leader of a new nation may yearn to pick and choose – to insist upon a rigid concept of 'national independence' or 'socialism', even if the one disorganizes production and the other necessitates the refusal of foreign capital.

The underdeveloped countries are not alone as true believers convinced of the absolute truth of their ideology. The Americans sincerely believe that private ownership of the means of production is the system most favourable to increased productivity and the dissemination of well-being among the people; the Marxist-Leninists are just as convinced that the system of collective ownership best serves these ends. Although both sides justify their respective systems in terms of efficiency, their preferences are not determined ultimately by economic arguments and are thus impervious to proof. They are the expression of a definite and uncertain interpretation of society, history, and human existence.

Let us accept, then, that the nationalism of the new states has certain characteristics of its own, and that the underdeveloped countries usually accept Marxism-Leninism as offering the interpretation of history most satisfying to their self-esteem. Does this mean, by contrast, that the nationalism of developed countries is about to disappear? Are not other economic and social ideologies taking the place of capitalism and Marxism-Leninism? In short, if civilization's tendency toward *universality* is being blocked by *nations* and *regimes*, are these obstacles outmoded survivals? Or hallmarks of industrial civilization itself? Can this civilization avoid being torn asunder by a science and a technology that are genuine and efficacious for all men, opposed by collectivities that endeavour to retain their singularity, and ideologies that do likewise, even when they claim not to?

## The Third World

In the next chapter we shall try to answer these questions, that is, determine the degree to which national and social ideologies, which are essentially aggressive, are a necessary consequence of industrial civilization, despite its universalist character. In this chapter we still must deal briefly with the following problem: *the influence of inequality of progress and the nationalism closely related to it on the international order*.

Let us first dispose of the myth (when applied to the present) and the nightmare (when applied to the future) of an aggressive world-wide coalition in which the poor would unite against the rich, the coloured against the white. Representatives of most of the countries of Africa, Asia, or Latin America will doubtless eventually manage to organize a common front in trade negotiations in order to wrest certain concessions (stabilization of the price of raw materials, tariffs, etc.) from the industrialized nations. This unity, however, is bound to be precarious, even when its objectives are modest and purely economic. After all, people who sell the same products are basically in competition with one another despite a temporary coalition whose purpose is to increase their common bargaining power.

Viewed from a perspective of several decades, on the diplomatic level the underdeveloped countries have displayed neither the intention nor the means of achieving any unity of action. They do not share the same ideologies, they engage in numerous quarrels among themselves. (We may call these disputes petty local quarrels, but as seen retrospectively from Peking or New Delhi, the recurrent disagreements over the boundaries of France and Germany might also have been called local quarrels.) These countries do not have the same form of government, and they all maintain inescapable relationships with their former mother-countries, whether these be strained or friendly. Finally, even if firmly allied, they still would have no determining influence over the more advanced nations. The threat of not selling raw materials presupposes a foolproof solidarity which does not exist. Militarily, all these countries are strong at home and weak externally, adequately protected against invasion, but incapable of offensive strategy. Individual arms have furthered the liberation of impoverished peoples, but the weapons of massive destruction are enough to prevent the great crusade which some of the ex-colonials dream of and others dread; the divisions among the great powers would disappear forthwith in the face of coloured hordes mounting an assault against the accumulated wealth of the whites.

Even today, the concepts of the Third World and the non-aligned nations, which are often confused, do not overlap. An African or Asian country identified with the Third World may actually have close relations with the West (the Philippines, Thailand, many Latin-American countries) or, more rarely, with the Soviets (Cuba). From time to time the Third World appears to be united – more by words than by deeds – in opposing colonialism, or in the effort to further certain commercial demands. And it might still become unified on occasion in order to mediate some disagreement between Communists and anti-Communists. But the configuration of world politics will be determined tomorrow, as it is today, not by the attitude of a score or more of powerless states but by the relations between the great powers – essentially the Soviet Union, the United States, China, and perhaps Western Europe and Japan. In relation to the present configuration, the major changes to be expected between now and the end of the century will come either from Europe between the Russian border and the Atlantic, from the rise of the People's Republic of China, or from the renewed vigour of Japan.

By the year 2000 China will have a nuclear force that will be inferior to that of the United States but none the less substantial. Whatever the disparities in the technological domain, there will probably be less difference in strength between the two nations than there is today; each will be able to employ the threat of nuclear arms. On the old continent it is conceivable that the countries of Eastern Europe will free themselves gradually from Soviet domination, that the Russian and American armies will retire eastward and westward respectively, and that the direct consequences of the Second World War will finally be wiped out.

In abstract terms, five principal factors determine national groupings on a world-wide level: *national interest* (space, resources), *ideological affinities, the geometry of power relations, kinship of culture,* and *inequality in development.* Since 1945 the Soviet Union and the United States have been enemies because of the geometry of power relations and ideological differences. If two great powers in an overall system cannot rule together they become enemies (no matter what they say). Today they are resigned to accepting the status quo, each anxious not to quarrel, but still unable to work out any lasting agreement with his adversary. Two predictions (or should we say prophecies?) seem plausible. As the standard of living rises in the Soviet Union, it will become increasingly difficult for her to preserve the role of spokesman and leader of oppressed, destitute, and revolutionary peoples. This will increase the hostility between the Soviet Union and Communist China, as China seeks to head the historic drive for world Communism, and may demand territories in Asia that were once incorporated in the empire of the Tsars and are now Soviet Socialist republics.

We can attach little importance to such facile and illusory speculations. The more one thinks about the diplomatic future in terms of the past the less one has a right to misconstrue the uncertainty of events dependent on so many social and even individual factors. No configuration can be lasting so long as the history of nations proceeds according to the immemorial rule of power. These remarks were made merely to demonstrate that the decisive influence of the level of progress on the international order during the next few decades will be exerted by the two great Communist powers, one of which is far more advanced on the road to what they both call the establishment of socialism. Most underdeveloped countries will adapt themselves to the circumstances created by the great powers, just as small countries have always done throughout the past. It would be useless to outline a diplomatic policy common to all, except to note their inclination toward non-commitment. But this inclination is hardly significant so long as the conflict they want to stay out of, symbolized by the

Warsaw Pact and the Atlantic Alliance, is situated in a distant theatre of operations where they have little interest and no means of action.

Must it be said, at any rate, that the underdeveloped countries increase the instability of the international system by their 'nationalism'? Let us recall the two meanings of this word: the desire for independence, and the consciousness of being a unique community, these resulting in a social organism in which individuals wish to participate and to which they attribute an infinite value.

In this last sense, nationalism appears praiseworthy when it is called patriotism (loyalty to a political unit), odious when it is called chauvinism and is expressed by a lack of appreciation for the merits of other nations, by contempt or hostility toward them. It is easy to slip from one meaning of the term to the other; my patriotism may seem like chauvinism to another, just as his patriotism seems like chauvinism to me. In the case of some underdeveloped countries the simultaneous emergence of nations and nationalism seems more to be hoped for than feared. In North Africa, the more the Kabyles and the Arabs acquire a sense of belonging to the same nation the greater the likelihood that Algeria will become unified. The new states in Africa are all heterogeneous. The single party as it has usually emerged is inherently autocratic; it is ordinarily composed of members of a single tribe who will have nothing to do with other tribes and arbitrarily deny them a share of influence and position. Such a system necessitates continuous despotism and intensifies internal tensions even if it represses them for a while. But the spread and the strengthening of a sense of citizenship that accompanies even this deplorable process answer a historical necessity. The more national the new states become the better off they and others will be.

By being national the new states will not necessarily become more aggressive towards the outside world. Indeed, when the nation itself has acquired a measure of stability, its rulers may well be less and less inclined to regard outside aid or foreign investments as a threat to national independence. One is reluctant, however, to make a categorical statement for quite a different reason. In certain parts of the world, in Africa south of the Sahara, for example, the new states are so numerous and so patently artificial that one hesitates to take a position on the nationalism of Senegal, Sudan, Ivory Coast, or Gabon that would repress the existing feelings of participation in linguistic or tribal communities. On the other hand, the worst thing that could happen would be a revision of boundaries or a wave of so-called nationality disputes (in the European sense of the term).

Can it be said that the same desire for independence that maintains the anarchy of power politics in the atomic age is also inconsistent with the logic of world economy? The comparison is only partially valid. One can conceive of a world agency that would preclude any form of violence or, at least, the use of mass weapons of destruction; prudence would dictate the subjection of humanity to a single military power if this could be obtained peacefully. But inequality of development, combined with the principle of nondiscrimination, precludes government on a world scale for the simple reason, among many others, that the administration of things is always and at the same time a government of men by men. In other words, cooperation among nations is required by the rationality of the industrial age, but the plurality of states is not only an inevitable but a rational consequence of the inequality in development.

Postwar experience in Europe bears out this thesis, although it is frequently alluded to in an effort to prove the very opposite. To be sure, an obvious, symbolic contrast exists between the determination of any African state to be independent and the professed desire for unification on the part of the European Six. Genuinely national countries, secure in their political and moral autonomy, no longer manifest in an aggressively childish manner their fear of foreign interference. However, the ultimate outcome of the European Economic Community remains uncertain. Even in the unusually favourable circumstances of postwar development, it is not yet certain that men will be able peacefully to overcome the persistence of 'national states' – of sovereign states that are the expression of a nationality aware of itself. In Western Europe inequality of development does not constitute a barrier to the establishment of supranational power; despite the somewhat lower standard of living in Italy as a whole (the standard of living in northern Italy is, however, comparable to that of the other countries of the Community), experience has demonstrated that a common market between the Six is economically possible. The bulk of public opinion in the several countries, according to the polls, now favours a common diplomacy.

The uncertainty, however, remains, and fortuitous circumstances are partially responsible for it. West Germany is only a fragment of a nation. Seventeen million Germans live on the other side of an arbitrary boundary line. Can the Five then enter into definitive agreements with a state whose rulers do not and cannot accept the status quo and whose diplomacy is necessarily 'revisionist'? The European Community was conceived during the Cold War when the Soviet world seemed monolithic, mysterious, and aggressive. The Sino-Soviet schism, the international evolution of the Eastern European states, and the growing autonomy of those states in their relations with the Soviet Union have altered the climate of international relations. To the extent that the attempt to unify Europe was aimed at consolidating the advanced positions of the Atlantic world against the Soviet threat, it apparently no longer has the same urgency. Furthermore, would it not stand in the way of another unification – that of the two Europes which are now separated by what has been called the iron curtain?

Even if we set aside these circumstances, important as they are, and the special proclivities of the current national leaders, nothing would be settled. There is no precedent whatever for a state, organized peacefully and by mutual consent, which would deprive nations like Germany, Italy, and France of their roles as historic protagonists. Empires have been built by force; federations come into being slowly, as the confirmation of an interdependent destiny to which a long past bears witness (Switzerland) or as a compromise between ethnic groups (Canada). A European federation would be the first to be constructed by great nations who were once enemies in order to put a definitive end to their rivalry.

In fact, the undertaking may result in less than a federation in the full sense of the word, without having to be considered a failure in its highest terms. A common market that would not create obstacles to the free flow of goods, money, and people, as do the present administrative constituencies in France or the *Länder* in Germany, would require a common coinage and, in many respects, a common administration of the economy. This might be done by a form of federation without, however, *necessarily* requiring a single diplomatic authority or a single and identical political destiny. In short, even the Common Market does not imply that a 'European State' will come into being – that is, a single authentic historical entity, responsible for a common foreign policy of the Six, or, rather, substituting one diplomacy for that of six.

Furthermore, if the purpose is to overcome chauvinism or extreme manifestations of the desire for independence, a change of scale from national states to a multinational state will provide no guarantee. An increase in the dimensions of the new market as well as of the population would favour economic expansion, but it would not necessarily improve the quality of government or the standard of living. Would a new, enlarged European state that sought to compete with the two great powers on the international scene, or to counterbalance the Soviet Union or draw Europe away from the United States, necessarily behave any better than Germany or France? Tsarist Russia and the Soviet Union, both giant multi-national states, have been no more respectful of the law than the truly national states.

The objection will immediately be made that the empire of the Romanovs or of Lenin and Stalin was founded and maintained by force, that the federal constitution of the U.S.S.R. is still naught but fiction. The United States of Europe would be a genuine federation; the member nations would retain their autonomy save in two areas: a single market for goods, capital, and individuals, and a common diplomatic front. I do not deny this difference; indeed, I emphasize it, for it raises the question of progress and purpose.

Yes, a federation by mutual consent, devoid of a federating agent, would probably be peaceful and rational, but would it be so deliberately or because it was powerless? Would such a federation ever see things through to the end, to the radical separation of two kinds of nationalism – one defined by an awareness of historic community, the other by a resolve to be politically and militarily independent? Such a separation is not impossible: it has been achieved here and there. In Switzerland every citizen recognizes two national groups of reference, the canton and the confederation, and also a third, intermediary – the linguistic community of which he is a part. But the Swiss confederation is small and it survives because of its neutrality. Would a federated Europe of the Six have to be neutral? Could it mobilize on behalf of a single cause the patriotism of peoples who have been long-time enemies?

# 9 The Heterogeneous Order of Values

The instruments of destruction have temporarily consolidated the plurality of sovereign centres of decision; the means of production have brought the scattered parts of the human race closer together physically, but they have substituted inequalities in the standard of living for the diversity of living conditions. Instead of the historic contrast between masters and slaves, between conquerors and subject peoples, we now have the disparity of wealth among peoples, a disparity which is both more and less accepted.

To the extent that this disparity can be imputed not to nature but to society, it may be regarded as temporary.Twenty, fifty, or a hundred years from now Asians and Africans also will have a refrigerator and a car per household. But those on top are not concerned with such prophecies; their own superiority is confirmed by statistics and they do not question it – but instead enjoy their status in good conscience since it has been achieved by work, not by war, in a competition supposedly open to everyone. The superficial unity created by the universality of science and technology has not yet obliterated nationalism, in the two meanings we have attributed to the word. Individuals belong to a nation or to an ethnic group before belonging to the human race, and some of these ethnic groups aspire to an autonomous existence which can be achieved solely by the assertion of sovereignty.

The obstacles to mankind's unity, insurmountable as they might be in the long run, remain in a certain sense external to industrial civilization itself. Our preceding analyses have presupposed that industrial civilization has the same tendency towards universality as science and technology, and in a certain sense the hypothesis is well founded. Geometry is true for all men; technology, when appropriately applied, works as well in South America as in North America. Hygiene can increase the average life span in every latitude. However, it is possible that certain nations may prove to be incapable of adapting themselves to industrial civilization, or capable of doing so only by sacrificing those qualities that constituted their uniqueness. The path of human history, as we know, is strewn with the wreckage of cities, of empires, of cultures. But these are merely extrinsic obstacles.

In this chapter we shall concern ourselves with a re-examination of our initial hypothesis: Is it legitimate to relate the universal truth of science, the universal efficacy of technology, to industrial civilization's tendency toward universality? Industrial civilization perhaps entails certain immanent value judgements or ideals to which we have referred in the first two parts of this work. But the two notions of equality and individuality (or liberty) are vague and ambiguous. Are they convincing to non-Western minds? Do they suffice to define the common goal of all industrial societies, whether Soviet or Western, American, Chinese, or Indian? Does not every society need its own principle of cohesion, its unique system of beliefs, in short, either an ideology derived from 'civil society' and the state or a religion?

## The Mixed Regime

The kinship between Soviet and Western regimes (socialist and capitalist) and the convergent evolution of each towards a mixed regime are leading subjects of current political speculation. The ideologists in the Soviet Union, whose task it is to interpret official doctrine, still make a great show of attacking 'the theory of industrial society' as the supreme justification for a capitalist system at bay. Actually, in certain Eastern European countries this theory, although not accepted as such, is now being discussed rationally. After all, how could the Marxists refuse to deal seriously with a question as simple as this: Given the same productive force – a force which is scientific and technological and inevitably more or less the same in all developed societies – to what extent will relations of production and social organization be different?

We can take certain facts for granted. The Soviet methods of planning, as they evolved during the first five-year plans, are not suitable in a complex economy. It would seem impossible, even with the help of electronic machines, to include in a plan elaborated by central organisms the virtually infinite variety of decisions implied by the rational combination of the means of production and the organization of trade on all levels. Moreover, an arbitrary price system and a refusal to take into consideration the relative scarcity of goods – in particular the scarcity of land and capital – rule out any rational allocation of resources. The way in which the Soviet planners had interpreted *Capital* partially explains their resistance to the notion of marginal utility and many other concepts associated with the very nature of the market. But as of now the Soviets are winning out, if we take the long view. The doctrine of growth at any and all cost, a growth obtained by a high percentage of investments, by merciless discipline, and deprivation of their people – 'economic Stalinism' – has been rather effective during certain stages of development. But economic Stalinism cannot constitute a permanent regime because it creates, by its successes as well as by its failures, obstacles for itself. We are not suggesting in this connection a theory of the 'self-destruction of socialism', similar and opposed to the theory of the 'self-destruction of capitalism'; both theories are as ambiguous as the terms socialism and capitalism. *Stalinism* hardly deserves to be described as socialist; it destroys itself in the precise and limited sense that its failures (in agriculture) and its successes (the creation of large-scale industry) force it to change.

Capitalism, too, is changing. Perhaps it owes to the challenge of Soviet planning its own recourse to non-authoritarian planning based on economic 'projections'. Or, on the contrary, it might have been that economists and statesmen, even without the threat or example of the Soviets, would have discovered their capacity, even their obligation, to exert some control over the entire economy in order to regulate global demand and to prevent depressions and attenuate the ups and downs of the cycles without having government regulate businesses in a high-handed way or paralysing the mechanisms of the market. As the history of the twentieth century unfolds, it resembles a dialogue, sometimes between deaf people, but a dialogue that will, none the less, be valid and fruitful in the end. The last word has not been spoken; the debate over the superiority of the many aspects of existing systems still continues. But it now appears that the illusion of total planning has been dispelled, along with the illusion that it is possible simply to dispense with money, prices, the autonomy of business enterprises, rates of interest, and the like. The dialogue continues, but it has turned to the advantage of the liberals – although this might change if the electronic computers make it possible to obtain artificially the essential economic information the market alone supplies today.

The dialogue over public or private property and the means of production has preserved an essentially ideological character. Superficially it is easy enough to say that all modes of regulation borrow from both planning and the free market. On the other hand, the attitude of Soviet theorists is uncompromising on the question of ownership. They see private ownership of the means of production as the very definition of capitalism, just as public ownership defines socialism. Between these concepts the gulf still yawns wide; if the theorists of both camps seem naïve or fanatical they nevertheless continue to wield great influence.

Why should we regard them as naïve or fanatical? The obsession with property has come down to us from past centuries when property was confused with wealth and wealth itself was a more or less constant quantity. Property was therefore a basic cause of inequality; agrarian reform, the division of land holdings, was one of the first symbols of socialism, and socialists were called 'sharers'. But now it is industry, not agriculture, that is the primary economic activity, the one that absorbs the majority of workers and creates most of the wealth. In an industrial society the lot of the workers is not appreciably changed by the state's legal ownership of the means of production as against ownership by stockholders. The workers themselves are primarily affected by the quality of management; it is on the basis of efficiency that the respective merits of the two differing modes of ownership now must be judged.

Private property, moreover, in so far as it relates to large corporations, is mostly a fiction. At least, to use a commonplace, property and power are dissociated. Most stockholders have little if any influence on the selection of directors and none at all on the management of the concern. It is not uncommon to increase the number of stockholders and disperse the ownership of shares among thousands of families. A large corporation thus belongs, in one sense, to no one; in another sense it belongs to an oligarchy of directors, chosen by a system of co-optation. The situation under public ownership is not intrinsically different; the state, which represents everyone, may be dominated by the few and so the enterprise is not really owned by anyone.

The so-called private property regimes have, in the end, one advantage: they tolerate the notion that property can have a varying status depending on the sector of the economy – agricultural, commercial, or industrial. Thus they avoid the total bureaucratization that has accompanied the nationalization of all the means of production. They allow centres of autonomy to persist that serve as a check on the omnipotence of the state and that open many avenues to social advancement. Finally, there is no lack of occupations that can be properly carried on solely by individuals who are motivated by their own self-interest. Despite their efforts, bureaucracies have not always succeeded in providing the prerequisites of such self-interest.

The traditional debate on the ownership of the means of production is, according to all the evidence, on the decline in developed societies. But the classic capitalist position provides no completely effective answers to three principal arguments. The first is that of inheritance. As long as private ownership of the means of production persists, some heads of industry will be chosen not because of their competence but because of the accident of birth. The logic of an order whose hierarchy must reflect merit necessarily condemns inheritance. The Saint-Simonians, who were the first to conceive of a *meritocracy*, were more hostile to inheritance than to property. In the eyes of many contemporary critics private ownership is discredited when it permits the handing down, within a family, of the right of management along with that of possession.

Moreover, personal as well as real property implies profits that have no relation to ability – at least ability in science, technology, and administration, which the industrial order values. Profits derived from market speculations, or from manipulations made possible by the increasing scarcity of certain commodities, have no justification in relation to the system of values and can hardly be separated from private ownership of the means of production. Such personal holdings not only place vast wealth in the hands of the few (this inequality of wealth is hardly in harmony with the philosophy of Western societies) but they result in inequalities of income that have nothing in common with the income patterns otherwise established by bureaucratic societies.

To be sure, inequality of income is not always greater in a Western society than in societies of the Soviet type. The top of the pyramid of wages or salaries varies greatly from one Soviet country to another; it has also varied during different periods within the Soviet Union itself; at times the ratio between the lowest wages and the highest salaries was 1 to 4 or 5, at others it was 1 to 20 or 40. Moreover, in a Soviet regime the material advantages associated with certain positions (a villa, or a car and chauffeur) are so considerable that a rough scale of wages and salaries has but limited significance. In the West the range of public and private salaries has decreased within the last century; a judge no longer earns twenty-five times as much as his bailiff, as he did a century and a half ago, but something like five to ten times as much, depending on the country and the moment. But, granting all this, it is still true that ownership of the means of production and mobilization of ownership in the form of securities superimposed on the equality of income (which theoretically reflects the inequality of industrial ability) a further inequality which in many circumstances is not only greater but has a different foundation.

Finally, a third argument is the exact counterpart of the one we have outlined in support of the opposite theory. The consequence of private ownership of the means of production, particularly in huge industrial organizations, is to give a few individuals enough power to oppose or dominate the collectivity. From one point of view this can be regarded as a limitation of the power of the state, from another as a bondage of the many to the few – or at least the creation of a state within a state. To say that the 'monopolists', or 'Wall Street', rule the United States or freely manipulate the political system is to give credence to a caricature still firmly entrenched in radical circles. It is true, however, that the state cannot be master of its own decisions so long as strategically placed minorities, capable of opposing the will of those who claim to represent the people, are made possible by the private ownership of the means of production.

The preceding analyses suggest that behind the question of the status of property there are issues of greater scope. Whether large corporations are managed by directors who elect each other or are appointed by the state makes little difference to the ordinary man, to workers and salaried employees, or even to intellectuals. If one of these two methods of selection gives better results in terms of productivity, there is no apparent reason to object to it. Actually, however, the choice indirectly involves a basic question: the survival of a commercial order, *essentially individualist*, in an industrial age necessarily poses the issue of limitation or expansion of the authority of the state.

Soviet society, as it has existed until now, has been despotic, and in its effort to undertake rigid planning it has often seemed almost absurd. There is an element of caricature here, too, however, and it is not impossible to imagine a purely industrial social order that is rigorously rational and more like the Soviet regime than it is like capitalism. To be sure, it may be argued that those features that are usually criticized as antisocial characteristics of capitalism – the profits of scarcity and those that result from trade, luck, or inherited property – might be eliminated from Western society, or might appear in another form in Soviet society, or finally, might even perform an essential social function in either, that of innovation. When a planned economy restores market prices and the autonomy of financial concerns, certain modes of profit linked to individual initiative will have to be accepted. On the capitalist side it certainly is not revolutionary to consider reducing the size of inherited fortunes through taxation, or even national-izing all land, as some liberal economists have suggested, because its scarcity as a result of population growth is creating a value that will enrich many owners without regard to merit or con-tribution to the general welfare. As for the innovators, they presumably always will derive profit from a purely industrial social order.

Veblen made the mistake of thinking that the industrial order –

the order of production – was sufficient unto itself. In his opinion capitalists were parasites responsible for all the ills of society; on the other hand, producers, engineers, and workers were animated by a different spirit, that of reason, efficiency, and peace. But this leaves out the fact that the productive order is necessarily subject to the requirements of economic calculation and that the man who does the calculation, who uses the means of production most effectively, is by definition the head of a business, whatever his intellectual training might be. The Soviet economy recognizes the necessity of such economic calculation (and therefore of a market where certain prices are regarded as authentic) and thus in effect concedes the importance of the function of the manager.

There are two possible directions an industrial society can take. In one, with the means of production, and of land in particular, collectively owned, the accumulation of private fortunes is impossible; the hereditary transmission of ownership and sometimes of management of business enterprises disappears. The power of the state is consequently unhampered; the worker serves the collectivity, not some private entrepreneur or stockholder; and the planner, although he uses market prices in his economic calculation, does not feel he is the slave of the consumers' desires. This is in contrast to the most advanced of all the Western economic systems, that of the United States, which is also the system that most clearly is characterized by a commercial spirit concerned not only with satisfying but with arousing the desires of the consumer. In an ideal Soviet society, producers and planners have the say. In the ideal Western type of society, sellers and the consumers are dominant; in order to operate at full speed, the economic machinery must pour out its products, and the man who sells, promotes, and advertises is the indispensable agent of prosperity.

In comparing these two ideal types it is difficult to determine how much should be ascribed to the phase of development of each and how much to their contrasting social objectives. No society of the Soviet type has reached a threshold of opulence, even by the standards of Western Europe. Were Czechoslovakia outside the Soviet orbit it would certainly again have reached this threshold; there can be no doubt that it has been prevented from doing so by the direction central planning has taken in setting a series of objectives that are artificial, given the traditional framework of the economy. Nevertheless, the direct and indirect consequences of public or private ownership of the means of production are such that the dialogue over the status of property continues to have an essential meaning: *the industrial order* versus *the commercial order; the state, master of the economy,* versus *the state, limited by the individual right of ownership and profit-making*. These alternatives do not imply that the supporters of one must be mortal enemies of adherents of the other or that the controversy can be resolved only by a death struggle. Within Western societies these alternatives can be vigorously, even passionately, debated, while the historical dialogue between the contrasting societies continues. As of now, the ideals of such societies are neither strictly contradictory nor fully compatible.

### The Industrial Image

Are there any differences between Western economic systems that enable us to characterize ideal types? Do Europeans and Americans, or the French and Germans, set different social goals for the same means of production? Are they building societies that are plainly different from one another? A little book published by French planning experts entitled *Reflections for 1985* is instructive in this respect. The editors of this study had constantly before them the question: 'To what extent is America today an image of our own probable or desirable future?' The answers perhaps necessarily seem contradictory. On the one hand, the task is 'to sketch the characteristics of a new society ... one that seems truly preferable to us and to other Europeans because the wealth of traditions in Europe could alone almost guarantee that the structure of consumption would continue to reflect a scale of values different from those that prevail on the other side of the Atlantic'. On the other hand, the experts concede that 'the desire to compete will doubtless lead us (especially in the realm of mass production) to imitate an economy that is ahead of Europe in growth but with which Europe intends to keep pace in technological progress'. And a little further on: 'Scientific civilization tends more and more to attenuate national traits and idiosyn-crasies.' The planners seem to be at once eager, yet unable, to define the originality they want to preserve in French and Euro-pean society as distinguished from American society.

Let us briefly recall a banal idea: some social transformations brought about by economic growth have already become so universal nobody questions them. Among these are: the reduction of the agricultural labour force (and, more generally, a redistribu-tion of the working force among the standard three segments of the economy); the reduction in the proportion of individual income spent for food (in France this was down to 39.4 per cent in 1960 and will drop to 24.7 in 1985); increasing urbanization; prolongation of the educational process; a shorter working day; rapid development of certain new industries (electronics); diffusion of means of transportation and communication; and a more than proportional increase in spending for research and development. Such a list, which is by no means exhaustive, serves to illustrate the theme of the *tendential laws that are common to all Western societies* – laws that are the consequence of scientific and technological dynamism as well as of human reactions to this dynamism.

It goes without saying that these common tendencies are not incompatible with quantitative and qualitative differences in the style of living and the nature of cities from one continent to another, or from one country to another. Given the same income level, the Frenchman eats more meat than the German and less sugar and milk than the Englishman. For some time he has spent proportionately more money for an automobile and less for lodgings than his European neighbours. But the most striking result of statistical studies is not the persistence of such differences but rather the tendency of any social group in any given nation, once it has reached a certain income level, to desire the same material goods that had attracted groups which had moved upwards earlier.

Nevertheless, this tentative conclusion remains paradoxical. Knowledge is power, as Francis Bacon put it. Increase in power cannot but increase the range of possible choices. Why should all societies necessarily make the same choices? And will not diversity of choice bring about a diversity in social organization? In fact, it is possible to define various types of societies on the basis of their response to certain fundamental alternatives.

The first of these and the most obvious is the choice between *national power* and *material well-being*. Compared to Western nations, the Soviet Union has regularly devoted a higher percentage of its gross national product to national defence, a higher percentage of industrial investment to heavy industry, and a lower percentage of its labour force to commerce. On one side of the iron curtain the use of resources is different from that on the other. (And the preference for power is not the only reason.) In any event, in Eastern Europe the ownership of a car is still a luxury reserved for the privileged few. The Soviet Union manufactures annually approximately one seventh as many passenger cars as France, although its population is more than four times greater. Yet cars are no less popular there, as is attested by the long list of those who have the means to own one and are waiting their turn.

The politico-economic regime of the Soviet Union makes it possible to refrain from producing what the consumers would like to buy. If the goal of society is to satisfy as well as possible the desires of its members, of what good is such omnipotence of the state? From the point of view of material well-being, why go against the logical operation of the market, even if subsequently one has to control and restrain it in order to finance certain tasks necessary to society? A market economy certainly does not rule out the mobilization of political power; the United States is proof of this. But a market economy, combined with a democratic political regime, limits the power of the state to substitute its own preferences for those of the consumer.

No Western society could seriously consider recourse to the stringent measures taken by the Soviet Union to obtain distribution of the national product in conformity to the interests of the state; to do so planners and rulers of the Communist Party must reserve for themselves the supreme right to decide what these interests are. All the Western economies are oriented towards material well-being. Can we, then, perceive the possibility of some other choice over and above the fundamental one between power and material well-being? Sociologists have suggested a number of alternatives.

Some say we are approaching the point where the choice may be between a *consumer* and a *leisure* society. I do not believe that this alternative suggests two ideal types. To be sure, at a given level of productivity, it is not impossible to consent to a slowing down of economic growth in order to provide immediately for greater leisure. Experience suggests, however, that for many reasons the range of choice is limited. The demand for greater leisure is not likely to outstrip the demand for a continued rise in the standard of living. No economy involved in international competition can pay wages that are not in harmony with the productivity of labour. Moreover, to pay the same wage for a shorter working week is equivalent to raising the hourly rate of pay and this would lead to inflation (France experienced this in 1936) unless it was accompanied by a corresponding increase in productivity. So far, differences in the weekly work hours are relatively minor from country to country when the level of productivity is the same; they are certainly not great enough to isolate the ideal types suggested by the *consumer-leisure* comparison.

Another alternative has been suggested: *individual consumption* or *public service – gadgets* versus *solidarity*. It has been said that a society completely given over to the law of the market tends to produce more and more goods at less and less cost – but that these are the goods that heads of businesses, making use of technological innovations, decide to impose on the public. Now, the goods which producers cannot persuade the public to buy without large-scale advertising campaigns are not always those which are most useful to society. Who should make the determination of priorities? Granting that state planners are subject to the risk of attributing an absolute validity to their own scale of values, the need for certain public services, such as roads, urban renewal, hospitals, and schools, is generally agreed upon. Yet these needs do not create a market demand as does the need for food, cars, and private housing. It is therefore inevitable that public authority must take from taxes a sufficient percentage of the national product to finance such services. Here some theorists see another possibility of two divergent paths. Those societies that accept a controlled market and political democracy will move in the direction of a substantially different way of dividing the national product between private consumption and collective needs.

This alternative is actually less meaningful and far more ambiguous than is suggested by the simple formula, private consumption versus public services. In every country, a rise in the standard of living entails a more than proportional increase of certain types of spending, such as those for education, medicine, and highways. These expenses can be financed in varying degree, either by the state or by individuals, and the formula chosen will have some bearing on the society's professed concern for equalization of incomes.

Aside from the Scandinavian countries, the reduction of inequalities in income through taxation has not been pushed in Europe any more effectively than in the United States. If any difference exists it is in the climate of opinion; profits and individual wealth are still accepted in the United States as proof of, and legitimate reward for, success. On the old continent, the dominant ideology sometimes encourages hypocrisy and the concealment of concentrations of wealth which, on a European scale, are probably as great and as numerous as comparable individual or family holdings in America.

With regard to social security – used here to mean general state support of public services – there has been and still is a perceptible difference between most of the countries of Western Europe and the United States. The United States reserves a smaller proportion of a larger gross national product for social security; furthermore, many educational institutions, particularly colleges and universities, are still supported in large part by private endowment. This difference, however, is rapidly disappearing as a consequence of a twofold evolution taking place on both sides of the Atlantic.

American prejudices against the public sector have been often condemned in recent years and appear to be finally undermined. Leading voices in the United States cite the intolerable conditions that result from failure to understand the contribution that public expenditures can make to the well-being of the people and to the quality of their lives, and denounce the tendency to confuse private consumption and general welfare. Within the last decade public expenditures and social legislation have acquired a popularity reflected in significant votes in Congress. The federal government is now financing a growing part of the cost of primary and secondary schools and universities and is moving rapidly into health and other fields previously left largely to private philanthropy and state and local government. Even the great private universities receive large sums from the federal government through research contracts.

In Europe, on the other hand, and particularly in France, planning studies show that the mere continuation of present social legislation plus the current volume of governmental functions will, within twenty years, require that public expenditures be multiplied by five, whereas national production, even according to the most optimistic estimates, will increase only threefold. Certain expenses, particularly those financed by the state, are rising faster than the standard of living; among these are expenditures for public health, medicine, and education. Countries like France which have gone further on the road towards social security and financial support for certain public services may be forced very soon to turn to an increased role for private financial support.

The difficulties of adjustment will be greater in Europe than in the United States. The latter is working out its social legislation at a time when the per capita production is two or three times greater than it is in Western Europe. The United States can undertake the process of increasing its social services without running into insurmountable economic obstacles. France and other European countries are already committed to providing most of their population with health insurance, family allowances, accident insurance, and old-age pensions. They will find it difficult to retreat in search of a more practical solution that recognizes that, while it is natural and necessary for the state to protect the destitute from misfortune and even guarantee to all a minimum income, it is absurd for prosperous people to receive free of charge services that are becoming more and more scarce, as in the case of medical treatment.

Therefore, I do not think that the alternative – private consumption versus public services – can be considered a choice between ideal types. Still less do I think that one represents Europe and the other the United States or that in this regard American society of today prefigures French society in 1985. Differences will persist even on a purely economic level. Division of the national product among the various sectors and the ratio between expenditures for social security and private consumption as determined by public administration will not be the same from country to country. Distrust of state intervention is and continues to be greater in the country that exalts free enterprise than among the grandnephews of Colbert. Whether successful or not, resistance to certain aspects of American commercialism will continue in Europe, at least verbally.

This analysis is intended to show that national differences, which are both probable and desirable, do not lend themselves to the elaboration of ideal types. All Western societies are of one type. Whether they like it or not, they are all caught up in the same dynamism of economic growth and scientific research. They consume the same products. Their techniques of management tend to be similar. Nowhere does the state passively permit the national product to be distributed by the sole mechanism of a market subject to the influence of large concentrations of industrial and financial power. And nowhere does state intervention succeed in wholly upsetting the way of life that technology and the rational organization of businesses are creating.

### Regime and Culture

In order to show that economic systems marked by a similar obsession with growth and productivity, utilizing the same methods of production, and sharing the same fundamental values[1] can seem essentially different, we must identify a radical difference either in *means*, in the *social order*, or in *objectives*. The Soviet regime insists on *the effectiveness of planning, the elimination of private property and classes*, and a goal that transcends historical

1. In spite of a dissimilar stress on the two objectives of rewarding each according to his work and providing a minimum for everyone according to his needs.

experience – *the creation of a new type of man* in a society that is homogeneous and without conflict. Once the utopian concept is set aside, the means no longer seem so original; the elimination of classes in the social order is a matter of terminology and the evident stratification that still remains reduces the contrast with the West. Only the status of property and the contrast between the commercial and the industrial order remain, in spite of everything, and continue as a real theme of ideological debate and historical dialogue.

Among Western societies neither the means, the order, nor the goals are essentially different. The means all involve a combination of planning and the market or to put it more simply, a controlled market system; private ownership of at least some of the means of production still persists and, consequently, social stratification and the eventual formation of socio-occupational groups into classes or class parties; the proportion of private consumption and public services, respectively, is not sufficient to define a type.

The opposition between industrial societies of the Soviet type and those of the West springs from the economic-social regime. The *differentiation* between countries that have the same socio-economic regime is based on their culture. A regime defines a particular order of industrial civilization; a culture is the totality of values, beliefs, and customs, which includes those inherited from the past as well as the specific traits that can be attributed to industrial civilization. A regime finds expression in ideologies, a culture in a tradition, in a personal mode of relationships, sometimes in a religion. The Soviet countries are those that claim to deduce from their ideologies the legitimacy of power, the ultimate purpose of their own action, and the goal of humanity itself.

The word 'ideology' is ambiguous as we know, but we are using it here in a precise sense. *An ideology is a more or less systematic interpretation of society and history, regarded by its supporters as the highest truth.* All men hold opinions today about the kind of economic, political, or social organization they deem desirable. Many are firmly convinced of the superiority of this or that status for property or of this or that method of regulating the economy.

Depending on our interests or our philosophy, each of us leans either toward the right or the left, toward 'liberalism' (in the American sense) or conservatism. If we broaden the meaning of the term 'ideology' to include opinions and preferences, whatever the degree of elaboration, every country, every class, and every regime has its ideology. But national socialism or Marxism-Leninism are ideologies *par excellence*, or rather they constitute *a particular kind of ideology*. They claim to be *superior to transcendental religions* and *they take the place of religion*. They have been called secular religions, and this very term raises the fundamental problem of a social order in a secularized civilization.

Development, that is to say, the rational organization of production, can validly claim to be an indispensable means to any end. But neither production nor consumption is an end in itself. Production is a means to material well-being or power, and material well-being is a prerequisite for the good life. But in what does the good life consist? What authority, be it government, party, church, or public opinion, is to define the good life as such or delineate the kind of man who should serve as a model for everyone? A possible answer is given by secular religion, which, as the religion of the state, is held up as the highest embodiment of truth.

At the beginning of the last third of the twentieth century, secular religions, gospels of collective salvation by a class or a race, appear to be on the decline, at least in the developed countries. It is difficult to understand how dogmatic ideologies, whose intellectual and even spiritual poverty now seem obvious, exerted, and occasionally still exert, great influence on superior minds. But the trend is difficult to assess. Twenty years ago Westerners tended to overestimate the historical significance of secular religions; they could be inclined to underestimate them today.

The Fascist and National Socialist movements were at once backward-looking and revolutionary. They were nostalgic for the heroic ideals which democracy and modern civilization tend to eliminate from daily life, yearning after those organic communities which industrialization has inexorably destroyed. This rejection of the rationalization of contemporary society by a fraction of the intellectuals and the common people came to be embodied in movements that borrowed their method of action from the Social Democratic and Communist parties. Hitler's diabolical genius enabled him to exploit his country's mass resentment and revolt, and to draw Germany into an apocalyptic adventure.

Many National Socialist regimes, that is, regimes inspired by socialist forms and tending to exalt a narrow nationalism, still exist after the Second World War, even though, as ideologies, National Socialism and Fascism do not seem to have much chance of flourishing again in the foreseeable future. An oligarchy that knows how to manipulate the masses can acquire authority in the name of democracy and proclaim its devotion to all of humanity even though its sole concern is for its own self-interest. It would appear that the material progress of industrial civilization in Europe and America during the last quarter-century has definitely subordinated nostalgia for the pre-modern past. If an economic crisis like that of the 1930s were to occur, the demagogues would probably try to mobilize the masses in the name of ideologies that might be nationalist but would also tend to be 'futurist'.

The secular religion that has had the most spectacular success obviously is Marxism-Leninism; its zealous pursuit and geographic spread is often compared to that of Islam. It has by no means reached the end of its historic career, but now, a half-century after 'the ten days that shook the world' and resulted in the seizure of power in Petrograd, a provisional assessment is not impossible.

The faith that Marxism-Leninism inspired in the country of its origin has been corroded by time and by the experience of the regime that was based on it. Contemporary Russian physicists and biologists are not really interested in Marxism-Leninism; writers and artists rebel against socialist realism; economists take liberties with the literal interpretation of *Capital*; among the recent winners of the Lenin Prize were mathematicians, who are certainly more interested in introducing linear programming and the use of electronic computers than in paying due heed to the labour theory of value. The sociologists of the U.S.S.R. themselves, although they accept the classic doctrines (class struggle, socialism versus capitalism, the final and inevitable triumph of socialism), are beginning to study the actual condition of the proletariat instead of merely extolling its liberating mission. It may be objected that dialectical materialism remains the official philosophy and that if the doctrine were stripped of its pathological excrescences (why should Marxism bear within itself the true theory of heredity?), if it became more flexible, more centred on the essentials, it would emerge greatly strengthened by such a revision.

I personally do not believe this to be true. Only the future offers a transcendence perhaps comparable to the authentic transcendence of great religions. As the official credo of a society on the road to stabilization, Marxism-Leninism is no longer but 'a spiritual point of honour' (the expression which Marx himself applied to Christianity), the universalist and egalitarian credo of a hierarchical and nationalist order.

The new faith – as Communism was called after 1945 – has lasted an even shorter time in the Eastern European countries dominated by the Soviet regime because of the presence or proximity of the Russian armies. Public opinion, even among members of the Party, is veering towards a kind of scepticism tinged with nationalism. Certain features of the doctrine, such as collective ownership and planning, have been preserved, but they are treated more as opinions than as articles of faith. The ruling minority, intent on maintaining its power, still has a certain sense of ideological solidarity with the parties and countries that are its brothers in socialism.

It does not follow that the Marxist-Leninist parties have lost their power to convert or to conquer. Revolutionary enthusiasm is subsiding in those countries that have had their revolutions and are beginning to achieve comfort if not opulence. But sometimes religions gain from the outside what they lose in the country of their origin. The Communist parties of Western Europe are condemned to a permanent and sterile opposition so long as they merely echo the characteristic doctrines of the Bolshevik party and promise that victory will bring a twofold 'Russification': submission to Moscow and an imitation of the Soviet regime. By giving up an intransigent universalism they adapt themselves better to the diversity of national conditions. The apparent return to French and Italian orientation by the two largest Communist parties west of the iron curtain is not enough to ensure eventual victory. But it is a significant development nevertheless.

Finally and most importantly, a new destiny looms for Marxism-Leninism since its adoption in Communist China as the official creed of some 700 to 800 million people – about one fourth of mankind. Here it is no longer the revolutionary doctrine of a working class on the road to becoming middle-class, as it was before 1914 during the era of the Social Democrats; it is not an ideology needed as justification or camouflage for the revolutionary technique of Lenin or the totalitarian technique of Stalin. It is too early to know what the Chinese will do with it. For the present they are using Marxism-Leninism to condemn simultaneously 'Western Imperialism' and 'Soviet revisionism'. Thus the doctrine, whose creator was a Rhenish scholar and whose prophet was a Russian intellectual, may become the gospel of the poor and the coloured peoples against the rich and the white.

This function, polemical in nature, seems today the most obvious if not necessarily the most important. It did serve, in the West, the emotional needs of intellectuals without a firm commitment and of uneducated and semi-educated people uprooted by industrialization. But the culture of the Western countries, at least among the upper classes, was not basically opposed to industrial civilization. Industrialization, it is true, has transformed ways of life and destroyed traditions, even in the West where it began. However, the gap between indigenous culture and the demands of industrial civilization in no instance has been nearly so great in the West as it is in China and India. Although in many technological domains China had been several centuries ahead of the West, she derived no profit from this but maintained a social order in harmony with the cosmic order. She cultivated the art of living but did not develop the means of production. In India, respect for sacred animals, belief in metempsychosis, the caste system – indeed all the elements of Indian culture – have so far precluded the manner of thinking and acting that seems to be indispensable to an industrial civilization.

It may be that the Chinese version of Marxism-Leninism will serve to impose or facilitate a mental and moral conversion. The language of science, technology, and productivity does not warm the heart; occasionally it is convincing, but it is never moving. But everything is altered when the same transformations and the same demands are expressed in the language of secular religion. It is no longer a matter of producing but rather of building socialism and creating a new kind of man. The philosophical values proclaimed by the Enlightenment have been translated in terms of ultimate goals and integrated in a total ideology that can win the fanatical support of the masses and the intellectuals. No one can predict how the synthesis of Marxism-Leninism with Chinese tradition will work out in the long run. On the other hand, the brief history of secular religions already enables us to discern another key aspect of the dialectic: universalism.

## The Universal Appeal

Marxist inspiration is proclaimed to be for all of humanity; it is for mankind everywhere that the Russian proletariat fights and sacrifices. All the ideologies of the past have either expressed or concealed man's exploitation of man, as manifested in the class struggle. According to the gospel, reconciliation will be possible only in a classless society, after a revolution. But until the final stage is reached (or the end of prehistory), this revolutionary drive will degenerate into an ethic of war. Those who stand in the way of the benevolent march of history are not responsible for their blindness – since every man is the prisoner of his condition – but they do not have the right to live at the expense of the revolution. The opposition must be, and is destined to be, eliminated in one way or another since it has no place in the society of the future. The amorality which is imputed to the true believers in the Marxist version of temporal salvation is the logical result of the structure of their dogma as well as of the mission of the party-church. The dogma is merged with a vision of the world according to which the will of individuals is subject to objective necessity. How could militant churches or activist parties, devoted unconditionally to a temporal goal and inspired by a primitive faith, acknowledge the right of the individual's conscience to resist? By sanctifying a particular doctrine of ownership and a certain method of administering it, Marxism-Leninism attempts to transform what should be a rational dialogue about the respective merits of different social orders into a death struggle between good and evil. In theory, at least, it begins by tearing mankind asunder and dividing it into two hostile camps on the pretext of leading the way to an ultimate reconciliation.

As a secular religion, Marxism-Leninism is more threatened by success than by failure. The goal, which constituted the supreme value, seems to recede as the movement progresses. Through no fault of men but because of the weight of history, this ideology, which teaches action and revolt against injustice, is being used little by little to justify an established order. At the same time it is losing its power of persuasion, since it is no longer able to condemn contemporary reality and to proclaim a future without precedent. For these reasons it cannot recapture its tendency toward universality.

As the regime erected by the revolutionaries turns its attention to the concerns of daily life, totalitarianism, the complete control of all individual or collective activities, tends to slacken. The ideology does not die, it merely changes. It continues to be the basis for the state-church, the principle of legitimacy, or, to revert to Gaetano Mosca's concept, the *formula* used by the political class. The Communist Party remains the incarnation of the proletariat, unless the state, in a later phase, should be declared the agency of the entire people. But individual morality resumes its rights. In a socialist regime a good Communist respects the established order: respect for order does not entail hopes for a radiant future, and perhaps such expectations might lead to doubt. For purposes of teaching civic virtues to the Komsomol or to Soviet citizens, would not a reading of the Ten Commandments be more effective than a reading of *Capital*?

Auguste Comte, who gave sociology its name, was dogmatically atheist. His prime conviction was that the mode of theological thought belonged to the past and would be supplanted by positivist or scientific thinking; he died in the belief that he was the first high priest of mankind. Atheism was also the starting point of Karl Marx's intellectual journey. Religion is the opiate of the people, he proclaimed; man fictitiously casts his essence into a transcendent being because he cannot realize this essence on earth. Marx's critique of religion was the model for his 'critique of political economy', the oft-forgotten subtitle of *Capital*. Both Comte and Marx believed in the universalist trend of modern civilization and both wondered about the destiny of a humanity bereft of religion, in the traditional meaning of the word. For a century and a half philosophers and sociologists have continued to ask the same question: what will fill the gap left by the death of God? Will God's death upset the social order?

For a time it was possible to believe that economico-social ideologies or nationalist passions would discharge in modern civilization the traditional function of the gospels of salvation: to unite men's souls and provide the supreme value or ultimate goal of human existence. A similar dialectical relation appeared between the traditional order of society and gospels of personal salvation on the one hand, and the promises of the modern order and secular religions on the other. In the past, gospels of salvation appealed to the individual, although each was, in fact, the prisoner of his condition. Secular religions promise collective salvation today, whereas the social order, however far it may be from attaining its ideal, attempts to give every individual an opportunity for advancement and accomplishment. Gospels of personal salvation were the complementary negation of a theoretically stable hierarchy. They restored in the sight of God the equality of all men who accepted as normal the obvious inequality they found on this earth.

Secular religions claim that through collective action they are hastening the advent of an order which is in harmony with the final requirements of the new civilization. Philosophers counter this rapprochement of secular and transcendent religions by maintaining that the specific content of religious faith – God, transcendence – is not to be found in any set of economico-social beliefs. Ethnologists and sociologists have a different objection. Every society possesses a culture, a more or less coherent whole, ways of living and thinking which command respect, sometimes as duties or prohibitions. Gospels of salvation were but one of the elements of culture; this element has grown weaker, or at any rate, those who are responsible for socio-economic organization no longer recognize the authority of religious dogmas. None the less, the secularization of industrial civilization does not create a need for a substitute religion. Social imperatives, whose religious imperatives were but a case in point, continue to control collective life.

Secular religions represent an extreme form, adapted to times of crisis, of a phenomenon obviously related to industrial civilization. This civilization no longer entails an order sanctified or sanctioned by the Church. It is in a state of perpetual change and is critical of itself in terms of self-assigned ends it never succeeds in attaining. Individuals no longer regard the position they occupy in society as definitive; behaving as if they had no other life save the one they lead on this earth, they attribute vital importance to the political, economic, and social regime in as much as this regime controls the only life they have. This is why in every country where there is an industrial civilization, opinion about public affairs tends to become an integral part of the culture, even when such opinion is not elaborated in a system and manipulated by political parties of totalitarian inspiration.

## Politico-Social Opinion

The role of politico-social opinion still varies widely from country to country. Politics, religion, and culture hardly seem to constitute an integral whole towards which the future of all peoples must converge as if it were an inevitable end. At the present time certain national ideologies require fixed principles of economico-social organization, while others are presumably compatible with any political preference the people might display. A communist in the United States engages in activities and holds beliefs that are considered un-American; in France, a Communist, or even a National Socialist, does not cease thereby to be French or to be regarded as such. Frenchmen are proud to have their society defined by a dialogue, even at the risk of civil war. Americans are not against a dialogue, but they exclude morally anyone who challenges the very foundations of their Constitution, in other words, the political unity of the nation itself.

It is not surprising that an integral facet of American patriotism, as of Soviet patriotism, consists of politico-social ideology. The people of America who emigrated from every country of Europe (to say nothing of the Negro minority) did not become a nation in the same way as did the peoples on the old continent, by the slow action of history. Adherence to a politico-social creed was necessary for 'acculturation', a conscious adherence that accompanied the unconscious absorption of behaviour patterns and values. Similarly, although in quite a different context and manner, the nationalities within the Soviet Union are loyal to Moscow only when their Soviet patriotism, which is partly ideological, has been aroused.

This observation reminds us of the complexity of the relations between 'ideologies' and 'nationalisms' in our time, both phenomena being outgrowths of industrial civilization. In a mobile society the individual cannot be indifferent either to his linguistic and cultural community or to the political parties that promise an equitable social order for all. He is therefore naturally sensitive both to social ideas and to the idea of nation. This is the first fact that strikes the observer.

A second fact, which is no less incontestable, is the superiority of social ideologies over nationalism when it comes to intellectual elaboration and system. The contrast between the rapid breakdown of National Socialism and the triumphant progress of Marxism-Leninism throughout the world might suggest that it is ideology, not nationalism, that is the ruling idea of our time. But the real lesson of the recent past is that only those ideologies which do not deny the aspiration toward universality immanent in modern civilization are likely to spread across boundaries and oceans.

The eventual primacy of nationalism is to be found at an entirely different level. National Socialism and Marxism-Leninism, it is often said, are ideologies – that is, systems of representations and politico-historical values – whereas nationalism is a collective experience gradually formed in the course of centuries. Ideologies are temporary; they are part of a clear consciousness and a confused mind; nationalism is permanent, or at least long-lasting, rooted in the collective unconscious. There is no contradiction between the power of national experiences and the weakness of Fascist or Hitlerian ideologies.

In our time the majority of ordinary men still belong to a country rather than to a political party. If there is a conflict between the two loyalties, the former usually wins out. Such was the decision of the masses in 1914, and such was also the decision of the majority of socialist leaders. During the Second World War there were traitors in every European country, motivated by ideological conviction, but their numbers were relatively small. Yet it is also true that in 1914 Lenin and his supporters chose revolution rather than national defence. From 1939 to 1945 in a number of countries the cadres and some of the troops who belonged to Communist parties faithfully obeyed orders from Moscow, even when those orders were contrary to national interests and patriotic duty. Politicians interested in the short run would be wrong to underestimate the influence – perhaps temporary but effective – of political parties dedicated to the realization of an ideological dream.

The Sino-Russian schism and the attempt of the Eastern European states to achieve autonomy are two solid arguments to support the same thesis. These arguments are not, however, precisely of the same nature. While Communist China is virtually a great power, driven by a will to independence, the Sino-Russian conflict is ideological as well as national. If the leaders of the two countries did not wish to be and did not believe themselves to be Marxist-Leninists, they might quarrel none the less but it would be in a significantly different manner. Leadership of international Marxism-Leninism, one of the key issues in the current controversy, is meaningful only to states that claim to embody an idea. Common adherence to a doctrine that has a universal tendency, then, has not lastingly united the two great Communist powers; rather, it has deepened a conflict that might well have been provoked by rivalry between national interests. Once again the division has resulted from an impossible claim to universality.

The nationalism of the countries of Eastern Europe is a natural reaction to the violence they have experienced. Their regimes were imposed on them by an outside force, whether it is considered an occupier, or neighbour. Stalin ruled as a despot, unmindful of the feelings and the respective interests of brother countries. National claims were expressed variously – in one place by an insistence on industrialization (Rumania), in others by abandoning the compulsory teaching of Russian, and everywhere by demands for an increased freedom to rule, that is, a strengthening of internal sovereignty. The party in power derives a twofold advantage from this: having returned from exile in the military trucks of the foreigner, the leaders' popularity is doubly enhanced when they stand up to those who gave them power. And like all rulers in all times, they would rather command than obey.

However important these phenomena may be from the point of view of interstate relations, they do not resolve the internal problem of relations among culture, nation, and regime, a problem that in turn springs from a more fundamental one: To what extent does industrial civilization impose values and goals upon all of mankind, *de jure* and *de facto*?

We have granted as a starting point that equality – equality before the law and access of all to jobs of every kind – represented an immanent norm in modern civilization. The social order of an industrial civilization, to use Talcott Parsons's concept, tends to be *universalist*. There is no difference in kind between individuals, each is judged according to his achievements; individual or collective life is splintered into specific activities.

The social order of industrial civilization is therefore not neutral in regard to the values that govern other social orders. A caste society is at the opposite pole of an industrial society even when the latter seems to be divided into classes or ruled by an elite. Classes are seen as an outrage in so far as they seem to persist through the generations; and they do not prevent young people of every class from meeting in the same schools or on the same playing fields. It is the hereditary transmission of membership in a caste, much more than the curse which weighs down the untouchables, that is sharply at variance with the normative implications of industrial civilization. The rulers of the state, convinced of the need for progress and subscribing to values of modern society that are Western in origin, cannot fail to condemn the caste system. Officially, the status of untouchability no longer exists, although prejudice changes more slowly than laws, whether we refer to the untouchables of India or the segregated Negroes of the United States. Similarly, respect for all life, the ban against killing monkeys or cows that characterizes some Eastern religions and cultures, constitutes an obstacle in the road to economic progress. Whether the goal is production or material well-being, animate or inanimate nature serves human needs. Animals are treated not as 'inferior brothers' or 'companions', but as a source of nourishment.

Legally, industrial civilization does not interfere with creative freedom in the arts or with recreation, or in any of the domains unrelated to rational and productive work. But in fact, diverse activities, whether remunerated or performed free, whether or not subjected to the inflexible exactions of self-interest, react upon each other. The working man and the man of leisure are one and the same; he discovers different aspects of his personality in each of his activities. These related aspects are not always cohesive. Much more than traditional societies, modern societies comprise too complex a process of historical sedimentation to constitute an organic whole, intelligible in terms of a single purpose.

To assume a conflict between the normative implications of industrial civilization and free creativity is an over-simplification. The norms of industrial civilization do not entail, on the institutional level, a single definite expression. They allow, so to speak, a margin of variation. Moreover, rarely does an activity have a single purpose, or, if a purpose is stated, rarely is there only one method of achieving it. Specialists in organization have opposed the myth of a single valid method, 'the one way', in workshops, administrations, or businesses. How much more absurd this myth would be if one applied it to teaching methods or to various interpersonal relations in family, political, university, or religious life. Industrial civilization, viewed as a whole, is much too complex to be understood from a single design or ideal.

Despite an inequality in development, on both sides of the Atlantic, in the United States as well as in France, concern for the *quality of existence* is beginning to rival concern for *per capita production*. John Kenneth Galbraith in the United States and Bertrand de Jouvenal in France have both developed this theme.

Galbraith takes as his point of departure the contrast between traditional problems of poverty and the problems posed by an affluent society. Relentlessly he attacks what he calls conventional wisdom, for which it would perhaps be difficult to find qualified spokesmen. But in the course of combat devoid of peril leading to a victory devoid of glory, he has brought to light ideas which, to say the least, had been in the background of contemporary thought. After attaining a given gross national product, Galbraith contends, the important thing is not to produce still more but to distribute as fairly as possible the surplus production. The flood tides of poverty will not all disappear of themselves in the next stage of growth; it is therefore more important to improve public services than to provide a third car for households that already have two. The ugliness of cities does not detract from the value of the national product any more than the beauty of a well-maintained landscape or public monuments enhance an individual's income. But for the living, and even more for those who will come after us, is not this beauty a more precise measure of our civilization than the statistics of our national accounting?

Once he has set out on this line of reasoning, the critic has no choice but to continue. Does not the attempt to produce as much as possible, which implies the transformation and manipulation of living or inanimate nature for the sole purpose of satisfying human needs, in fact destroy the priceless riches of our heritage from the past?

We have now returned, by this bypath, to the problem we touched upon at the end of Part Two: the world in which industrial man must live has lost its enchantment. 'All at once an entire universe has paled, our repast has lost its flavour, our natural psychic *élan* has been stricken, reversed, betrayed, discouraged. And we needed so much to be undivided in our vision of the world!'[2] Before there was science men often dreamed; they continue to dream, but without the heartening illusion that their dreams coincide with reality. Modern man is faced with the chilling knowledge that he can encounter reality only by making use of mathematics.

2. Gaston Bachelard, *La Formation de l'esprit scientifique: Contribution à une psychoanalyse de la connaissance objective*, J. Vrin, Paris, 1938, p. 241.

Even relations between individuals, not only those between man and nature, obey in turn the inexorable laws of objectivization and rational calculation. Human tastes are an inflexible factor in the total cost of production. From this point of view, productivity and rationalization are universal means, but, one might say, secondary ones. They are the instrumentalities of production, but production itself is a necessary, if sometimes a contradictory condition for the achievement of authentic values. Manipulation of nature or of workers is in itself barbaric, but it is indispensable if all individuals are to escape the curse of poverty and share in the collective life and in a flowering civilization. What must remain inviolate is not progress or the rate of growth, but culture – that is, the totality of works of the mind (including of course, positive science).

By the same token, the universality of modern civilization, at least as it is interpreted today, is open to question. Science and technology are the common adventure of all humanity. But one essential part of culture remains distinctive. And the eventual obliteration of diversity seems a threat, not a hope, the nightmare of the 'brave new world', not the dream of a humanity that preserves its heritage as it overcomes it. If the true goal is culture – a unique way of life, a singular expression of creative freedom – will we not once again take this roundabout way back to nations and nationalisms, the spectre that again arises to haunt the world just as the spectre of communism and its secular religion seem to be fading in the distance?

This does not mean that cultural units coincide with political units. There are, as we have seen, multinational or multitribal states. Nor does it mean that modern cultural communities – such as the French or German nations – are completely homogeneous in the same way that small societies of several hundred people used to be. It would not be difficult for an ethnologist to find multiple cultural units within the French nation: social strata, regions, occupations, each being the expression of a certain existentialist attitude. And it is no less true that among these cultural units, systems of belief, and ways of living – the nation, in the European sense of the word – has its special place. This is true because the nation unites language, the vehicle of tradition, with the *state*, the agency by which the individual achieves citizenship and with it an awareness which may be illusory that, although he is but one among many, he is helping to forge, not simply submitting to, the social order.

## National Coexistence

We must repeat that it is impossible to foresee what inroads the spread of modern technology will make on the desired diversity of cultures. It would be even more idle to speculate about the future of cultures than to speculate about possible diplomatic realignments in the year 2000. Our final remarks will be concerned with the contradictions between universality and nationalism.

Four instances of these contradictions are:

1. *The desire for nondependence*, therefore the determination not to be dependent upon others for one's security.

2. *Inequality of development* which is responsible both for tensions between ethnic groups within a political unit and the desire for economic and political autonomy on the part of new nations and resuscitated ones.

3. *Theoretical conflict and confusion in fact between secular religions with universalist pretensions and national loyalties*, which explains why both the Russians and the Chinese have a tendency to confuse *their* version of the Communist doctrine with universal truth, even though Communism has been profoundly marked by the requirements of a singular tradition.

4. *Desanctification of the universal technological adventure* and *the sanctification of what is unique in a work, in a culture, and especially in a national culture.*

Do not these four factors of the dialectic culminate in a conclusion that is as disappointing as it is paradoxical – that the age of universal technology is also an age of conflicts which are successively or simultaneously national and ideological? There are some like André Malraux, who, disenchanted with the revolutionary ideology, now exalts his homeland, France; such men promise, as did the democratic nationalists a century ago, that peace will come through the independence of all peoples. The great wars of this century, they say, were not the product of the desire for national independence, but of the desire for conquest or hegemony, the drives of imperialism.

But this is an eternal illusion, all the more dangerous because it fosters a half-truth. National states, confident in themselves and their identity, and satisfied with their boundaries, can in fact coexist without giving up their sovereignty. But how easily national pride degenerates into chauvinism, and chauvinism into contempt for others! How could state sovereignties, contemptuous of any international law, avoid the temptations of power politics? How could nations, each concerned exclusively with its own interests, and proudly indoctrinating its citizens with the slogan, 'my country, right or wrong', be able to settle their quarrels peacefully?

Westerners, to be sure, are delighted that nationalism in the countries of Eastern Europe is upsetting the hegemony of Moscow and the solidarity of the Soviet bloc. On the other side of the iron curtain, chiefs of state who assert an independent attitude toward Washington are acclaimed. Power corrupts, it is pointed out – and it even corrupts democratic governments. A relative weakening of the United States' influence over the Western world might even be in the best interest of the United States itself.

It would be unfortunate to confuse these contemporary vicissitudes of world diplomacy with a realistic outlook for the future. Mankind is now divided and will remain so because of the widespread if not universal desire for national independence; because of the inequality of development; because of the prevalence of an essentially particularist nationalism; and because of the tensions created by ideologies held by their adherents to be universal. For the time being, the anarchical order of power, as we have analysed it in an earlier chapter, may safeguard mankind from major catastrophes. Inequalities of progress can only be overcome slowly. Industrialization will not automatically and universally efface the diversity of systems of norms and values, as they are called today, or customs and manners, as they were called in the eighteenth century. Science will never answer those final questions man is forever asking; and the answers provided by the various religions, secular and otherwise, are not unanimously accepted. The West is justifiably proud of its hard-won tradition of not dictating to the individual the means of his personal salvation, of allowing him sole responsibility for his own destiny. Secular religions – the sanctification of a task that is often necessary and of a regime that is always imperfect – are, *par excellence*, in Western eyes sins against the human spirit.

In the face of these divisions, some of them the legacy of centuries, others created by a false claim to universality, how can one envisage an order that would be at once peaceful and all-encompassing? Ideally, mankind should willingly bow to the exigencies of rational administration in regard to problems that clearly affect the whole of humanity (air pollution, the preservation of natural resources, birth control). Other problems, those affecting the economy or general progress of the nationalities, might logically be dealt with, according to their scope, at different levels, wherever global, continental, national, or regional authorities, cooperating with each other, could be seen to possess the necessary competence. A peaceful community is not necessarily a homogeneous one, but it would require that cultures be separated from drives for national power; they would become like religions, a private affair. National sovereignties would have to be subject to laws; inequalities of development would have to be erased or so treated as no longer to give rise to resentment; and the patterns of economico-social organization would have to be insured against transfiguration into ideologies that claim to be universal.

In short, the eternal problems of politics and economics, of legitimate power and abundance, would have to be resolved. Scientific truth, technological efficacy, and the equal dignity of all men would have to be acknowledged by acts, everywhere and forever. Apart from doing a reasonable amount of work, all individuals and groups would have to be free to pursue their own way of life, their creative and leisure activities. History, as it has evolved over several thousands of years, would have to have run its course. It has not done so.

The new ecumenical spirit, the respect that representatives of the great religions have lately displayed towards each other,

attests perhaps a conversion to the universalist spirit at the heart
of modern society. But we cannot be sure that the peace between
gospels of salvation does not constitute a counterpart of the war
between secular religions.

# 10 Technology and History

Anyone born in the early years of the twentieth century feels that he has lived through several epochs of history. Thanks to the stories told by his parents and to his own childhood memories, he knows something of the pre-1914 world. The twenty years that separate the two wars are those of his youth, and they divide quite naturally into postwar and prewar. The first period was marked by the general revulsion against senseless slaughter, by the vain attempt to return to what was called, not without irony, 'the good years', and by new hopes awakened by the revolutionary fires seen as 'the great light in the East'. Then came the prewar period that began with Hitler's accession to power. After 1930 and the Great Depression, 'history was again on the move', to use Toynbee's expression, but mankind, despite the unmistakable presentiment of impending catastrophe, in the end was surprised by events which it foresaw but would not face.

How different the present work would have been had it been written in 1913, or 1928, or 1938! Before the assassination at Sarajevo a treatment of the social order might have predicted, in the manner of Spengler, the coming of wars and dictators, but there would have been no inkling of the destiny of Marxism, of the vast experiments in economic and social planning, or of the rivalry and common denominators of the regimes conditioned by action and reaction inspired by the new secular religion. Had it been written before 1939, it might have prophesied the disintegration of European empires and the rise of the Soviet Union and the United States to predominant position (after all, such predictions had been current in Europe for more than a century); but it would not have foreseen the junction of Marxism (which was to become Marxism-Leninism in its passage through Russia) with the Chinese tradition, the diplomatic unification of the planet, the spread of the notion of development, the balance of terror, and the revival in rationalized form of earlier modes of combat.

Now, over twenty years after the end of the Second World War, are we in a better historical position to take our bearings? Are we any more likely to avoid provincialism, to escape being contradicted by the turn of events in the near future? The answer is probably not available to those who cannot expect to see the dawn of the next century. Still, it is not unreasonable to assume that today we have a better chance of seeing the contemporary world and its prospects more clearly than we would have had fifty or twenty-five years ago.

Our historical awareness has been broadened by the discovery of our more distant past, the history of mankind as an animal species and the history of our most archaic societies. Our backward view is no longer limited by a naïve ethnocentrism or by a dogmatic theory of history. We are no longer forced to make a categorical choice between cycles of culture such, as those which Spengler and Toynbee have described, and the progress of science and technology, which is demonstrated daily. Complex societies no longer strike us as totalities whose various parts develop according to a single law. It may be that the technological revolution of our time has opened an unprecedented phase of the human adventure, in which the patterns supposedly observed over thousands of years – from the era of the first European empires to the detonation of the atomic bombs that devastated Hiroshima and Nagasaki – will never again be re-enacted.

But the same revolution forces us to recognize the limits of our knowledge, the uncertainty of our foresight, and the possibly intrinsic uncertainty of mankind's future. Thus constrained to be modest enough to confess our ignorance, we are less likely to deceive ourselves. Our ignorance is, so to speak, well grounded, since it is acknowledgement at once of something we cannot know in the present state of human history, and of all that we have learned from the past.

Biologists, paleontologists, and ethnologists teach us to consider man and human societies as part of nature. But there is no contradiction between the views of biologists and any faith *that accepts the fact of evolution*, or, if one prefers, the fact that on this planet (itself formed in the course of time) life has had a history; that over hundreds of millions or even billions of years, there has been a progressive development of increasingly complex forms of life issuing from anterior forms in accordance with processes we understand only imperfectly. Industrial societies regard themselves as being in a state of flux. Biologists and sociologists are agreed on a philosophy that exalts the process of becoming, although they are equally amazed as they discover the complex internal structures of bacteria, languages, or social systems.

Not only is evolution itself firmly established, but the evolutionary point of view is likewise universally accepted. André Leroi-Gourhan has written:

Whatever explanations they may give for it, evolutionists are unanimous in believing that the stream which carries us along is indeed *the* stream of evolution. The lichen, the medusa, the oyster, or the giant tortoise are, like the gigantic dinosaur, nothing but eddies in the mainstream that flows towards us. If it is insisted that the creatures behind us represent only one of the branches of evolution (the one which leads to intelligence, the others leading to other no less honourable forms of ultimate development), the evolution towards man still subsists, and the choice of illustrative linkages is legitimate. Whether, like Bergson or Teilhard, one sees in evolution the sign of an *élan*, the general quest for awareness culminating in *Homo sapiens*, or (what amounts to the same thing on a material level) the play of a determinism culminating in living forms that are increasingly responsive to the motives for exploiting matter, the comportment of the mass from which man has sprung remains the same. Beneath the superstructure of explanations, the infrastructure of facts resolves itself into the same system.[1]

The popular success of Teilhard de Chardin's works, in which most biologists find little scientific value and professional philosophers very little precision or originality, may probably be explained by this *infrastructure of facts*. Although the rest – vocabulary, figures of speech, pseudo-explanations out of Lamarck or Bergson – are worth almost nothing, the whole gives the illusion of being a synthesis of science and metaphysics (or religion). It is a false synthesis, since scientists do not explain

1. *Le Geste et la parole, technique et langage*, Albin Michel, Paris, pp. 85–6.

evolution in terms of an internal thrust on the part of life or an aspiration toward 'hominization' or toward the noosphere (an explanation which they regard as comparable to the one symbolized by the soporific power of opium). Yet it is an understandable illusion, since evolution, or at least one branch of evolution, actually leads to man as its final outcome.

Man is a part of nature, both in respect to basic cellular structure and the vital interaction between living being and environment. The physical and chemical use of matter involves two extreme modes, 'one of which entails the harnessing, so to speak, of matter by the direct confrontation of the molecule that is being used with the molecule that is using it, as in the case of viruses, whereas the other entails a hierarchical kind of "consummation" that makes use of inert matter through a chain of living beings, as in the case of man eating beef at the end of a long line of successive eaters and eaten'.[2] Even if today's philosophy of biology is rigorously scientific and deterministic and regards mutations and natural selection as a satisfactory explanation for the evolution of species, yet it makes no attempt to *reduce* the higher to the lower. It fixes the human species at the final stage of the evolutionary process, but acknowledges the specificity of other kinds of organization at every level of the animal kingdom, the reciprocal relations of the components of every unit – cell or higher animal. In short, the teachings of biology stress rather than minimize the specificity of mankind and human society.

It is the biologists themselves, relating human history (or the evolution of society) to the evolution of life, who emphasize its novel quality. Language, literature, and the transmission of past achievements make possible an evolution of mankind not to be confused with biological evolution. Intellectual ability, genetically considered, is probably no greater than nor basically different from what it was a thousand or five thousand years ago, but the technico-social environment is vastly different and the knowledge transmitted to children continues to increase. Those philosophers from Dilthey to Sartre, for whom man has a history rather than a nature, express in a striking and seemingly paradoxical way an idea that is at bottom quite banal. In transforming its environ-

2. ibid., p. 86.

ment the human species transforms itself. Divided into societies, each of which is inseparable from a culture, mankind can survive only by subjecting all individuals to a discipline that becomes internalized in the form of moral obligations and inquiries. Technological achievements, plurality of cultures, and moral awareness – from these three and from their interrelations emerges the socio-historical dialectic, certain contemporary aspects of which we have analysed.

In the minds of biologists and ethnologists, of physicists and chemists, technical achievements constitute a revolution comparable to the Neolithic revolution. For some time paleontologists and archaeologists have been using changes in technology to mark out epochs as they prefer to measure them. Historians have never followed this example, holding that the history of cities and empires from Sumer to Hitler has evolved on the basis of a stagnant or very gradually changing technology. Marx correctly sensed a sudden acceleration of technological change. In the *Communist Manifesto* he stressed the role of the bourgeoisie who, in one century, had done more to alter mankind's living conditions than other ruling classes had done in a thousand years. But, carried away by polemical ardour and revolutionary zeal, he scrambled into a single concept the relations of production, tools (or material techniques), the status of property, and the organization of work. Out of this confusion Marxism was created – that mighty arm of revolutionary propaganda and conflict whose fascination resides as much in its ambiguities as in its promises.

Since 1945 the progress of science and technology has been so greatly accelerated in capitalist regimes that it is impossible on the scientific level to establish a simple correlation between means of production and relations of production (or economico-social regime). In the West one is inclined to make use of one of Marx's ideas, that of the primacy of the forces of production, either by applying the term to technology alone or by using productivity of labour as an index of progress and thus of the effectiveness of labour.

There is no doubt that scientific and technical progress affects all the characteristics by which the human quality of man has been defined throughout the ages: language and communication, tools, mastery of the physical environment, knowledge or reason. But even so, the history of mankind has never been reduced to mere progress in science and technology.

The size of a community traditionally depended on the resources which men were able to procure in a given area. Social organization has been a function of the mastery men were able to gain over the environment, or, to be more precise, mastery of the environment has marked the limits within which various kinds of social organization were possible. Even so, Paleolithic man was not exclusively *Homo faber*, a toolmaker. An 'ethical animal', to use the expression of a contemporary biologist, man has internalized into moral obligations the real or imaginary requirements of collective discipline; he has translated into words, myths, and narratives his interpretation of his society and of the cosmos. In the realm of science and technology, mankind may be compared, as Pascal put it, to a single man who would never stop learning. In the domain of artistic creations, religious beliefs, and even of the social order, mankind has never been as one and has never displayed any consistent awareness of unity. Would mankind consent to renounce 'intraspecific' conflicts – in other words, wars – if the price of peace were the loss of cultural diversities? Biologists like the great scientist Konrad Lorenz, in his *Natural History of Aggression*, bring out how ill-adapted to the present stage of history is the aggressive human behaviour that might have been useful in an earlier phase of evolution; but they sometimes leave in obscurity the peculiarly human aspects of the rivalries between states or churches. As citizens and as believers, men have repeatedly demonstrated that they may prefer their faith to their life, and do not yield even if the battle is hopeless. Should one now want mankind to conform to the rationality of economic calculation?

An 'ethical animal' – religious, artistic, and playful – social man has never before our time had as his conscious objective the total mastery of his environment; perhaps even today technological power may prove to be but a means to other ends that are not yet clearly defined. To be sure, science and technology are obviously at the origin of a number of phenomena characteristic of our age: the great increase in population, the lengthening of the life span, the growth of cities, etc. But the development of global societies cannot be likened to the progress of science and technology; and that progress itself, although in retrospect it seems cumulative, has been in fact a history in the literal sense of the term.

The word 'history' is rich in ambiguities. In several languages it means, as everyone knows, both reality in process and the science of that process. Let us discard the latter meaning. We mean then by history, in its most superficial sense, a series of directed changes that have affected some definite reality. The earth has a history in the sense that our planet, through the ages, has traversed a series of different phases and is continuing to do so. In this same sense the solar system has a history. We try to decipher the history of life and of living species by uncovering the mechanisms of change and then reconstituting our heritage.

The idea of history acquires additional significance when the succession of states or forms seems, in retrospect, not to have been determined from the beginning. I have heard biologists ask themselves whether, if life had been created out of inorganic matter on other planets, the net result would be the same as that on earth. Most of them have answered this question in the negative. The role in the evolutionary process attributed to mutations, that is, to chance phenomena, suggests, to be sure, that life might have taken a different course, at least in some of its specific aspects. The French philosopher Cournot contrasted order and chance; he defined chance as the convergence of independent series, and regarded the influence of chance or, to put it another way, the efficacy of chance phenomena, as the essence of the historical phase, which in his eyes, constituted only a fragment of the human adventure on this planet.

The concept of history takes on a still richer meaning when applied to human societies in a state of flux. Societies not only change in the course of time and the changes are not solely the joint effect of massive facts (the growth of population, the use of machines, etc.) and of circumscribed realities (the unforeseeable convergence of series, the role of great men); human history is also made up of relations, in turn peaceful and bellicose, between collectivities each of which has its own gods and perceives no meaningful life outside its own universe. The behaviour of some animals reminds one of human behaviour from which certain historical processes result: a feeling for one's land, defence of one's frontiers, the capitulation of the vanquished, acceptance of the verdict of battle, the ritualization of certain attitudes. With language, that form of communication by symbols which makes possible the preservation of accumulated experience and an accompanying sense of values – in short, with awareness and moral consciousness – a new dimension of history appears, a dimension that includes the *plurality of more or less incompatible cultures and the search for an existential truth.*

Human societies are unequally historical, or so it is said. Lévi-Strauss speaks of 'cold' societies which change slowly and 'warm' societies that change more rapidly and yet conserve what they have. We know and shall always know very little about the history of preliterate societies. Although these societies have been historical (in the sense of changing in the course of time), they have not attained a historical consciousness, that is to say, a full awareness of both the plurality of cultures and the plurality of epochs within the life span of the same culture. Once he is aware of this double plurality, man becomes *essentially* historical, regardless of whether he resigns himself to the anarchy of values or seeks to surmount it.

Modern societies are historical In all the senses we have just enumerated, and their historical awareness is more *forward-looking* than *backward-looking*. They have less respect for tradition than for the future. They are dominated by the sense of a break between pre-industrial and industrial societies and of an increasing acceleration in scientific, technical, and economic progress; whether it is the number of scientific journals, the rapidity of transportation, or the power of explosives, the graphs all show the same exponential trend. It took only ten years to 'progress' from a capacity of thousands of tons of TNT (A-bombs) to a capacity of millions (H-bombs). The intervals between developments of this kind grow ever shorter: from railroad train to aeroplane, from piston aeroplane to jet, from jet to supersonic, and from supersonic to rocket. The rate of growth of the economy, like the increased rate in the number of researchers, cannot continue indefinitely, nor even remain at the present level.

Scientific and technological progress continues to be historical in all the meanings of the term. It is part of the global movement of societies; it takes place within national communities that compete with one another even though to a certain extent scientists themselves constitute a 'transnational' community. It entails that combination of necessity and accident which, it would seem, characterizes all human undertakings; supported financially and morally by the state and by the people themselves, this progress continues to depend on the will of men, a will that is given impetus by individual beliefs and is oriented toward a variety of goals.

At the same time scientific and technological progress is cloaked in a kind of fatality. When states decide to make supersonic aeroplanes in order to gain three hours in the New York –Paris hop – even though the time saved might be lost in the bottleneck between the airport and the centre of town – those responsible in both the public and private sectors can only reply with the meaningless phrase, 'You can't stop progress'. Sometimes it seems that societies themselves have less and less mastery over their destiny as they employ technology to increase their mastery over their physical environment.

It may be that we are reaching the final antinomy of modern society or of the historic consciousness of our civilization – an antinomy in which the dialectics of equality, socialization, and universality were but passing moments. The most obvious if not the most basic characteristic of modern societies is their spectacular progress in science, in the creation of labour-saving devices, and in productive capacity. Why should such societies not be moved to apply to themselves the methods of thought that have given them an increasing mastery over their physical environment? The question raises another: Can the mind of man tolerate the idea that scientific and technological progress will not be determined by a technology based on science – that instead the development of scientific societies is historical, in the literal meaning of the word, that is to say, *not* subject to techniques that are themselves at the service of a reflective human will?

Let us pause for a moment to consider the distinction we have made between *history* and *technology*. Any activity, peaceful or warlike, psychological or material, that has as its end either the production of goods or persuasion, is defined as technical when ends and means, after rational elaboration, can be determined, or when, the end having been determined in advance, effective methods can be scientifically apprehended. Strictly speaking, the ends that technology determines – whether it be the best way of running a business or a cure recommended by a physician – are never the final ends, but they are sometimes clearly presented as necessary means to an ultimate end (such as productivity or profit in one case or restored health in the other). Actually, *the history of societies taken as a whole has never been the object of a technical undertaking.* Even today there are few sectors where the social sciences (in the broad sense) have reached the operational stage at which they can impose a technique of action. And certain psychosocial techniques, always limited to one sector of existence, excite quite as much anguish as they do hope.

Let us return to the contradictions of equality. It is permissible to say, as we have suggested, that they can be ascribed to the extravagance of modern man's aspirations. How could one put all children on a footing of equality at the beginning of social experience when the process of socialization taking place through the family promotes the development of some and paralyses that of others? But economic progress disappoints the best minds for a deeper reason.

Why, despite an increase in productivity that has exceeded the hopes of the most optimistic, is it incorrect to say that even in the richest countries the problem of production has been solved? The first and immediately obvious reason is that needs or desires have increased along with productivity. If men had preserved the mode of life that existed a hundred years ago, the growth of productivity would indeed have solved the problem of production and at the same time that of economic equality. But this hypothesis is self-contradictory. If the mode of life had not changed, the productivity of labour would not have increased so rapidly, for the process requires a concentration of effort on goods costing less and less.

There is no reason, abstractly speaking, why a human society cannot be imagined which would be less concerned with increasing the potential of its machines or of its productive energies than with assuring to everyone the minimum requirements for a decent existence. This was the teaching of Rousseau. But economic history has been quite different. The will to power and wealth has carried the day. The demand for equality has gone beyond the formalism of equal rights, or the opening of all occupations to everyone, only as a direct result of the increase in the collective resources. Even today most criticism of the so-called affluent society stems from this realization. The becoming of these societies is not subject to a conscious social will. It proceeds in accordance with the unforeseeable vicissitudes of history and in many respects still appears to be immoral and irrational.

What is the major charge which may legitimately be brought against all developed societies of whatever regime? Not one of them makes use of its resources in the way an all-powerful sage would have them do; not one of them respects the priorities that seem obvious to men of goodwill. It is an outrage to the conscience that there is so much misery in societies which command so great a productive capacity and have the requisite means to assure the indispensable minimum to everyone. It is outrageous that the Soviet Union can spend billions to photograph the hidden side of the moon and yet has to buy grain abroad. It is outrageous that the United States, the Soviet Union, with Britain, France, and China in their wake, are engaged in an armaments race which consumes tens of billions of dollars while hundreds of millions of men live in complete deprivation. A philosopher of Hegelian training cannot but condemn a scientific rationalism employed in the service of irrationality. A satirist of our time could write a tale on the theme of 'modern rationality' in the same way that Voltaire in *Candide* dealt with 'the best of all possible worlds'. Is there anything rational about the world of Hitler and Stalin, the world of genocide and cold war, the world of organized waste and of destitution for two thirds of humanity? Is it a rational world in which two great powers accumulate bombs of ever-increasing destructiveness and missiles of ever-increasing swiftness for the sole purpose of mutual paralysis, and yet are still unable to avoid the insults of Albania and Cuba?

This is an accusation which, depending on the temper of the individual, will be either irate or ironic, but its only virtue is to disclose to us the ultimate cause of what I shall call the *disillusions of progress* (after the title of the book by Georges Sorel, *The Illusions of Progress*). The three values which seem to me to be immanent in modern civilization are *equality*, *personality*, and *universality*, and each of them admits of divergent interpretations. All three are perhaps subordinate to the ultimate inspiration of the modern age which I shall call the *Promethean ambition* – the urge, to borrow a Cartesian expression, to become the *masters and possessors* of nature.

Science and technology are the tools of this ambition. Man-made satellites, the exploits of the astronauts, the Apollo project (sending men to the moon) are its symbols. But is it not exasperating that in that same Soviet society, where physicists can calculate the exact point at which a missile will make impact on the moon, no one is able to predict how much wheat will be harvested in one or five years? Is it not intolerable that satellites obey the will of the planners but the peasants do not? If one replies by saying that nature can be mastered only by obeying it, a further question automatically arises: What social or human nature should planners obey?

No answer can be given to this question since men and their societies have a history, not a nature that is fixed once and for all. Yet, though human and social nature may not be immutable, it does possess certain permanent characteristics that limit the omnipotence of politicians, if not the imagination of writers of science fiction.

It is possible that the distribution of intellectual aptitudes is about the same in the various classes of a society – in the Negro minority and the white majority of the United States – and in the various peoples of the world. But individuals in every social or ethnic group are unequally endowed, and such factors as social status, family, school, age-group, exposure to media of communication, advantage some and disadvantage others. Many reforms, some immediate, others long-range, will make it possible to attenuate but not eliminate the effects of a socio-familial continuity that cannot and should not be destroyed.

Awareness of mankind's unity would perhaps be the appropriate answer to the technical unification of the species. Man has remained a *social animal*, and the human species is not a society, or at least, it is a society so remote, so abstract, so inorganic that for no individual does it fulfil the function of a kinship group – village, religion, class, race, or nation. The technological unification of the planet is but one of the elements in a diplomatic history, modified in some respects but not transfigured by the unlimited power of atomic explosives and ballistic missiles.

The dialectic of universality is the mainspring of the march of history. It is not a problem to be solved nor is it an ensemble of contradictions to be overcome by the intelligence of scientists or the courage of a few rulers. No single person has the capacity miraculously to eliminate racial prejudices, to bring about equality in the standard of living, to increase agricultural production on the earth to the level which proven techniques could enable us to attain, to separate consciousness of one's own culture from the sense of belonging to a political unit, to take away from nations their desire for non-dependence. In short, international relations proceed *historically*, in the full meaning of the word. Technology provides the material tools – weapons and means of communication – for acts whose configuration and unforeseeable results are in the end irrational, despite the partial rationality for which each of us strives.

In the duel between nations that possess thermonuclear weapons the rationality of the participants ought to produce rational results. Escalation should stop long before it reaches the highest rung of the ladder of violence. The nation endowed with the greatest resources will not exact from its rival excessive sacrifices or a loss of face. Such would not be the result of a duel between a guerrilla army and a regular force, even if each of the two made the best possible use of its techniques – the techniques of partisan subversion on the one hand, the technique of repression on the other. The variance between ends and means is such that each is in a sense invincible, and neither has a vital interest (as is the case in a duel between powers that have thermonuclear weapons) in bringing armed conflict to a halt as rapidly as possible.

Whatever the method employed by the protagonist – entrepreneur or strategist – to make the optimum decision, the dialectic of decision-making, even in the abstract, does not always guarantee a rational outcome. The protagonists, whether they be generals or politicians, no more resemble the *strategicus* of game theory than consumers or entrepreneurs resemble the *Homo oeconomicus*.

In other words, as regards equality or universality, disappointment arising from at least a partial failure is inevitable. Man has not become, he cannot become, master and possessor of social nature, which does not lend itself to manipulation as does inorganic or organic nature. It becomes transformed in another way; it is a free creation based on psychosomatic data which either remain constant or change gradually.

Since there is no universal state, there can be no all-powerful planner. To do away with the plurality of states would mean, on the political level, the end of a certain kind of history, a technical solution. But if this solution were imposed by a single state, that is to say, by a single man, it would resemble the construction of past empires – precarious, perhaps odious. As long as a plurality of state-protagonists persists, with partially contradictory, partially compatible interests, the whole of becoming will remain historical, and techniques will serve a future created by all but willed by no one, unforeseeable, perhaps irrational.

The obstacles which Promethean ambition encounters when it purports to give form to a new type of man or to enable each man's personality to attain fulfilment are still greater, and of a different essence. The desire for an egalitarian order, or for the proportionality of status to merit, clashes with the inertia and complexity of collective life, one might say with social chance. Each man's fate, in life as in games, is the result of both ability and accident. The ideal of personal self-fulfilment involves a contradiction between liberation and adaptation. At one pole stands the spectre of anomy, at the other that of conformity. Critics of modern society condemn the one no less passionately than the other.

In more general terms, one discerns several kinds of social regimes, just as one discerns several kinds of economic regimes. All economic regimes represent compromises between the power of the state and that of the consumer, between the primacy of industry and that of commerce, between the objective of power and that of welfare. But perhaps the compromises, as different as they are today will tend to become more alike, as Soviet ideological rigidity relaxes and as the mechanisms of the market (free or controlled) are accepted (in accordance with common sense) as *politically neutral*, offered to all with an eye to whatever goal the planners may have in mind. To be sure, to recognize the need for these mechanisms is to allow the consumer's choice to have an influence on scarcity and therefore on price and investment. Hence, one must admit that an entire economy cannot be managed like a factory (Lenin thought it could) and in the end give up the illusion of the planners' omnipotence. In spite of everything, it may be argued that in this case what experience has condemned is not so much Promethean pride as a false conception of technical capacity. Planning is an attempt to reduce guesswork, to lessen the role of chance; it can do this only through the study of a complex reality made up of hundreds of millions of individual decisions which the planners can influence and up to a certain point foresee, but cannot replace with official decrees or those provided by electronic computers.

As for the social order, the contrasting terms are not so clearly defined. They refer to cultures rather than to political regimes, to diversity rather than to clear-cut antitheses. Despite these reservations, if our analysis is correct, the modern age involves on the social level a few basic alternatives: What part should the family and the school respectively play in the process of socialization? Does one counterbalance the other or do they multiply each other's effects? Do the media of communication tend to make society more homogeneous? Or is the gap between mass culture and learned culture as great today (and will it be as great tomorrow), in a society where everyone can or soon will be able to read and write, as it was yesterday, when there was a relatively small cultivated class and a huge majority of uneducated people? How can society manage to harmonize the impersonality of relationships within organizations, the anonymity imposed on so many professional activities, with the yearning for identity? Is modern society, in the last analysis, threatened by anomy or conformity, or by both at once, and in what degree by each?

The answer that each particular society gives or will give to these questions depends on traditions rooted in the consciousness and unconsciousness of peoples. We would go beyond the scope of this essay if we did more than sketch some typical patterns. For the time being, family and school in most societies are working together. The reforms instituted in the schools and the increase in the funds devoted to the training of the young will provide a greater opportunity to gifted children from the lower classes. However, a society in which social status depends on college degrees – a 'mandarin' society – entails more continuity from generation to generation and less mobility than one would ordinarily think.

An offsetting factor lies in the fact that social mobility means the die is not cast at the very outset and that merit will be measured less by success achieved upon being admitted to or graduated from college, and more by commendable performance on the job. In a civilization where the hierarchy is based largely on education and intellectual ability, a society might conceivably have either very little mobility or a great deal, or at least a considerable degree of variation in mobility from one generation to another, depending upon circumstances.

At present, the cultural homogeneity produced by the media of communication seems to me largely an illusion or a myth. A significant part of the population has no access to so-called learned or higher culture. The radio and television programmes offered to everyone and consumed, so to speak, by the entire population, create a common culture that is both limited and superficial. Is it conceivable that in the future the various societies will resemble either the preponderantly homogeneous model or the one in which heterogeneity predominates? It may be that the model of homogeneity will always be unattainable in any strict sense, but a more or less extensive range of variation is likely.

There are also several possible solutions to the antinomy between anonymity and identity: a more or less fictitious personalization of relations that are essentially impersonal; cooperative enterprises that encompass and animate impersonal relations; the preservation or reconstruction of local political or religious communities. If we think of a business enterprise as the centre or symbol of occupational life, we note once again two opposite types: at one extreme is the Japanese concern, which looks upon itself as one big family responsible for the social advantages elsewhere provided by a civil service; at the other stands a type of business in which most of the workers have no *esprit de corps*, regarding themselves simply as employees of the firm, and not integrated with it or given any sense of security. The Japanese type will not remain just as it is, but integration of working personnel into the firm and a form of 'company patriotism' are developing here and there in Europe and the United States.

It is obviously impossible to imagine either a completely integrated society or one that is completely unintegrated. If the assent of most people to the value judgements accepted in their milieu is labelled conformity, then no society is possible without conformity. Where does one draw the line between *conformity* and *consensus*, the latter being indispensable to a society, the former despised by intellectuals? In this case I do not believe in the existence of two models, one of which is characterized by conformity and the other by the absence of consensus. But the distinctions in which writers of the last century delighted are still meaningful. In one place the constitution enjoys a consensus, in another it is perpetually challenged; here society itself imposes a stricter discipline, there it is the state which condemns certain deviations. The fact is that all contemporary societies are waylaid simultaneously by anomy and conformity. The swift changes in ways of working and living, the plurality of milieus and values within a large and complex society, create the danger of anomy; the potency of the means of persuasion and the specialization of everyone's knowledge create the danger of conformity – all the more so since the internalized values themselves are based less on God or conscience than on particular social imperatives that are often recognized as such. Yet it has not been shown that these dangers are now greater than they were in the past.

Even more than the dialectic of equality and quite as much as that of universality, the dialectic of personality eludes technology and remains essentially historical. Traditional culture dictates the solution given to the typical problems of modern socialization

No technician, in the last analysis, can 'manufacture' a personality at once integrated and autonomous. The technician brainwashes people, seduces buyers, and even, at a pinch, imparts knowledge. He creates the conditions in which individuals will have a better chance to achieve self-fulfilment; no technician can deliver the individual from the responsibility and freedom of attaining self-realization. Even the psychoanalyst helps the patient without serving as his substitute.

Unlike the technician who resorts to drugs and chemical products, or the stockbreeder who selects certain animal breeds, sociologists and psychologists can only help men to become conscious of themselves. The attainment of such consciousness is transforming the behaviour of individuals and peoples, but it has not yet changed the essence of their life experience. Every man's life, like that of every society, is still historical in the broad sense in which we have used that term; it is the dialectic of inherited nature and of circumstances, of tradition and moral judgement; it is, in our era, the dialectic of an inevitable scientific and techno-logical progress and of a humanity which does not know with certitude what it is or what it wants.

It may be that the present-day penchant for predicting or, as the French say, for 'prospecting', reflects the unresolved antithesis between technology and history, between Promethean ambition and the uncertainties of the future. Accidental events are deliber-ately disregarded, rates of economic growth are extrapolated, the processes of production and consumption in the most economic-ally advanced societies are noted in order to assess the future of less progressive societies; scientists are questioned about impend-ing discoveries and an attempt is made to picture what industry will be like in the twenty-first century and what use will be made of a hypothetical gross national product. One speculates about the future of political and economic institutions in the era of the computer. These speculations are legitimate, occasionally instructive, and always exciting, but they also entail some in-tellectual and moral hazards.

There is no doubt that men have never known the history they were making, and there is no reason to assume they know it any better today. It is a good thing to think about the future rather than to regard it as predetermined. But this sort of thought should result in a call to action, based as much on awareness of the limits of our knowledge as on that knowledge itself. No technical experts can create the society of tomorrow. All mankind will create it in a future whose diverse characteristics are unpredictable. Each man's share of responsibility is so small it seems almost ridiculous; but if the responsibility of the few turns out to be decisive, how many others thereby would be reduced to mere objects, doomed to bitter passivity?

History is dramatic. If the time should ever come when a few men were, or believed themselves to be, 'masters and possessors of social nature', then perhaps the drama would be over. But the individual would have forfeited his sense of liberty. Would a life subjected to a rational and purposeless organization still be human?

# Index